Childhood Speech, Language, and Listening Problems

What Every Parent Should Know

THIRD EDITION

Patricia McAleer Hamaguchi

WILEY

John Wiley & Sons, Inc.

To my husband, Norihito, for his unwavering support
and patience throughout this project.

And to my father, Frank McAleer, who taught me
the power of words, and my mother, Joan McAleer,
who taught me the value of listening.

Published by John Wiley & Sons, Inc., Hoboken, New Jersey
Published simultaneously in Canada

Library of Congress Cataloging-in-Publication Data

Hamaguchi, Patricia McAleer, date.
    Childhood speech, language, and listening problems : what every parent should know / Patricia McAleer Hamaguchi.—3rd ed.
        p. cm.
    Includes index.
    ISBN 978-0-470-53216-4 (pbk.)
    1. Communicative disorders in children—Popular works. I. Title.
    RJ496.C67H35 2010
    618.92'855—dc22

                                                                    2010006501

Printed in the United States of America

10 9 8 7 6 5 4 3 2 1

Contents

Acknowledgments

With this third edition, there have been many balls to juggle and keep in the air while writing. Without lots of support, it could never all have gotten done, so there are many people to thank! First, my husband, Norihito; children, Justin and Sara; and friends who have been there to give me moral support and pick up my kids when needed, Christina Gluhaich and Nasreen Ahmed.

I could not have managed to take the time off over the summer to get this together had it not been for the master multitasker who runs my front office at the practice, Michelle Talerico-Hurst. Michelle, a huge thank-you to you! You are the best! The rest of the "Hamaguchi Office Friends" keep me energized with their passion and love for the children we work with, with our collective experiences serving as a backdrop for many of the issues discussed in this edition: Gail Ballenger, Michelle Turkoglu, Jennifer Minton, and Kristen Moore. Another thank-you to Amie Reese, who is going to be the most amazing speech-language pathologist when she graduates.

A big thank-you to June McCullough, who is not only a fantastic audiologist and a professor at San Jose State University, but also a very dear friend who has been a great resource for all things related to audiology. Deb Ross-Swain has been another great resource and friend who has been very generous sharing her thoughts on auditory processing and autism spectrum disorders over the years, as well as collaborated on a number of writing and speaking projects. I have a very special group of online friends who have given me great professional support over the past few years and help keep me current with all the latest cutting-edge thinking in the field of speech pathology, but more than that, they are a great sounding board for everything related to private practice: the American Academy of Private Practice Speech-Language Pathologists & Audiologists (AAPPSPA). Thanks to Barbara Moore for letting me pick her brain on school issues; to Yvette Tazeau and Sharadha Raghavan, who have given me invaluable insight into neurobiological disorders; to Henriette Langdon on issues related to bilingual language learning; and to my "COA Friends," who keep me on my toes with all things related to sensory-integration and OT issues: Teri Wiss, Barbara Fourt, Pam Joy, Patti Volpe, and Glenda Fuge. You guys are the best!

Lastly, thanks to John Wiley & Sons and my editor, Christel Winkler, and production editor, Rachel Meyers, as well as to my agent, Alison Picard, for helping to put this current edition together.

Introduction

Sometimes when I try to think of what I want to say, uh . . . the words get um . . . jumbled up in my head. . . . When the teacher calls on me in class, I can't think of it fast enough, so uh . . . I just say "I don't know." I wish I wasn't so stupid.

—Jared, age 9

Sometimes I don't understand what Miss Rodriguez is talking about. I've heard the words before, but I forget what they mean. When I have to write my spelling words in sentences, I hate it! I kinda know what they mean, but not exactly. When I read stories, I don't understand what's going on. And when I take tests in class, I forget everything. All the names and places start to sound the same. Maybe my teacher is right: if I really tried, I could do better.

—Janet, age 10

"Little Red Riding Hood" is about a wolf and-and-and he putted on Grandma's clothes and she's pickin' flowers and she doesn't know it's him so he's—uh, she's—in the closet, and boy is she scared! She thinks it's her, but she gots tricked, so the wolf chases her. . . . Is that your game on the shelf?

—Michelle, age 7

Yesterday Mrs. Sauer was telling us what to do, and I couldn't remember what she said, so I asked Jamaal 'cause he's smart. When she caught me askin' him, she got really mad because she said I should pay attention better, but the words just fly out of my head like a bird.

—Tamina, age 5

Jessica is a very bright child, so I know there can't be anything wrong with her. Besides, we've given her so much stimulation from the time she was in the womb! Still, my sister keeps telling me that maybe she should be saying more than a

1

few words at two and a half years old. My pediatrician doesn't seem concerned, so I guess I'll just wait a few years and see if she outgrows it.

—Mother of Jessica, age 2½

I know Tatiana is a bright girl. She gets straight A's in math and is a whiz in art, music, and PE! I think that's because she likes those classes better. She just sits and stares at the paper for half the period during language arts. If I prod her, she'll put a few words down every once in a while, but it's like pulling teeth. If she had a learning disability, she wouldn't be such a good reader, right? So she must just be lazy, I guess.

—F. G., teacher

Most of the time I can figure out what Ben wants from us. We've developed a "code," if you will. For example, I know when he says, "Gogga" he wants me to take him somewhere in the car. I feel bad when other people don't understand him, but we've learned to be good translators. It's not a problem for us, so why bother subjecting him to speech therapy? I wouldn't want him to feel like he's different from the other kids. Besides, I heard that most kids outgrow this stuff. If he doesn't, they can work with him when he gets to kindergarten.

—Father of Ben, age 4

Caleb is talking okay, after a little bit of a slow start. He's amazingly bright! At age three, he is already starting to learn to read. He's incredible on the computer and a whiz with puzzles. I just wish he had a little more interest in the other children. His eye contact is poor—I have to keep reminding him to look at me. His preschool teacher tells me he just wanders around or goes in a corner by himself. He doesn't seem interested in the other children. Sometimes he even talks to himself. His teachers are concerned, and so am I. Is he just shy or is it something more?

—Mother of Caleb, age 3

These are the voices of children with communication disorders—and the adults in their lives. If their words sound familiar, then you have found the right book. I wrote it for parents like you. Perhaps you suspect your son or daughter has a speech, language, or listening problem, but aren't sure. Or maybe you *are* sure but would like to have more understanding and information. Armed with knowledge, you are in a better position to help make your child's life more fulfilling and far less challenging. Despite all the other caregivers, teachers, and specialists who touch a child's life, parents need to be the most educated about their children and what they need. You are your child's best advocate!

If you suspect or have been told that your child has a speech, language, or listening problem, you are far from alone. The most recent estimates indicate that more than 1 million children (1,137,934) between the ages of 6 and 21 receive speech and language special education services in U.S. public schools. Another 641,713 children from birth through age 5 receive speech therapy services (according to the U.S. Department of Education's latest figures from 2007). In addition to these children, there are undoubtedly more who could benefit from receiving therapy services or who choose to utilize private therapy in lieu of the available public services.

A Note on Definitions

The basic formula underpinning this book is C = S + L + L, or Communication equals Speech plus Language plus Listening. "Speech" is the process of producing meaningful sounds or words; "language" is the content of speech, the desire to interact and use language, the meaning of words; "listening" is the process of receiving and understanding those words. I've tried to use terminology that is familiar to most people and, at the same time, consistent with professional usage. You'll discover as you read the book that this balancing act is not always easy. For example, what I call "listening disorders" are sometimes referred to as "auditory disorders" or "receptive language deficits." You'll have to put up with a bit of jargon here and there, but I'll try to translate as we go along. In any case, learning the vocabulary will help you better understand your child's communication problems.

About This Third Edition: What's New?

It's been nine years since the last edition of this book was written, and it's amazing how much has changed! I listened to many of you and tried to include more in-depth information on the topics that are on your mind. Here are just a few highlights of the changes in this edition:

- Current research, philosophy, and terminology
- A new section on social language and pragmatic issues
- Expanded information on topics related to toddler and preschool speech and language development
- Additional information on the nature of speech (articulation), including terminology that is often used in reports and how parents can help at home
- Updated information about the Individuals with Disabilities Education Act (IDEA)
- A new chapter (chapter 9) called "Answers to Your Questions," which highlights miscellaneous questions that parents ask me on a regular basis

- Information on neurobiological disorders that impact the communication process, including anxiety, selective mutism, obsessive-compulsive disorders, sleep apnea, and Tourette's syndrome
- Updated resources and readings

How to Use This Book

Part I contains general information that any parent who has, or might have, a child with a communication problem needs to know. Chapter 1 introduces you to the field and expands on the definitions of speech, language, and listening. It explains how children learn to communicate—defining the parent's role in that process—and identifies the skills and behaviors common to children of various ages. Chapter 2 tells you when to get help from trained professionals and details the warning signs of potential problems for your child. Chapter 3 helps you decide which professional to see and describes what services are available at the different institutions (schools, hospitals, private clinics, and so on). It also walks you through the often confusing evaluation process. An explanation of the data and jargon in the evaluation report is provided in chapter 4. This chapter also describes what happens after the evaluation; that is, what your responsibilities and options for therapy are. You'll probably want to read all of Part I carefully.

Part II examines particular communication problems in much more detail. You may be more selective in your perusal of these chapters, but please understand that many of the conditions they describe are inter-related (C = S + L + L). Chapters 5, 6, and 7 cover speech, language, and listening problems, respectively. I explain the diagnosis, characteristics, and treatment. I describe how your child might be affected socially, at home, and at school, and I explain how you can help your child cope and improve. Chapter 8 discusses causes or related conditions associated with speech, language, and listening problems, such as lead poisoning, frequent ear infections, head trauma, cleft palate, Down syndrome, autism, cerebral palsy, and others. And chapter 9 is new for this third edition, with answers to the most common questions I've received over the years.

Children with speech, language, or listening problems can look forward to less frustration, self-doubt, and misplaced blame for their limitations if they are properly diagnosed and treated and if their family is informed and supportive. No child should dread going to school or having a simple conversation! There is much that you can do to help your child be well adjusted and reach his or her full potential.

PART I

What You Should Know and How to Get Help

1

Speech, Language, and Listening

How They Develop

When you said "Good morning" today and someone answered in kind, the exchange didn't strike you as particularly complicated. In fact, you were using your highly developed powers of speech, language, and listening—all part of your hard-won ability to communicate. As a parent, it is important to remember that communication is not always as easy for your child as it is now for you as an adult. After reading this chapter, you'll have a deeper appreciation of just how complex a child's path to effective communication really is.

Children start on the road to successful communication as soon as they are born. However, they progress at different rates. Some advance seemingly overnight from speaking single words to forming complete sentences that make sense. Other children take a slow, steady course with small steps, gradually adding words and building up to sentences. Often, both types of travelers reach their destination—learning to communicate equally well—in their own time, without any special attention. Members of a third group, however, need a little extra help along the way.

How is your child's communication journey going? Is he or she traveling more or less in step with one of the first two groups; that is (the dreaded question), is he or she "progressing normally"?

When discussing childhood development, the word *normal* projects a powerful aura of good and right, perhaps because *abnormal* is not a label we want attached to our children. Please understand, however, that *normal*, as used by educators and therapists, is a nonthreatening statistical term, better defined as *typical* or *average*. Developmental standards for what the professionals call normal have been established after years of observation and study of children who are considered to be free of such handicapping conditions as deafness or cerebral palsy. Indeed, within the parameters of normal, you will find a wide range of proficiency.

How can two children who exhibit different language abilities both be considered normal? Because, even within each age group, each child has an individual developmental timetable. For example, Roberto may acquire the language behaviors of the 2-to-3 age group just before his second birthday, whereas Mark may only be beginning to display those behaviors as he approaches his third birthday. Both of these boys fall into the normal category. Just because two children of the same age have markedly different communication patterns does not mean that one of them has a problem, particularly in the younger age groups.

Later in this chapter, I explain how children learn to communicate. Then I detail the important communication milestones for the many age groupings, ranging from birth to adolescence. First, however, we need to share a common vocabulary. Just as we "pros" have our own sense of normal, so, too, do we have our own definition of *communication*. Actually, our communication is much like the everyday variety. It is best understood through the three central skill components: speech, language, and listening. Knowing what's involved in these three areas is the first step in understanding what difficulties your child may be having, and thus is the beginning of being able to help.

What Is Speech?

Speech refers to the sounds that come out of our mouth and take shape in the form of words. You realize just how complex the speech process really is when you study it or if you lose the ability to produce speech effortlessly.

Many things must happen in order for a child to speak:

- There must be a desire to communicate.
- The brain must have previously heard and learned words in other contexts.
- The brain must create an idea it wants to communicate to someone else.
- The brain must then send that idea to the mouth.
- The brain must tell the mouth which words to say and which sounds make up those words. Intonation patterns and accented syllables must be incorporated.

- The brain must also send the proper signals to the muscles that produce speech: those that control the tongue, the lips, and the jaw.
- These muscles must have the strength and coordination to carry out the brain's commands.
- The lungs must have sufficient air and the muscles in the chest must be strong enough to force the vocal cords to vibrate. The air must be going out, not in, for functional speech to occur.
- The vocal cords must be in good working condition for speech to sound clear and be loud enough to be heard.
- The words produced must be monitored by his hearing sense. This helps him review what is said and hear new words to imitate in other situations. If words are not heard clearly, speech will be equally "mumbly" when reproduced.
- Another person must be willing to communicate with the child and listen to what he says. If no one is listening and reacting to his speech, he will not be motivated to speak.

For most children, these processes happen naturally, if proper stimulation occurs, without conscious thought. For some children, this sequence breaks down. Once the source of the breakdown is identified, these steps can be facilitated in a direct and conscious manner.

What Is Language?

Language refers to the content of what is spoken, written, read, or understood. Language can also be gestural, as when we use body language or sign language. It is categorized into three areas: receptive, expressive, and social. The ability to comprehend someone else's speech or gestures is called *receptive language*. The ability to create a spoken message that others will understand is called *expressive language*. The way in which language is used with others is called *social language* or *pragmatics*.

In order for children to understand and use spoken language in a meaningful way, these things must happen:

- Their ears must hear well enough for the child to distinguish one word from another.
- Someone must show, or model, what words mean and how sentences are put together.
- The ears must hear intonation patterns, accents, and sentence patterns.
- The brain must have enough intellectual capability to process what those words and sentences mean.

- The brain must be able to store all this information so it can be retrieved later.
- The brain must have a way to re-create words and sentences heard previously when it wants to communicate an idea to someone else.
- Children must have the physical ability to speak in order for the words to be heard and understood when used.
- Children must have a psychological or social need and interest to use these words and communicate with others.
- Another interested person must reinforce attempts at communication.

Children with receptive language problems may have *auditory (listening) disorders* as well, since listening is the most common way we receive language information. It is our brain's input. A child with a receptive language problem may find activities such as listening to classroom lectures, comprehending stories heard or read, following conversations, or remembering oral directions confusing and frustrating at times.

If a child's receptive language is not developed, the entire language learning process stalls before it even begins. Parents tend to be more concerned if their child isn't talking the way they expect, but speech-language pathologists also want to find out if the child is hearing clearly and understanding language. If not, meaningful speech (expressive language) is not going to develop efficiently. That is why "speech" therapy often focuses on strengthening receptive language skills, even if the concern is that the child isn't talking properly.

Speech is the physical process of forming the words; expressive language is what that speech creates—the output, or the product. Even if we have the capability to produce understandable speech sounds, we cannot communicate if what we say is meaningless or confusing to others. We must use words that others can comprehend and put them together in sentences that have order and flow. These words and sentences can be spoken, written, or gestured. Children with expressive language problems may use words incorrectly (e.g., "He falled down"); they may have difficulty organizing and sequencing their thoughts, as well as learning the names of things; and they may dislike engaging in lengthy conversations. It is also not uncommon for children with expressive language problems to have difficulty pronouncing words.

Many children with language problems have difficulty with both receptive and expressive language. They may also possess weak listening skills, since strong listening abilities are needed to receive and develop language.

What Is Listening?

Listening is an active process of hearing and comprehending what is said. As with speech, several steps must occur for a child to listen to speech:

- The child must attend to the speech signal.
- Sound waves must carry the spoken words to his ears.
- The sound must travel through the outer ear canals without obstruction.
- The sound must then pass through the eardrum and the middle ear without being distorted by fluid from colds, infection, or allergies.
- It then must travel through the inner ear, which must be functioning properly as well.
- This sound must travel via the auditory nerve to the brain.
- The brain must try to compare what it hears to previously stored sounds and words to make sense of the message.
- The brain must take in visual information (e.g., lip movements, facial expressions).
- The brain must hold on to the information long enough to process it.

Good listening is as critical a part of the communication process as are speaking clearly and choosing the right words, because communication is a two-way process. One person sends a message, and, ideally, someone else receives it the way it was intended. Who likes to talk to someone who doesn't pay attention to what is said? Who enjoys repeating things over and over without the desired response? Who wants to be misunderstood? No one, of course. A child with a listening disorder will certainly test your patience, but she is probably even more frustrated than you are.

Your child's frustration may translate into behaviors that can be misunderstood as ignoring you, not paying attention, or stupidity. A child with listening problems will have difficulty coping in a classroom situation, because so much of the information teachers give to students must be heard. With the right help, however, a child can learn to cope and to improve listening skills.

If the brain can't stay focused on the task of listening long enough to translate the information, the message will be lost. This is what happens with an *auditory memory* problem. With an *attention deficit* problem, the brain works on too many projects at once and can't stay with a message long enough to finish comprehending it. If the brain has difficulty storing old information, it will not know how to integrate the new information or make sense of it. An *auditory comprehension* or *auditory processing* problem may result. These are examples of just a few listening disorders.

How Do Children Learn to Communicate?

You may think communication begins with a child's first words, but a great deal of preparation must take place before that first word is uttered.

Communication Begins with You

Babies need someone to interact with them and encourage them in a loving way. Placing a baby in front of a television exposes a child to some language, but it's a passive process. A baby needs to be actively engaged with people in order for the communication experience to be meaningful. I can't overstate the importance of a parent's interest in and interaction with a child, from infancy on, in developing a child's communication skills.

The receptors in a child's brain need to be stimulated, particularly during the early learning years. These receptors are stimulated when the child is touched, spoken to, and shown pictures, objects, places, and people. Without proper nurturing, a child may experience learning delays or speech, language, or listening disorders.

In many cases, a parent's stimulation can make the difference between a child with below-average communication skills and one with above-average communication abilities. Information must have a way of getting into the brain. If no one helps to put information in, the brain will not be adept at processing it once information is received in school. *Unfortunately, many children do experience communication problems, regardless of the amount or quality of early stimulation.*

The Communication-Learning Process

Babies practice using their brains to produce the sounds that come out of their mouths. For infants, the first sounds are crying. As infants' lungs and mouths develop strength and control, they can make the cries sound the way they want. They learn to intensify their cries when they are really upset and to temper them when they are just uncomfortable or hungry.

At 3 to 6 months of age, babies experiment with their mouths and find they can make some babbling sounds, which often elicit a lot of attention from the people around them. If they get noticed, they will do it more. They have even more fun when people repeat the sounds back to them. Babies listen to the words people say and try to figure out what they mean.

Sometimes a problem in one of these areas can affect a child's rate of speech and language development. For example, when a child who has had frequent ear infections coupled with a delay in speaking is brought to me, I might suspect that some residual fluid is lingering in the middle ear. This problem needs to be medically resolved in order for meaningful speech to occur. I would urge the parents to take their child to an audiologist and an ear, nose, and throat doctor. If eating and walking were difficult for the child in addition to pronouncing words, a motor problem (difficulty moving muscles normally) might be the underlying culprit. In this case, I would refer the family to a physical or occupational therapist, or even a neurologist.

Your daughter or son must always be seen in terms of the "whole child." By focusing exclusively on individual parts of the child, we cannot know if all the other parts are doing exactly what they should. That is why team evaluations are such a good idea, particularly for infants and preschool children.

Speech, Language, and Listening Milestones

Your child will probably begin to exhibit the following behaviors at the ages shown in the following lists. Use these as a general guide. As stated before, every child is unique. If some skills have not yet developed, read chapter 2 to see if you need to consult a specialist at this time.

Birth to 3 Months
- Reacts to sudden noises by crying or jerking body
- Reacts to familiar objects, such as a bottle, or familiar people, such as parents
- Differentiates the cry of pain from the cry of hunger
- Coos; begins to form prolonged vowels with changes in intonation ("Ahhhh-AH-ahhh!")
- Watches objects intently

3 to 6 Months
- Begins to babble, using syllables with a consonant and a vowel ("Baa-ba-BA-ba-ba!"), and uses intonation changes
- Laughs and shows pleasure when happy
- Turns the head to see where sound is coming from
- Reacts when his or her name is spoken
- Uses a louder voice for crying and babbling than before
- Shows delight when bottle or breast is presented

6 to 9 Months
- Begins to comprehend simple words such as *no*, and looks at family members when they are named

- Babbles with a singsong pattern at times
- Controls babbling to two syllables, which sometimes sounds like words such as *Mama,* although meaning is, typically, not yet understood by the baby
- Understands facial expressions and reacts to them
- Attempts gestures to correspond to "Pat-a-cake" and "Bye-bye"
- Shakes head to show *no*
- Uses more and more sounds when babbling, such as syllables with *da, ba, ka, pa, ma,* and *wa*
- Typical utterances at this age: "Ga-MA-ma-ga!"

9 to 12 Months
- Has fun imitating simple sounds and babbling
- Begins to say "Mama" or "Dada" or another word, sometimes
- Begins to understand that words represent objects
- Jabbers loudly and will try to "talk" to you with some intent, even though the speech is not meaningful yet
- Responds to music
- Gives or seeks a toy or a common object when requested
- Imitates common animal sounds
- Gestures and whines to request something
- Looks directly at the source of sound immediately
- Will watch and imitate what you do—loves your attention!
- Typical utterances at this age: "Ah buh-BUH-buh . . . ooooh!"

12 to 18 Months
- Understands 50 to 75 words
- Uses 3 to 20 "real" words, even if they are not produced completely clearly
- Will point to the right place or answer ("Bed") when asked questions ("Where's your pillow?")
- Points to known objects when named, such as in a photo book ("Where's the cat?")
- Points to a few simple body parts, such as eyes and nose ("Where's your nose?")
- Babbles and uses nonsense words while pointing
- Follows simple one-step commands
- Makes animal noises when asked ("What does the cow say?")
- Uses words like *more, all gone, mine,* and *down*
- Imitates words
- Wants to show you things and share experiences

- Pronounces some understandable words
- Typical utterances at this age:
  "Mama!"
  "No!"
  "Daddy, doppit!" (stop it)
  "Appuh" (apple)
  "Gimme da!" (Give me that.)
  "Baw" (ball)
  "Too-duh" (toothbrush)

18 Months to 2 Years

- Comprehends about 300 words
- Uses about 50 recognizable words, mostly nouns
- Speaks often with mostly "real" words now, but still babbles and uses jargon some of the time
- Uses language to get needs met ("I want . . . "), to protest ("No, Mommy!"), to exclaim ("Uh-oh!"), and to entertain parents or seek a reaction, often with "silly talk"
- Wants you to read the same stories over and over again or wants to play the same game with you ("More!" or "Again!")
- Can point to pictures in a storybook when asked simple questions such as "Who's sleeping?," "Where are the shoes?," "Who has a balloon?"
- Uses a rising intonation pattern to show a question, even if the words are mostly jargon. The question is directed to someone specific much of the time.
- Nods or shakes head to answer yes/no questions and looks for your response when asked a question such as "Do you want more milk?" rather than simply grabbing the desired item when it's offered
- Can nod/shake head or tell you yes/no when you hold up a common, familiar object such as a spoon and ask a question about its name, such as "Is this a ball? (child shakes head); "Is it a *cat*?" (child says no); "Is it a *spoon*?" (child nods or says yeah/yes)
- Can follow two related commands, such as "Come here and give me your cup" if in the mood or attending to you (cooperation is variable at this stage)
- Points to the body parts of other family members or stuffed animals in close proximity when asked ("Where are Mommy's eyes?," "Where's the cat's nose?"). Cooperation and attention may be variable, but the key here is that your child differentiates "Mommy's eyes" from his or her own eyes, which requires attending not only to the word *eyes* but also to both the location and the body part.

- Uses language functionally and in situational contexts, not just for rote naming of objects or letters in a familiar book. For example, your child spontaneously says "cow" when playing with a toy cow, not just when looking at flash cards or at a book he has "learned."
- Begins to use some verbs (*eat, want, go, sleep, gimme*) and adjectives (*big, little*) in addition to nouns
- Joins two related words to make one word, such as "Geddown!" for "Get down" or "Stoppit" for "Stop it."
- Starts to ask the names of things that are unknown, such as, "What dat?" or "What dis?" or "Dis?" with an accompanying finger point and rising intonation
- Speaks at an appropriate volume (e.g., not whispering or mumbling so much that speech is rarely distinguishable, though it's still often very difficult to understand)
- Can answer "What's your name?"
- Joins in nursery rhymes and songs, but often gets just a word or two at the right time
- Attends to your facial reactions—shows unhappiness (or delight if in a devilish mood) if you are upset or mad, and often checks to see what you think of his actions. For example, he bangs a pan loudly with a spoon, then stops and looks at you to see your reaction.
- Speaks with many pauses between words; speech may be choppy and halting much of the time
- Typical utterances at this age:
  "Dawddie bad!" (Doggie bad.)
  "Go 'way!" (Go away.)
  "No, Mommy."
  "See . . . horsey . . . . Daddy . . . horsey cry!"
  "Danwit . . . goo' . . . Mommy." (Sandwich good, Mommy.)
  "Nigh'-nigh' now?" (Night-night now?)
  "Go dore?" (Go store?)

2 to 3 Years
- Understands about 900 words
- Uses about 500 words
- Speech is understandable 50 to 70 percent of the time
- Usually engages in eye contact during conversations with family members
- Uses language to seek information ("What is it?"), to express frustration or reluctance ("I don't wanna go!"), to clarify what was heard

("Mommy, we go store now?"), and to make observations about what's happening or what she sees ("That's a big cat!")

- Understands *my/your* ("Where's *my* foot? Where's *your* foot?") and makes the association with the person it is referencing without you pointing or using the child's name to clarify
- Makes frustrations known more with words and less with temper tantrums and crying
- Can find an object you describe by function ("Which one can you read?") from a group of three to four common objects, such as an apple, a car, a book, and a doll
- Wants to show you things and get your attention constantly, using words ("Look . . . Daddy . . . in dat little car!")
- Answers simple questions beginning with *who, where,* and *what* ("Who drives a fire truck?") about picture books or general knowledge
- Understands and uses prepositions such as *in, on,* and *under*
- Begins to ask yes/no questions ("It raining?")
- Understands basic categorical words ("Can you find an *animal*?")
- Prefers to play with other people much of the time and seeks them out for interaction if available; parallel play typical in the 2-year-old (side by side with others—watching what they do, copying) blossoms into more interactive play by age 3
- Uses toys for simple imaginative play (driving a car, giving food to a teddy bear, having a doll sleep on a bed) instead of just throwing them, stacking them, or swinging them around
- May talk to self while playing, but will also relate to nearby children and adults without prompting
- Begins to use auxiliary verbs such as *is* ("Ball is red.")
- Begins to use past tense verbs (*walked, kicked*)
- "Stutters" when excited sometimes, by repeating whole words ("I-can-I can-I-can play now?")
- Pronounces these sounds consistently in words: *m, n, p, f, b, d, h, y, m*
- Typical utterances at this age:
  "Daddy's tar so big!" (Daddy's car so big.)
  "Mommy put dat downdairs?" (Mommy put that downstairs?)
  "Oh no! My-my-my jeth iddirty!" (Oh no! My dress is dirty.)
  "You wanna'nana, An' Pat?" (You want a banana, Aunt Pat?)
  "I doe wannit!" (I don't want it.)
  "Mattchew's yeg beedin'!" (Matthew's leg bleeding.)
  "Duh wabbit eated duh cawit!" (The rabbit eated the carrot.)

3 to 4 Years

- Begins to use *is* at beginning of questions
- Understands about 1,200 words
- Uses about 800 words
- Uses eye contact more consistently during conversations
- Asks many questions, usually *what* or *who* questions
- Understands and uses pronouns such as *his/her, he/she, we/they* ("Give this to *him*.")
- Understands positional words such as *in front, behind, up, down, top, bottom*
- Starts to use *s* on verbs to show present tense ("He *runs*.")
- Uses contractions *won't* and *can't*
- Uses *and*
- Uses plurals consistently (*books, toys*)
- Uses *are,* or contracted form, with plural nouns ("Kids're playing outside.")
- Initiates conversations, making comments or observations directed to someone specific
- Asks many questions, sometimes the same one several times in a few minutes
- Understands negation ("Which one *isn't* on the bed?")
- Follows a simple plot in a children's storybook; can look at the pictures and tell you the story in a simple way
- Sits down and does one activity for ten to fifteen minutes
- "Stutters" less frequently
- Pronounces the beginning, middle, and ending sounds in words, except for consonant blends (e.g., *bl, fr, cr*)
- Speaks understandably 70 to 80 percent of the time
- Uses *k* and *g* sounds correctly, but *s* may still be somewhat "lispy" sounding; *r* and *l* may be distorted; *v, sh, ch, j,* and *th* still may not be used consistently
- Engages most often in motor-based play (taking turns on the slide and ride-on toys) and building (towers, Legos, Play-Doh), but is drawn to participate and copy what peers are doing
- Uses language to negotiate turn-taking ("First I go, then it's your turn") and influence outcomes ("I'll clean up later! I'm tired now!")
- Typical utterances at this age:
  "The bider ith cwawlin' up duh twee!" (The spider is crawling up the tree!)
  "Dad, the tiddy-tat breaked the diss." (Dad, the kitty-cat breaked the dish.)

"Is Mom-Mom comin' today?"

"Where's the hop-sital?" (Where's the hospital?)

"Yesterday my dog Wainbow ate six bixkits." (Yesterday my dog Rainbow ate six biscuits.)

4 to 5 Years

- Comprehends 2,500 to 2,800 words
- Uses 1,500 to 2,000 words
- Speaks clearly 80 to 90 percent of the time
- Uses language to retell events and reminisce about things that happened in the past ("Mommy, remember when we went to Grandma's and she made banana bread?"), to wonder ("Why is the sky blue?"), and connect two ideas or events ("After we went to the game, we went out for pizza.")
- Can look at pictures in a storybook and make up a simple story or retell it, with mostly complete sentences ("Then the monkey ate the banana. The monkey said, 'Hey, where's my banana?'")
- Makes up stories, sometimes with stuffed animals, dolls, or action figures ("Judy's cold, Mommy. I need to find her blanket! Here you go, Judy. Okay, Judy, what should we get for Bear's birthday?")
- Uses all pronouns (*he, she, I, you, them*) correctly
- Describes what you do with common objects, such as a hat ("What do you do with a hat?" "You wear it on your head!")
- Uses past, present, and future tenses of regular verbs (*watch, watched, will/gonna watch*)
- Uses many irregular verbs (*drank/ate*) and irregular nouns (*teeth, feet*) but sometimes mixes up the correct forms ("She falled down.")
- Follows commands with three to four critical elements ("Find the yellow truck and put it behind your chair.")
- Knows common opposites such as *big/little, heavy/light*
- Likes to chitchat with others throughout the day
- Repeats a sentence with 10 to 12 syllables, such as, "The big boy sat on the green chair by the door."
- Listens and attends to stories, conversations, and movies
- May mispronounce *s, r, th, l, v, sh, ch, j,* and consonant blends such as *st*
- Typical utterances at this age:

  "Daddy, I wanna go to Joey's house after lunch 'cause he's got this great new truck I wanna play wif [with]."

  "Is this your pocketbook? Could I thee [see] what you have inside it? Do you have any gum in there?"

"I found all these wed [red] marbles on José's floor, Mommy. Can I have them? I wanna play with them for a little while."

5 to 7 Years: The Refinement Years
- Refines pronunciation, sentence structure, word use, attention span for listening, and memory for directions
- Increases vocabulary; incorporates new words into spontaneous speech
- Retells stories; explains experiences more, in a cohesive, sequential manner and with greater elaboration
- Participates in group discussions and takes turns in conversation; comments are more relative to topic being discussed
- Begins to learn language relationships: opposites (*big/little, sad/happy*), synonyms (*big/large, sad/unhappy*), associations *(bread/butter, pencil/eraser)*, and classification (*shirt/pants/socks* belong in the category of *clothing*)
- Typical utterances at this age:
  "Last week Daddy took me and Levonne to the Bronx Zoo."
  "You shoulda seen the monkeys and elephants!"
  "On the way home, we stopped at the hospital to see Mrs. Stro . . . strogin . . . hausen . . . something like that—she's Daddy's friend from work."
  "She has 'amonia and she's really sick, so she has to stay in the hopsital for another week."

When children begin school, language is translated into written symbols through spelling and is comprehended through reading. Written words are developed into sentences and stories. Children whose oral language is deficient (beyond the typical errors a child of this age displays) are at risk for reading, writing, and spelling problems. However, teachers are trained to teach children in a way that best suits their individual needs. So although communication problems may present a challenge, they certainly can be managed with a little bit of teamwork, creativity, and patience!

7 Years to Adolescence
- Possesses a functional and abstract language system
- Shows age-appropriate skills in reading, writing, speaking, and listening
- Shows less vagueness and groping for words
- Joins sentences to form coherent, descriptive thoughts and stories; listeners are not left confused

- Masters word relationships (synonyms, antonyms, association, classification, etc.)
- Pronounces multisyllabic words correctly once practiced a few times
- Comprehends information heard and read when adequately taught and explained
- Understands and uses more idioms (*"pain in the neck,"* *"out of your mind"*)
- Understands plots with increasing depth and complexity when read or watched in a movie or television show
- Typical utterances at this age:
  "I really don't understand how they put this model together, Mom."
  "Do you think anyone will notice if I wear my old shirt to the basketball game?"

Essentially, a child's language at this age mirrors an adult's, but with more simplicity.

These, then, are the milestones, the points of progress children should reach in their own style, at their own pace. The next chapter details the warning signs that signal your child may be having more than normal trouble in developing communication skills. Read on to find out how to recognize these signals and what to do to help your child deal with special problems.

2

Does Your Child Need Help?

The Warning Signs

If you have any questions at all regarding your child's speech, language, and listening development, it's almost always best to be on the safe side and pursue a professional opinion. This may sound simplistic, but it is important. Don't assume your child will "outgrow the problem," although many children do in time. Where do you find such a professional? Most likely at your local elementary school. All U.S. school systems must provide free screening for children if a parent is concerned, even before the child has entered school. The legal mandate comes from the Individuals with Disabilities Education Act (IDEA), Public Law 101–476. If you have health insurance or can afford to pay out of pocket, a private practice may also be a good choice. You have nothing to lose by seeking help, and everything to gain.

When to Get Help

Children usually learn to talk in a natural way, by listening and repeating what they hear. Learning speech and language, however, does not come "naturally" for every child. Your child may need a different approach if he or she has a speech or language disorder. And earlier is *almost always* better.

There are cases where a child *is* better left alone, particularly when stuttering or pronunciation problems are involved. But you should have a better idea about when to give a child some time to grow out of a speech problem after you read this book.

22

If you have concerns about your child's speech, language, or listening development, here are some good reasons why you should consider pursuing a professional opinion now, just to be sure:

- Research shows that a child whose language delay is identified early has a significantly better chance of developing necessary prereading and academic skills than a child whose delay is not identified early.
- Children who are self-conscious about their speech can develop self-esteem problems. That said, my experience shows that young children are often less aware of their speech problems. Thus they can be successfully remediated, in many cases, before they even realize their speech is different.
- From a practical point of view, it is better to assess and treat children prior to their entering school. Research continues to show that younger children have a keener ability to adapt to newly learned speech and language patterns. In many cases, children may not need therapy anymore by the time they reach kindergarten. By starting early, parents avoid the dilemma of having their child pulled out from class for services or the struggle to find time to implement therapy exercises after school, when homework and sports are scheduled.
- You may unintentionally hinder rather than help your child by insisting that she imitate sounds or words before she's ready. A professional can tell you how to help your child without causing frustration or loss of self-esteem.
- In many cases, the speech-language pathologist may simply put your mind at ease by telling you that your child's "problem" is a very normal stage of development.

What Is the "Right Age" to Seek Help?

Unfortunately, there is no universal age at which parents should seek professional help for a speech, language, or listening problem, because every child is developmentally unique. Also, some problems are less pronounced than others and only become noticeable when a child is a little older. Hearing problems or brain injuries can occur at any age. Nevertheless, your child's communication skills can be observed by speech-language professionals and compared to those of children who are "developing normally" for that age. Within that relative framework, your speech-language pathologist can help you determine whether your child's communication represents a typical maturational speech or language pattern or displays warning signs that you must investigate further.

Case Study: Tawana

I saw Tawana when she was 2 years old, and though she did not have advanced speech skills, she was still within that broad spectrum of what we call "average." Her language skills, however, were on the lower end of the average range, so I gave her parent some activities to do at home to give her a little boost. I asked to see Tawana again in six to eight months, just to make sure she was progressing as she should. When I saw Tawana again eight months later, she still basically spoke as she had at age 2. Of course, what is normal for a child at age 2 years, 8 months is a little more advanced than for a child who just turned 2. So Tawana's language skills were now considered below average. She had not kept up with her peers as we had hoped.

Should I have known Tawana would have problems? Should Tawana have been receiving aggressive speech therapy to prevent such problems? Did we wait too long? The answer to all these questions is no. Tawana received help at the appropriate time. Her development in other areas was age-appropriate, she had no health problems, there was no family history of communication problems, and her parents were educated, nurturing people. Tawana's parents brought her in to see me as soon as they became concerned. This early intervention allowed me to keep a careful eye on her progress and to introduce help when it was appropriate and could benefit Tawana the most.

Unfortunately, predicting whether a child will have problems at a later age is usually difficult, if not impossible. We can merely examine what the child is doing *now,* stimulate growth as much as we can, and monitor progress carefully. Subjecting a child to preventive therapy in the absence of the conditions I described in the preceding case is not helpful or appropriate.

The age at which a child needs therapy depends on the child and the nature and degree of the problem. Many times a child falls into a gray area—there may be deficits in a few speech or language areas, but the child is within normal limits overall. That child may in time catch up and pass her peers, or she may fall farther behind. Without a family history of problems or other variables present, there is no way to know what the future will bring. In these situations, the child's cooperation and the logistics and availability of services may determine whether or not to intervene.

If you are concerned, it's best to call a professional and schedule an assessment. Chapter 3 explains the assessment process.

Should You Wait until Your Child Goes to School?

When mulling over your concerns, bear in mind that a child who has a speech, language, or listening problem upon entering kindergarten will be at a distinct disadvantage for learning and participating in class.

The following are just a few of the ways speech, language, and listening skills are crucial to success in school:

- The ability to follow directions in a group setting requires an adequate attention span, knowledge of basic concepts, good hearing, and memory for spoken language.
- Learning how to sound out words and associate letters with sounds also requires good hearing, memory for sounds, and an understanding of how sounds make up words and change their meaning.
- Understanding the plot to a story requires the ability to process language and integrate previously learned words with new ones.
- Making up a story or explaining something as simple as "Show and Tell" requires the ability to put words together with organization and use a speech pattern that is understandable to others.

Getting help before kindergarten does not guarantee a trouble-free school experience. If there is a problem, however, early intervention will give your child a head start on working out a solution.

Can an Intelligent Child Have a Speech, Language, or Listening Problem?

Don't make the mistake of confusing intelligence with speech, language, or listening skills. Although children with limited intellectual abilities do have limited communication skills, children with delayed communication skills do not necessarily have below-average intelligence; in fact they can have average to superior intelligence. These children can be gifted and talented in many, many ways. *By pursuing a speech-language evaluation, you are not questioning your child's intelligence.* A psychologist performs IQ testing, which measures a child's intellectual ability. These are two related but separate issues.

Some parents in the United States are reluctant to have their child tested for fear of having the child "labeled" by the school system. In fact, a child who is being tested is *not* labeled as a "special education" student unless the evaluation shows a need for services and the parent consents. If your child does need help, please know *the label of "special education" has no relationship to the child's IQ.* These days, special education covers a wide range of services that meet a child's individual needs. In many cases, children with high IQ scores also have special needs.

Warning Signs to Look For

Most parents I see are quite perceptive about their children. They often discount their observations or fears but are usually right on target. *Trust those gut feelings.* You may not know the professional lingo, but you know when something is just not "right." In addition, the following warning signs can guide you in determining whether your child may need special help for a communication problem.

Signs of a Receptive Language Problem

As we discussed in chapter 1, receptive language refers to how well a child understands and remembers what is said. The following behaviors may signal a receptive language problem:

• *Your toddler doesn't respond to her name.* "Tuning out" is often the first sign that a child isn't attending to speech signals the way we'd like. You shouldn't need to keep repeating your child's name or physically turn her head to elicit eye contact when you are attempting to talk to her unless there is something unusually interesting going on!

• *Your toddler/preschooler finds objects much more interesting than people.* From the time babies are first aware, their greatest thrills should be to elicit reactions from those around them and to direct interest ("Look!") and attention to themselves. Making goofy faces and sounds together should evoke interest and giggles. A lack of interest in you will likely translate in less interest in or motivation for talking. If your child likes to pull out toys and objects but not necessarily to play interactively with you, that's a big red flag.

• *Your preschooler doesn't listen to stories.* While your child may like to flip pages or look at—and even name—the pictures in a book, letting you hold and read the story itself may be a challenge. These children may strongly prefer books without actual stories, such as books of animals, counting books, or color/shape books. This can often be interpreted as disinterest, but in fact the indifference could be due to difficulty processing the auditory information he hears, since storybooks require a higher level of language processing than do books that target single-word concepts.

• *Your child has difficulty with reading comprehension once she is able to read.* While remedial reading tutoring is helpful, the problem may be language-based and require additional expertise and treatment from a speech-language pathologist.

• *Your child withdraws from social conversation or tries to develop relationships through physical activities.* The athletic child who can play for hours on the playground with friends may be uncomfortable when the activities turn to conversation. As children become older, social interaction is less activity-related and the problem may become more pronounced.

• *Your child may be very "forgetful."* Your child might appear to hear what someone is saying but really does forget what he or she is supposed to do. This behavior can often be construed as willful disobedience or "laziness." I have met very few "lazy" children. Often a legitimate reason, beyond their control, accounts for their lack of follow-through. Once you know why your child is "forgetting," you can learn how to communicate in a way your child can understand and remember.

• *Your child misconstrues what others are saying to her.* This some-times causes hurt feelings or "acting out" behaviors. *Acting out* refers to any aggressive physical behavior, such as kicking, throwing, pushing, or hitting.

• *Your child has difficulty following directions.* Remembering what to do and doing it in the right order is hard for a child with a receptive language problem. Processing too much language at once can get confusing. Often the child may compensate by copying what other children are doing, pretending to know what to do (but often doing it incorrectly), or fooling around so he or she can avoid the task altogether.

Signs of an Expressive Language Problem

As discussed in chapter 1, expressive language refers to what the child is able to say and how it is said. The following behaviors may signal an expressive language problem:

• *Your child seldom initiates conversations and tends to give short answers to your questions.* This can sometimes be misconstrued as indicating a "shy" personality.

• *Your child overgeneralizes names of things.* For example, all drinks may be "juice" to a 4-year-old instead of more specifically "lemonade" or "iced tea." An 11-year-old may identify a bracelet as a "thing on your hand."

• *Your child may talk in circles.* This tendency makes it difficult to make heads or tails of a story or an explanation. The sequence of what happened may be backward or unclear. Very young children do this, but by age 6 or 7 this should be greatly improved.

• *Your child has difficulty remembering the names of people, places, and things.* This difficulty can be particularly noticeable in school when your child is studying for and taking tests. Filling in blanks becomes overwhelming.

• *Your child has difficulty putting sentences together with enough words or with the right words, or in the right order.* The words may have no endings to show plurals ("Three car outside"), possessives ("Sally house is nice"), or the past tense ("He work yesterday"). Some words may be left out; for example, "Mommy dress not on a bed." This type of sentence is typical for a toddler but not for a child 4 years old or older.

Red Flag: Recurrent Ear Infections

If your child has had frequent ear infections, you should be on guard for possible delays in speech, language, and listening skills. Frequent, protracted ear infections are sometimes associated with delays in these skills years after the infections have cleared.

More and more, research is showing that even a very mild loss or change of hearing clarity in one ear can significantly affect a child's ability to process speech. I experienced this firsthand with my son, who at age 5 began constantly saying "What?" In class he had difficulty following during whole-group instruction. Once we addressed the fluid in his ears, his ability to process language and focus returned to normal.

Red Flag: Play Skills

How a child plays can tell us a lot about his interests and communication style. In the early years, a baby's primary interest should be *you*: imitating you, touching your face, trying to get your attention, laughing at you, and following your lead in both noises and actions. While a baby is also intently interested in exploring the senses (touch, smell, taste), she is checking in with you frequently during that process. For example, if your 12-month-old picks up and tastes something that she thinks is "yucky," she should quickly look up at you and make a face, as if to say, "Hey, Mom, that's pretty yucky!" It's a shared experience along the sensory journey. Repetitive games, such as peekaboo and "copycat," should elicit a reaction or laughter. Why? Because normally developing babies should be seeking interaction with you. Baby wants to bang on a pan with a spoon? It's great fun! She should be looking back at you to "check in" and share the experience. Your baby should also be routinely pointing at something as if to say, "Hey, look at that!" by 15 to 18 months.

During the toddler years, your child should be able to put together simple wooden knob puzzles, finding the matching pieces and taking them out. Push and pull toys should be introduced, with your child curious as to how they work. When doing something is a challenge, does your child look to you for help? Or does he just discard toys and lose interest quickly, moving on to something else as soon as a task becomes frustrating? Toddlers who don't take those opportunities to interact with you to share their frustration or seek help are a concern. While our long-term goal is for independence, children who *prefer* to play by themselves or get whatever they want or need without assistance may lack appropriate communication skills.

During the preschool years, take a look at how your child is playing with toys. Is he making the toy cow say "Moo" or pretend to eat some grass? Or is he just lining it up, stacking it, or throwing it? How a child moves and manipulates toys such as cars and stuffed animals tells us how she is interacting with the environment. Typical play should have some imagination—making the toy act "real" and move. Your child should also be bugging you—or a sibling or a friend—to play too, at least for some of the time. With play at this age, there should be a bit of talking going on—perhaps even when no one is actually there! Spontaneous comments, including simple compliments and exclamations ("Wow, you did it!"), should be flowing naturally.

During later preschool years, "pretend games" are popular, such as, "You be the cat and I'll be the dog." This requires interacting with others and communicating with pronouns and some perspective-taking. It also requires some verbal negotiating and compromise. Simple board games such as Candyland are especially popular by ages 4 to 6, with the child understanding the turn-taking concept, as well as the concept of winning and losing. Is your child engaging in this kind of imaginative play? Can he sustain attention and patience to follow a simple board game with another child?

By the time your child is in grade school, there should be some development of special friends, with the children doing the initiating and organizing of the "playdates" more and more, with adult consent. However, a child with weak listening skills may find this confusing at times ("I think she said I'm supposed to sleep over her house on Thursday night . . . or was it Friday night?"), and a child with weak expressive skills may find it hard to have those kinds of conversations. Understanding the rules of games may be hard for children with processing problems

("I'm supposed to move this red piece—where?"). As conversational language becomes a bigger part of daily social interactions, children with weak receptive/expressive language or auditory processing skills can find it hard to keep up with the quick pace of fast-talking peers or to organize their thoughts quickly enough to jump in and explain what *they* thought of the movie last weekend. Red flags in this area of social pragmatic weaknesses tend to be related to children who act very differently around peers (much more introverted) than with family, or who act or think in a way that is different from their peers. (See chapter 6 for more information on this topic.)

Red Flag: Behavior Problems

Research shows that many children diagnosed as "emotionally disturbed" or who display other antisocial behavior have poor language and listening skills. It is sometimes difficult to know whether these communication problems *caused* the behavioral problem or whether they simply are a small piece of a larger puzzle for these particular children. Regardless, to help them develop their language and listening skills, they need the same understanding and treatment as is given to other children with communication problems.

Children with speech and language problems that go unaddressed sometimes cope by expressing their feelings and frustrations through their fists instead of through words. Their self-esteem can suffer, which can adversely affect their whole perception of themselves, their willingness to participate in class, and their ability to have a relaxed conversation with peers. Sometimes that "class clown" is merely trying to joke his way out of not understanding the question or conversation.

Therefore, whenever a child has consistently poor social behavior, a thorough learning disabilities and speech-language evaluation should be performed as part of any testing battery. These problems can be overlooked or referred solely to a psychologist. Although counseling and behavior modification are very appropriate methods of dealing with the behavioral symptoms, you may not be getting to the root cause of the behavior.

In my experience, many students demonstrate noticeable improvement in their behavior once their educational program is adjusted to meet their needs and they have been reassured that they are not "stupid" or "lazy." Once parents understand why their child is not following their directions or remembering conversations from breakfast, they are less apt to get angry or feel the child is deliberately ignoring them. After a language or listening problem has been properly diagnosed, a parent can learn how to communicate better with the child in a way that is less confusing and frustrating for both of them.

Other Warning Signs

Additionally, the presence of any of the following behaviors may be a warning sign of a possible speech, language, or listening problem. You should be concerned if your child:

Birth to 12 Months
- Avoids eye contact; prefers to look at objects rather than at people
- Rarely babbles; is unusually quiet
- Doesn't respond to whispered speech consistently
- Shows little interest in imitating gestures, such as waving "bye-bye"
- Cries or screams often
- Shows little emotion—is very "flat"
- Struggles with the transition to solid foods, choking, frequently spitting out food, or preferring soft foods only

12 to 18 Months
- Avoids eye contact
- Doesn't look up or attend when his name is called
- Doesn't look at parents' faces for feedback when sharing an experience
- Is quiet most of the time, rarely attempting to imitate or produce words
- Tunes out others frequently—ignores your questions or bids for attention
- Doesn't say "Mama" or "Dada" consistently yet (by 15 months) to call you and get your attention
- Uses primarily vowels ("ee-ee-oh-uh!") when vocalizing
- Is unable to point to common body parts when asked, such as with "Where's your nose?"
- Makes a lot of sounds, but does not have a consistent label for a variety of words
- Says one syllable and points to everything, such as "Duh!" (jargoning very limited in the variation of consonants and vowels used)
- Seems to "have" a new word, but often stops using it

18 to 24 Months
- Doesn't look at you for more than a few seconds at a time
- Can't name common household objects such as a phone, brush, chair,

or spoon; may be able to do so in a learned context, such as in a favorite book or on a flash card, but doesn't associate it with other representations of the actual objects

- Doesn't look at parents' or peers' faces for feedback when sharing an experience, such as looking at a lion roaring at a zoo and then at you, as if to say, "Did you see that?"
- Doesn't try to shake/nod his head when asked a question such as, "Do you want a carrot?" Instead, may grab it rather than communicating with you
- Has difficulty pointing to items you name ("Where's the bird?") in photographs, with actual objects, or in very realistic pictures
- Prefers to wander around the house, with little regard for what others are doing or where they are
- Does not call out to you to ask a question or show you things
- When you point to something, looks at your hand but not at the object you are pointing to; may ignore your pointing completely
- Repeats part of a question, but doesn't answer it
- Says only a few words, and tends to use the same phrases over and over, such as "Dih-dih duh!"
- Will name pictures in a book, but doesn't use the words out of that context
- Has difficulty sitting and attending to a book if you are holding it and telling a story
- Amount of speech is not growing as quickly as it should
- Drooling quite a bit; messy eater; mouth often open
- Uses primarily nouns with few verbs or connectors ("Boy . . . duck!" "Food . . . water.")

24 to 36 Months
- Doesn't say "Look!" or call your name to show you something
- Doesn't point to show you things
- Doesn't spontaneously exclaim, such as "Uh-oh!" or "Oops!" when a mistake is made or "Wow!" when delighted or amazed
- Uses mostly nouns when talking ("Dog . . . house . . . Mommy!"), leaving out action words and descriptors
- Is quiet when playing—very little chatter, commenting, or self-talk
- Doesn't try to make stuffed animals, puppets, or dolls "talk" when playing; may move them but doesn't incorporate meaningful speaking or imagination into play
- Repeats part of a question, but doesn't answer it directly with yes/no ("Do you want milk?" "Milk.")

- Doesn't put short two- to three-word phrases together; speaks in primarily one- to two-word phrases
- Has difficulty sitting and attending to a book if it has a story (prefers only nonfiction books with objects, letters, or numbers; may insist on holding the book and quickly flipping through the pages himself, sometimes while naming items)
- Is very difficult to understand when talking much/most of the time
- Doesn't play with toys normally (e.g., focuses on the wheels of a toy car and spins them repeatedly, rather than moving the car and making car noises; lines up cars or toys over and over instead of playing with them using imagination)

Preschool Age (3 to 5 Years)
- Speaks differently from other children of the same age; is difficult to understand
- Speaks in short phrases instead of complete sentences most of the time
- Has difficulty maintaining eye contact when listening or speaking
- Is disinterested or detached from other children of the same age when playing *or* is interested in playing with others but is mostly parallel playing (side by side) and not interacting or speaking much; generally prefers to play "alone"
- Talks and interacts normally at home, but verbalizes very little out of his "comfort zone"
- Doesn't talk much about things that happened in the past or "explain" well (such as why she's crying or what happened to the broken toy)
- Makes noises ("Dih-duh-duh!") or uses gestures to express needs instead of using words and sentences
- Leaves out functor words such as *the, a, is, did, to, for, from*, and *with* ("He playing a car!")
- Leaves off endings of words ("He jum ah the slie" for "He jumped off the slide.")
- Doesn't use plurals (says, "I have two car" instead of "I have two cars.")
- Doesn't use possessives (says, "Mommy hat is green" instead of "Mommy's hat is green.")
- Confuses basic positional words, such as *on/in, under/on, top/bottom, next to, in front, behind*. (When you ask him to put an object in the box, he puts it next to the box instead, unless you point.)
- Uses the incorrect pronoun for *he* and *she* (e.g., "*Him* took my ball!")

- Has difficulty at preschool during "Circle Time"; tends to tune out and not participate when in a group
- Has difficulty listening to a story read to a group during "Story Time" at the library or at preschool/day care
- Watches what others are doing; needs repetitions, demonstrations, or to see gestures before attempting to follow directions out of the normal routine
- Forgets or routinely confuses the names of familiar teachers, classmates, and family friends
- Overgeneralizes object names by using one word for all related items (e.g., all drinks are called "juice")

School Age (5 to 12 Years)
- Speaks differently from other children of the same age
- Experiences difficulty with reading, writing, or spelling
- Struggles with phonics, blending sounds, and rhyming concepts
- Has difficulty passing tests, even after studying
- Forgets the meaning of new words
- Gropes to put words together or avoids in-depth conversations
- Has difficulty comprehending written or oral information easily
- Mispronounces multisyllabic words or new words unless they are repeated and practiced many times
- Sounds "babyish" or awkward at times when speaking
- Is easily distracted
- Is animated at home, but extremely reserved or reluctant to talk in other settings
- Needs verbal directions repeated
- Often says "I don't know what I'm supposed to do" after listening to directions
- Uses vague language to retell a story or an event, leaving the listener confused (e.g., "That guy over there, and that big thing was next to that stuff.")
- Has significant difficulty "reading" facial expressions, body language, and tone of voice
- Jumps from topic to topic or makes unrelated comments during a conversation
- Has a favorite topic and steers most conversations to it—ignores disinterest
- Has difficulty "getting started" or answering at all when asked an open-ended question such as "Can you tell me about the movie?"
- Omits endings from words; leaves out or distorts sounds

- Displays behavioral or social problems—plays alone or has very few interests shared by other children the same age
- Sounds hoarse or uses too deep a tone when speaking
- Stutters

Again, if your child displays *any* of the warning signs discussed in this chapter, you should call a specialist to discuss your concerns. In the United States, talk to your pediatrician if other areas besides speech and language are delayed (particularly if your child is under age 2). Call a speech pathologist when your child's problem is only speech or language delays. Chapter 3 describes whom to call and how to find them. At that point the specialist can determine whether a personal meeting with your child is appropriate.

In Canada, talk to your physician if the child has not yet entered school, because speech therapy is handled as a Ministry of Education or Ministry of Health concern. Each province's protocol varies once the child reaches school. This is discussed further in chapter 3.

3

Having Your Child Evaluated

Once you've noticed some of the warning signs outlined in chapter 2, the next step is to talk to a professional. Many times a simple phone conversation is all you will need to put your mind at rest. However, in most cases the specialist needs to see your child in person to decide whether a full evaluation is warranted. But where do you start? Whom do you call? And how do you know this person is qualified? This chapter discusses how to choose the right person to give your son or daughter the appropriate help. First, I define the various types of professionals available and assist you in sorting out the different titles they may go by. Next, I identify the settings in which these individuals work—private practices, public schools, hospitals, college speech clinics, agencies—listing the advantages and disadvantages of each. Finally, I describe the evaluation process itself and detail the components of the informal and formal tests your child is likely to be given.

Whom to See

As discussed earlier in this book, many different professionals are available to help children experiencing communication delays. However, if your *primary* concern is your child's speech, spoken language, comprehension, or processing of spoken language, it makes the most sense to start with a *speech-language pathologist (SLP)*. Once an evaluation has been completed, the speech pathologist will know whether a referral to another professional is in order. For infants and toddlers, a team evaluation may be standard procedure in your area; this allows the professionals to look at your child from different perspectives and put their collective heads together. This eliminates a lot of running around and waiting for appointments.

In Canada, speech therapy is considered the domain of the Ministry of Education or the Ministry of Health. In most provinces you should talk to your doctor first or to the child's teacher if you have a concern. Some school systems in Canada have speech therapists assigned to the school through the Ministry of Education or work with the Ministry of Health, which provides the therapy at a hospital. Staffing is much more limited than in the United States, and in many cases SLPs have long waiting lists. Often other professionals in the school, such as the classroom teacher or a special education teacher, help facilitate speech and language development, with the speech pathologist acting as a consultant.

In both the United States and Canada, a special education teacher (also known in some regions as a *learning disabilities consultant*) may be consulted to see whether other *learning disabilities* exist that might get in the way of reading and writing the written forms of language. A psychologist can be helpful in assessing whether language use is being affected by emotional issues or whether the child has intellectual limitations. Usually a psychologist and/or a special education teacher are the primary professionals involved with *attention deficit disorder (ADD)* problems, with the speech-language pathologist contributing as a consultant or related service. This may also be true in some cases for children displaying autistic tendencies or those with mental retardation.

An *audiologist* should assist in treating a child with a hearing or *auditory processing disorder.* An *occupational therapist* is trained to facilitate development of fine motor skills, which can affect feeding as well as speaking.

Though these other specialists are important and integral parts of the team, the speech-language pathologist is uniquely qualified to properly diagnose and treat speech and oral language problems.

Speech-Language Pathologists, Speech Clinicians, Speech Therapists, and Other Labels

The terms *speech-language pathologist, speech clinician, speech pathologist,* and *speech therapist* are often used interchangeably in conversation. However, the American Speech-Language-Hearing Association (ASHA), which is the national organization that licenses speech-language pathologists in the United States, has made an effort to move away from using the terms *speech therapist* and *speech pathologist* toward using *speech-language pathologist* to better reflect the profession's orientation toward the diagnosis and treatment of language disorders. Most professionals now use speech-language pathologist on formal reports and documents. Although this is a more descriptive term, it is a bit cumbersome at times, particularly when writing a book! In the field, we sometimes shorten this designation by using the initials SLP.

In most states, speech-language pathologists are required to hold a master's degree in communication science or speech-language pathology. Licensing and certification procedures vary from state to state. School systems are required to hire only certified speech-language pathologists who also have training in school-related issues. ASHA tests and licenses on a national level and can direct you to an accredited program or a nationally licensed professional. The initials CCC-SLP (Certificate of Clinical Competency-Speech-Language Pathology) after a speech pathologist's name indicate a national license. You can find ASHA's phone number in appendix A.

In Canada, each province decides the educational qualifications needed to be a speech pathologist.

Where to Go

Once you have decided to consult a professional about your child's speech or language skills, the next step is to determine whom to call. In the United States you have several options.

Private Practitioners

Private practitioners are usually located in the yellow pages under "Speech Pathologist." Some private speech pathologists will come to your home, but most have a professional office. You should ask to see the SLP's state license; although a national license from ASHA is not required, it is desirable.

Some advantages of using a private speech pathologist include the following:

- *Specialized expertise and advanced training.* In certain situations, a private speech pathologist may be well worth the extra investment. For stuttering, swallowing/feeding disorders, voice problems, childhood apraxia of speech, augmentative/assistive devices, auditory processing disorders, cleft palate, or hearing impairment, advanced training and specialized materials are critical for adequate progress to occur. Group practices also offer extensive opportunities for more specialized mentoring of new graduates than do larger public facilities, where there is often limited supervision and time to help troubleshoot challenging cases.

- *Comprehensiveness of the assessment and report.* Private practices typically have access to a wide variety of test materials, but more important, they should have the time and interest to write a detailed, thorough evaluation of your child's needs and the time to explain it carefully to you.
- *Personalized care.* Individual treatment may allow children with serious problems to get more intensive and personalized therapy than they would in other settings. Communication with you is ongoing, materials specific to your child's needs and interests can be created, and sessions can be paced to uniquely suit your child's attention span.
- *Choice.* When your child attends private speech-language therapy, you can pick and choose which specialist sees your child. If you're not happy, you can move to another SLP whose personality or methods click with your child—or you—better.
- *No loss of school time.* Having your child pulled from the classroom to receive services can cause further fragmentation of your child's school day. Having the services after school allows your child not to miss valuable class time. That said, after-school appointments are typically at a premium and are often completely booked up at popular practices.

Some disadvantages of using a private practitioner include the following:

- *Cost.* Unless you have private insurance or are financially well off, private speech therapy can be quite expensive, costing from $120 to $200 per hour for individual treatment. Always ask what the SLP charges before making an appointment.
- *Isolation from school.* A private practitioner is in a difficult position to work with your child's teachers on a consistent basis, which can be important if your child has serious language or listening problems. Coordinating meetings can be expensive and logistically impossible. For this reason, it's often helpful to have both public school *and* private therapy for your child, particularly for disorders that include social delays, such as autism.

Public Schools

If your child attends the public schools, services are free; however, some states now require a contribution toward birth–5 services. You pay taxes for the services provided in the public schools, so don't hesitate to use them. Children who attend private schools are also entitled to access to public school specialists on a limited basis, typically for an assessment only. You should call your state's education department to find out your rights if your child attends a private school. In many states, public school speech-language pathologists have the same or greater training requirements as hospital or private practice SLPs.

Public schools provide evaluations and therapeutic services for children *before* they enter school if the child's delays are significant enough to qualify for services. Mild speed delays or difficulties usually will not qualify for services. Call your local school system and ask for the Special Education Department to find out what services are offered.

Some advantages of using a public school speech-language pathologist include the following:

- *Experience, materials, and comfort with children.* Because public school SLPs deal with literally hundreds of children, they should be comfortable and proficient with diagnosing and treating children's speech and language problems. Also, they have access to a vast array of materials designed for children.
- *Access and availability to other professionals.* For infants and preschool-age children, the speech-language pathologist usually works as a member of a team. Your child will have access to their areas of expertise as well. The SLP can more easily work with the teachers to help your child function in the classroom successfully.
- *Access to your child.* The school-based SLP has a bird's-eye view of your child at recess and lunch and in other situations and can readily see if skills taught are being used or if there are other issues that need to be addressed further.
- *Cost.* It's usually free!

Some disadvantages of using a public school speech-language pathologist include the following:

- *Lack of time.* Many school systems are pinched due to staffing shortages and budget cuts. Large caseloads mean less time for planning lessons, working with students, and talking to you. Also, with so many school vacations, assemblies, and other interferences, therapy is sometimes not as consistent as in other settings.

- *Lack of individualization.* Because of the preceding issues, many school clinicians are forced to group children who, perhaps in ideal circumstances, might be better served individually or in a more appropriate group.
- *Red tape.* Getting help in a public school setting can be a bureaucratic process, requiring lots of forms, meetings, and waiting.

Hospitals

To find out if your local hospital can help you, call the general information number and ask whether there is a Speech Therapy Department. SLPs in a hospital setting are always state-licensed and typically serve all age groups.

Some advantages of using a hospital-based speech-language pathologist include the following:

- *Access to technical equipment.* Hospitals have equipment on the premises that can be particularly useful when treating certain medically based speech problems such as hearing impairment, voice disorders, cleft palate, swallowing disorders, and stuttering.
- *Access to medical personnel.* This is important for children with more involved cases, particularly children with head trauma, a cochlear implant, serious psychological or psychiatric issues, neurological or biological disorders, prenatal defects, or facial deformities.
- *Specialization.* In hospitals that cater strictly to children, you can find some of the leading experts on speech disorders related to medical conditions such as those just mentioned. Many times, research is conducted at teaching hospitals, which helps staff stay current with the latest breakthroughs in the field.

Some disadvantages of using a hospital speech-language pathologist include the following:

- *Cost.* Unless you have insurance, costs can be quite high. Always ask before making an appointment.
- *Isolation from school.* A hospital-based clinician, like the private practitioner, is in a difficult position to consult with a child's teachers on a consistent basis. Also, recommendations given are sometimes difficult to implement in a public school setting.
- *Limited experience, materials, and comfort with children.* Since children are primarily served through the public schools, many hospital speech pathologists spend more time with adult patients. However, in a children's hospital or in a large city hospital, this is not the case.

College Speech Clinics

To find out whether a college offers services you need, call the general information number and ask whether there is a Speech and Hearing Department or a Communication Sciences Department. The administrative assistant in these departments can connect you with the professor who handles inquiries about the college speech therapy program, if there is one. A college with a student major in speech pathology will usually offer therapy services by trained students. A licensed SLP closely supervises the students, reviewing lesson plans, observing, and giving helpful suggestions.

Some advantages of using a student speech therapist from a college clinic include the following:

- *Cost.* In some cases, therapy costs may be reduced or eliminated for those with financial limitations. Regardless, fees are usually considerably lower than what a private practitioner or a hospital would charge.
- *Availability of services.* In many rural areas, a college speech clinic may be the only place a child can receive services.
- *Latest theory and practices utilized.* Because of the very nature of a college campus, professors are always looking at the most up-to-date information and research. Students have the benefit of their input and expertise.

Some disadvantages of using a student speech therapist from a college clinic include the following:

- *Lack of continuity.* Because students come and go from semester to semester or year to year, your child will have to establish a rapport with each new therapist. Also, the therapist needs time to get to know your child.
- *Inconvenience.* Most colleges have limited parking areas, so you may have to walk quite a distance with a young child in tow. Also, there is typically minimal flexibility as far as scheduling the sessions because the supervisor has to be present, or at least available.
- *Inexperience.* A student clinician brings extensive training to the therapy sessions, which should not be minimized. Also, many student clinicians have a natural "feel" for children and will do superior work. Nevertheless, they are still learning and may make some minor errors in judgment at times. Although good supervisors will be quick to remedy problems, they cannot be in all therapy rooms at one time and may not witness these moments.

Agencies

The term *agency* is somewhat broad. Sometimes an agency caters to children with specific problems such as cerebral palsy, mental retardation, deafness, or recovery from a brain injury. It can be a nonprofit, public, or private enterprise. Increasingly, if school systems are short-staffed, or are part of a regional program to service children under the age of 3 or 5 to comply with state or federal regulations, they are contracting out services to agencies. Typically, agencies provide a wide array of services, such as physical therapy and occupational therapy.

Some advantages of using an agency-based speech-language pathologist include the following:

- *Specialization.* Sometimes a speech therapist in this setting works predominantly with children having a specific set of problems, usually requiring specialized training. This focus is important if your child requires special attention.
- *Availability of other staff and services.* Because of its nature, an agency can coordinate services if your child requires them. This capacity cuts down on your running around and facilitates necessary teamwork.
- *Experience, materials, and comfort with children.* Like public school SLPs, agency-based clinicians deal with many children and so should be comfortable and proficient with diagnosing and treating your child's speech and language problems. Also, they have access to a vast array of materials designed for children.

Some disadvantages of using an agency-based speech-language pathologist include the following:

- *Isolation of skills.* If a child receives different kinds of therapy from several individuals, the program can become fragmented. It may be more helpful to receive therapy as part of one integrated "class." Many agencies don't offer this type of "school." Instead, specialists look at isolated parts of the child and work on their areas of specialty. For infants this is not a problem, but as children reach age 3, a different approach may be appropriate.
- *Cost.* Cost varies from agency to agency. Even a nonprofit agency, however, needs to charge fees to cover expenses. If a school system has made arrangements for the services, you won't have to pay for them. For certain problems, insurance may pay. Ask first.
- *Scheduling and convenience.* This is particularly problematic if your child will have to attend therapy after school hours. Many children

resent this and feel imposed upon. It also presents you with a lot of running around.

Appendix A lists the phone numbers of national organizations in the United States and Canada that can direct you to the appropriate, nationally licensed person or state association if you are still unsure about where to call. This listing may be especially helpful for people in rural areas, where services can be sparse.

About Insurance Coverage

Most people have either an HMO or a PPO health plan. At this writing, the U.S. government is actively working to create another option so that everyone in the United States has some kind of health-care coverage option. Currently, insurance coverage for pediatric speech therapy is very much a hit-or-miss affair. There is no single company or plan that consistently pays better than others. In my experience, the reimbursement or coverage is dependent upon the mood of the case reviewer and the willingness of the parent to appeal the denial. Remember, though, that most plans only cover therapy that is "medically necessary." That means therapy for mild articulation problems (such as remediating the *r*) would not be covered under most plans. However, what constitutes medically necessary speech therapy is highly subjective.

With an HMO plan, you must have your child's primary physician initiate the assessment and/or therapy, then select a private practitioner who is within your network. The SLP will collect the appropriate co-pay at the time of your visit. Even with the referral, there is no guarantee that your HMO plan will cover your child's evaluation or services. At times, the HMO may agree to pay another, nonparticipating SLP if there is no participating SLP within a reasonable distance of your home, if you appeal.

With a PPO plan, you do not need your physician's referral in most cases (check your plan). There are SLP providers who are "in-network" and have agreed to a negotiated fee with your health-care company. They will take your co-pay or work directly with your PPO for billing. However, these days, many private-practice SLPs work exclusively "out of network." That means they will provide you with a bill/receipt for services after you pay in full and it is up to you to secure reimbursement from the PPO. They do this because payment is often delayed, rejected for arbitrary reasons, or even denied after already having been tentatively approved.

The Evaluation (aka the Assessment)

Once you have decided *whom* you want to perform the evaluation, you'll want to know *what* to expect when you make that first phone call. What happens during an evaluation? What should I tell my child? Read on to find out the answers to these and other questions you may have about the evaluation process.

The First Step: A Screening

Before a formal evaluation takes place, the SLP may want to meet your child and do some informal testing, called a *screening.* The screening determines whether an evaluation is necessary or not, and if so, which tests would be the most appropriate for the child. A screening usually takes five to twenty minutes. A school-based SLP may want to observe your child in a classroom or interacting with classmates. In the public schools, some SLPs routinely perform screenings on all incoming kindergarten students and then again in a later, usually the second, grade. Children who have difficulty on this screening are typically monitored or referred for a complete evaluation. Permission from the parent for a screening may or may not be required, depending on the state and the nature of the screening. As a parent, you can (and should) request a screening if you have any concerns at all about your child's communication skills. Since the word *test* often makes a child uncomfortable and tense before walking in the door, as with all phases of testing, your child need only be told that "Mr. or Ms. Smith would like to meet you and talk to you for a while." If the child should ask why, it usually suffices to say, "Because it is your turn."

The Legal Process

Once you or the SLP decides to pursue a full speech-language evaluation, a certain legal process must take place. (*Note:* You may choose to skip the screening and request a full evaluation from the beginning.) When the evaluation is to be performed through a public school system, a meeting may be required first. Some states simply require the parent or guardian's written permission for the evaluation in lieu of a meeting. This process is a result of legislative acts that established Public Laws 94–142 and 102–119, which are federal laws that guarantee special education services for those students who need them. Public schools consider speech-language therapy services "special education" or a "related service" and therefore follow this process.

You must be notified before a meeting that concerns your child is scheduled. If your state requires this meeting, you will be invited to hear the concerns leading to the evaluation. Usually the meeting will include a school administrator, specialists working with the child, teachers (if the child is in school), and the parents. Informal strategies that have been implemented to attempt to remediate the problem, if applicable, are discussed. You will be asked to sign formal permission papers allowing the speech-language evaluation to be done. If you cannot attend the meeting, the papers may be sent home for your signature. (If a parent does not speak English, an interpreter must be provided by the school system.) *If you do not grant written permission, an evaluation cannot be performed.* It is important to note that granting permission for the evaluation does not mean you have granted permission to begin therapy.

What Is the Speech-Language Pathologist Looking For?

The speech-language evaluation seeks to answer these questions:

- Is there a communication "problem"?
- What kind of problem is it?
- To what degree is the child impaired?
- Should other professionals be asked to do evaluations? For example: a referral to a psychologist, neurologist, or learning disabilities teacher.
- How does this problem affect the child on a day-to-day basis, at home and at school?
- If needed, what kind of intervention will best help this child?
- What can the parents (and teachers, if the child is of school age) do to help the child?

Informal and Formal Tests

Both *informal tests* and *formal tests* will be used to answer the preceding questions. Informal tests (or "tasks") are activities initiated by the speech-language pathologist for a specific purpose. The activities are not manufactured by an educational testing company, nor are they necessarily asked in a uniform way for each child. The speech-language pathologist knows how a typical child at a given age should respond to conversational questions.

For example, I often begin my evaluation by chatting with a school-age student about any number of casual topics, such as what he or she was doing in class earlier that day. This may seem like a waste of time to an untrained observer, but this type of "chatting" gives a trained professional a great deal of insight as to how a child processes questions, stays on topic, articulates words, uses vocabulary, and puts sentences together. Following directions, telling stories, and describing pictures are other examples of informal tasks. Results are usually reported by noting the child's responses as "age-appropriate" or, if the child had difficulty completing the task, more descriptively (e.g., "Johnny described the busy construction picture with minimal detail and awkward phrasing. He displayed similar syntax deficits in his conversational speech. Ex.: 'I no want to have sausage on a pizza for lunch.'").

Formal tests refer to manufactured tests sold by companies that have developed a product. Data provided on a chart tell test givers what is a "typical" performance on a particular formal test. These norms are developed by giving the test to hundreds, and sometimes thousands, of children. The responses and performance of the typical 7-year-old children who took the test dictate what is expected (the "standard") for the 7-year-old child who takes the test once it is published. That is why formal tests are also called *standardized tests*.

What Will Happen during the Evaluation?

Most speech-language evaluations include a battery of tests that will take a half hour to three hours or more to administer, depending on the age of your child and the nature of the assessment. Often the evaluation is administered in several sessions instead of all at once. A combination of formal and informal tests will be used during the evaluation to provide a complete picture of the child's speech-language ability and use. The assessment should consist of the following components.

Background Information

The evaluator should discuss your concerns with you. The two of you will need to review your child's health and development as an infant and as a toddler. This developmental history is an important component of any evaluation. It helps identify any "red flag" areas such as delayed milestones for walking, a family history of language or learning problems, complications at birth, frequent ear infections, allergies, or other pertinent concerns that may signal a problem. The evaluator should also talk to your child's teacher to see how the child is functioning in the classroom. Samples of your child's schoolwork as well as scores in past reading tests should be considered. *Any time a child is evaluated for a speech or language problem, the results of a recent hearing screening should be included in the background history.* While the hearing screening can be done at the school, I would strongly suggest that you take your child for a more thorough assessment by an audiologist. Often you can ask your pediatrician to request a referral through your insurance company. If not, pay for it yourself. It usually costs $100 to $200 as of this writing and is worth every penny. Why? Because a screening only looks at a select number of frequencies and may not pick up a mild hearing problem. Fluid or wax (cerumen) affecting hearing may not be spotted.

Receptive Language Skills

As discussed in chapter 1, receptive language refers to what a child is able to understand, or comprehend. Receptive language is tested through a variety of pointing and direction-following activities. Some examples of receptive language tasks include:

- *Understanding word meanings.* This is typically done by having the child point to a picture that is named, with a group of four pictures to choose from. For example, if I ask a child to show me the leaf, does he point to the leaf, or to one of the other pictures, such as a tree, a feather, or a boy?
- *Understanding question forms.* Does your child understand the differences between "wh" question words (who, what, where, when, why), such as "*Who* is on the couch?" versus "*What* is on the couch?" When negation is paired with a question word (as in, "Why didn't the girl eat the sandwich?"), does your school-age child understand what you are asking?
- *Understanding positional terms.* The child may be asked to point to an object at a particular location. For very young children, it might be "Find the cat that is on the house." For school-age children, the direction might be "Point to the star that is between the house and the pencil."
- *Understanding grammatical language concepts.* Can your child find the picture of "*He* is eating" within a group of pictures, including a girl eating, a group of people eating, and a bird eating? Understanding of the pronoun *he* would be checked, usually after age 3. Another concept might be verb forms. If your child is asked to point to "He ate the apple," we would expect a 5-year-old to point to the picture of the boy with the apple core, not the picture of the boy still eating or holding an uneaten apple. Examples of other grammatical concepts include negation ("She *isn't* eating") possessives ("the *dog's* house") and plurals ("Find the *birds*").
- *Understanding story/narratives.* Once your child is 3 to 4 years old, we will want to know how much he or she comprehends when a short story is told. Sometimes it isn't the individual receptive language ele-

ments that are tricky, but sustaining one's attention and comprehending verbal information when it is in a longer context. With younger children, we include pictures, but older children are usually tested without pictures as well.

- *Understanding inferencing, idioms, humor, and sarcasm.* These are high-level skills that are learned during the elementary school years. Some children struggle to "read between the lines" by analyzing what is happening, "how" someone is saying something, double-meanings, and idioms, such as "Can you give me a hand?" by taking everything quite literally.

Expressive Language Skills

Tests of expressive language examine your child's spoken language. Some of this is evaluated through formal measures, but often informal measures (such as describing a picture, retelling a story, or simply chatting) can provide a seasoned specialist with even better information. Some examples of the types of expressive skills that would be examined might include:

- *Morphology ("Mor-FAH-luh-jee").* Morphology refers to the way a child uses morphemes, which can be a word or word "parts" such as a prefix (*un*happy) or suffix (teach*er*). Usually we are looking at endings such as plurals, possessives, and verb tenses. A 5-year-old child who is struggling with the morphological components of expressive language might speak this way: "I seed four boy go in Bobby pool." (I saw four boys go in Bobby's pool.)
- *Mean length of utterance* (MLU). In children who are still learning to talk, we want to know how much (actual quantity/length) the child is using language spontaneously. Some children will expand their phrases if prompted, but if left on their own may choose to pare down their expressions to just a few words or less. The speech pathologist will typically observe and record what your child says and calculate the MLU by determining the number of morphemes used.
- *Syntax ("sin-tacks").* Syntax refers to the order of the sentence, or the coherence of the overall sentence structure. A 4-year-old child who has difficulties with syntax might ask a question this way: "You did eat yet? Strawberries—my tummy—mm good!"
- *Semantics.* Semantics refers to the way words are used in a given context. Children who misuse words or select inaccurate words for the situation have difficulty with semantics. A 6-year-old with semantic difficulties might describe a firefighter putting out a fire with a hose

this way: "The man is watering the fire." In school-age children, we also look at their ability to name synonyms and antonyms and to understand more advanced categorical naming skills ("furniture" names all the pictures shown).

- *Word retrieval.* Someone with a word retrieval problem receptively knows—or understands—a word when it is used by others, but does not have the ability to pull out the word and use it himself when the verbal situation warrants it. Children with word retrieval issues may use lots of pauses, "ums," and filler language ("that thingy"), or they may compensate with incorrect semantics due to the fact that they can't "get to" the word that would work better in a sentence. A child with word retrieval difficulties who is 3 might be able to point to any picture you name, but when you say, "What is that?" shrugs or answers incorrectly. We often test word retrieval by seeing how fast a child can name familiar pictures with accuracy. Big gaps between a child's receptive vocabulary and expressive vocabulary, coupled with observations in situational language use, can also suggest a word retrieval problem.

- *Narrative language use.* This refers to how connected language is used for more sophisticated purposes, such as retelling a story or explaining "what happened." We look at how the information is organized, sequenced, and connected. Can the listener follow what's going on? Are the important details included, or is the information too vague? Are pronouns used so much that the listener is confused? Is the information too succinct and lacking in elaboration? How it's "put together" is what we examine during narrative language tasks.

Auditory Skills

Auditory skills tell us *how* your child hears, processes, perceives, or remembers speech. A child with normal hearing can still struggle with auditory skills. Auditory skills are critical to the development of both receptive and expressive language, and are important for academic success. You know that hearing should be checked at birth, but it should also be rescreened periodically during early childhood, with a complete assessment if there are frequent ear infections or a speech delay. However, a good, thorough assessment of your child (particularly after age 5) should include some aspects of auditory skills analysis if there are any concerns that might be caused by an underlying auditory problem. Auditory skills develop over time. Without adequate input and practice, they may not develop as expected. Sometimes children who have had temporary hearing loss (such as with frequent and early ear infections or a lack of early stimulation) may struggle with auditory skills later on, but sometimes there is no discernible reason why there are auditory difficulties. Children who are thought to have a pervasive difficulty with the auditory nerve pathways, such as an auditory processing disorder (also referred to as a central auditory processing disorder, written as CAPD or (C)APD), should be followed up with an audiologist who specializes in this area. The audiologist would be able to conclusively rule out or confirm a diagnosis when the child is school-age. Psychologists and special education specialists often do comprehensive batteries of tests, which can also pinpoint some gaps in auditory skills. The following are some auditory skills that would likely be included:

- *Auditory attention.* Is your child noticeably antsy and distracted when the test items have no pictures? Children who can't sustain their attention for short periods of time without visual support often struggle in the classroom because they can't stay "tuned in" long enough to hear the instruction. In younger children, we often find "Story Time" and "Circle Time" to be challenging as well. Older children may "zone out" during extended auditory instruction and do much better with "hands-on" learning experiences or those with visual support.
- *Auditory memory.* Can your child remember and repeat what is said? We often test auditory memory by having the child repeat a series of numbers or words, or point to a series of items. Difficulties with auditory memory can impact how your child processes and responds to school instruction and oral directions.
- *Auditory discrimination.* Is your child able to hear subtle differences between similar-sounding words? Do *beaver* and *fever* sound so similar when the child is listening that he confuses the two words? Are vowels—particularly "short" vowels such as bed/bad/bid—unusually difficult for your child to tell apart? When people are speaking rapidly or there is a little bit of ambient noise, children with auditory discrimination difficulties may be confused.
- *Phonemic awareness.* "Phonemes" are individual speech sounds. At around age 5 and older, your child should be able to identify the beginning or ending sounds in words, and to tell whether or not a word rhymes with another. An important phonemic skill is to be able to blend ("synthesize") a series of sounds. For example, if I say the individual sounds *g-i-f-t*, will your child figure out that it means *gift* when the sounds are put together? Difficulties with phonemic awareness can impact the ability to decode (read) and encode (spell) because you need to do this kind of blending and isolating for these skills. The

long-term storage of new words also relies on our brain's ability to "file" the word away, using the phonemic properties of the word as one of the "files" in which the word can be found. If there is little phonemic organization, retrieval of the word becomes much more difficult.

- *Auditory-figure ground*. When a child can focus on one person's voice, such as that of a teacher, and block out the other competing noises, he or she is using auditory-figure ground skills. It is a developmental skill that needs to be honed, typically by about age 7. When a child is overly attentive to all sound input, the teacher's voice becomes part of the background noise, and listening—particularly in a group setting, such as a classroom—becomes a challenge.

Social Language Use ("Pragmatics") and Play

Social language use refers to how we use language in "real life." While it's helpful to know how a child answers formal test questions, it's even more important to know if the child *uses* these skills in everyday social settings. There is more to how we communicate than merely the use of words. In fact, much of our communication is nonverbal, including gestures, facial expressions, intonation, pausing, and knowing how to negotiate the reciprocal give-and-take that occurs during a conversation. Currently, there are only a few formal tests that look at isolated aspects of social language use. Therefore, much of the information about a child's social language use is gleaned from observation and reported behaviors from those who see the child on a day-to-day basis, and is largely "described" rather than provided with hard data. For children with autism spectrum disorders, these issues are particularly important to examine and develop. The following are some pragmatic skills that might be observed during the testing process:

- *Eye contact*. We know that making eye contact while communicating is valued in our culture as a social manner, but a lack of eye contact can also indicate that the child doesn't know how to interpret your facial expressions, and hence has no particular reason to look at you. It also can signal difficulty synthesizing visual and auditory information at one time.
- *Play*. How does your child play? What toys, games, and activities are fun for her? How interactive is your child when playing? For the child in school, what is happening on the playground? How long does your child remain interested in a toy before moving on to the next? How your child plays is important information.

- *Comprehending basic gestures and facial expressions.* If you point out the window, does your child look at the object out the window when you point to it, or does he look at your hand itself? Or at nothing? When you rub your stomach and smile (to show anticipation of something tasty to eat) versus rubbing your stomach and grimacing (to show a stomachache) does your child know the difference? What do those gestures mean? In looking at picture books, does your child understand what the picture is trying to show? (E.g., that the child looking out the window is sad, because the other children are playing.) In kindergarten, taking a "picture walk" through a storybook without being able to interpret the characters' feelings, motivations, and interactions can make it difficult to understand the point of the story, and hence can cause difficulty answering comprehension questions.
- *Interacting with friends.* Does your child initiate joining others? If so, how? When playing, is your child willing to compromise, appropriately negotiate play rules, and pay attention to the desires of the other children? If another child looks disinterested, does your child continue telling joke after joke anyway? If your child is often confused about how to play with peers, left out, routinely bullied, or prefers to play alone, social skills may need further development.
- *Emotional regulation.* Children pay close attention to the facial expressions and emotions of their peers. If your child laughs too loudly or too long, or for no apparent reason, it can make peers uneasy, particularly as they get into elementary school years and older. If your child's facial expression is "flat" (lacking emotion), a greeting without a smile will seem odd and the other children may not know how to respond.

Likewise, children who cannot deviate from a set of learned rules for a particular game or activity ("That's not how you do it!") or cope with losing without becoming upset can struggle with friendships.

- *Situational problem-solving and white lies.* When is being "too honest" a social liability? It's a challenge for most young children, but some children never get the hang of how to handle awkward social situations. For example, if your child's friend sings a song, but has a poor singing voice, does your child point that out or simply applaud? Some children—long after the preschool years—struggle with what is appropriate to say out loud, in front of people, and what to keep in their head.

Articulation (Pronouncing Words)

Articulation refers to how your child pronounces words. The speech pathologist will look at how your child imitates speech, pronounces words, forms sentences, and articulates during conversational speech, and compare it to how typically developing children speak at the same age. Some of the aspects of articulation development that will be examined include:

- *Patterns, patterns, patterns!* The SLP will be carefully noting speech patterns to see if there are consistent errors or patterns of errors. For example, if a child consistently produces *k* sounds as a *t* ("driving in a tar") and *g* sounds as a *d* ("He dave it to me"), the SLP would note that as a "fronting" error. In speech pathology lingo, it simply means the child's tongue is making contact at the front of the mouth instead of in the back, where *k* and *g* sounds are typically made. These kinds of articulatory patterns are also called "phonological" speech errors because they follow consistent patterns.
- *Oral function.* The SLP should make sure that there is adequate mobility, strength, and control of the lips, tongue, and jaw. While there is still some controversy within our profession as to how much attention should be placed on the oral mechanism itself, certainly excessive drooling, tongue protrusion, poor lip contact, and a sliding jaw make clear speech production a challenge. Children with a lack of muscle tone (hypotonia) may have related speech difficulties, resulting in a slurring, breathy kind of speech pattern referred to as *dysarthria*.
- *Speed of production.* Children who speak rather slowly and laboriously often have a stilted or awkward speech pattern. The individual sounds may be technically correct, but the phrasing itself may cause the listener to have a hard time understanding the child. This may be due to a child's having a slower rate of linguistic organization (*What is it that I want to say . . . ?*), difficulty with motor-planning (*My mouth just won't move from one sound to the next quickly!*), weak muscles, or poor breath support. Likewise, children who are unduly fast, and speed through talking, may not take the time to pronounce their words clearly enough to be adequately understood.
- *Intonation patterns.* A natural-sounding voice needs to go up and down and use stress and natural phrasing. A child who has a "flat" or awkward melodic intonation pattern ("Do you want to play.") sounds different to peers. Speech patterns that are choppy ("The-dog-is-sit-ting-in-my-lap") sound a bit staccato and distract the listener.
- *Awareness of speech error.* Does your child realize he has a speech problem? Or does he think his *r* sound or slushy *s* is just perfect as it is? We want to know this because a lack of awareness may also signal difficulties with speech/auditory discrimination. Without a strong

awareness of correct versus incorrect production, it will be difficult for your child to change his speech pattern. This is often where we start with articulation intervention, especially for children age 5 and up.

• *Apraxia.* Children who are quite frustrated and cannot seem to move their mouth the way they want to—despite being keenly aware of the sounds they are trying to make—should always be checked for a possible Childhood Apraxia of Speech (CAS) diagnosis, particularly when there are multiple errors, difficulty at the phrase/sentence level, inconsistent errors, groping during attempts, and distortions of vowels.

Voice Quality

The speech pathologist should take notes on the quality of your child's voice. If a cold or a sore throat affects speech that day, your child should be checked on another day to make sure the voice returns to normal. Here are just a few things we would be observing:

• *Hoarseness.* Does your child's voice sound gravelly? Ongoing hoarseness can signal a vocal polyp or nodule. Children with loud voices and allergies are often susceptible to hoarseness.

• *Breathiness.* Your child should not be audibly breathing, straining to get the words out before running out of air, or whispering.

• *Resonance.* Children who constantly sound as if they have a cold are said to be *hyponasal.* Children who are hyponasal should be checked for nasal blockages or chronic allergies/sinus conditions. If they sound as if they are talking through their nose, they are called *hypernasal.* Children who are hypernasal may have a cleft palate or may have simply habituated an unusual speaking voice.

Fluency (Stuttering)

The speech pathologist will note if there are any concerns about stuttering. If the stuttering is an ongoing or severe problem, a more formal assessment should be made. Not all pediatric speech pathologists have a strong background in stuttering, so it's important to work with someone who does have extra training in this area if at all possible. The Stuttering Foundation (www.stutteringhelp.org) is a terrific resource for learning more about stuttering, as well as locating a specialist in the United States. The initial evaluation will screen for fluency disorders. The following areas will be observed:

• *Repeated words.* Stutterers typically don't repeat entire words. Children developing speech (around the ages of 3 to 5) often do, and it sounds much like a stuttering pattern to an untrained ear, but it's different.

• *Prolongations of sounds.* If this is happening, with which sounds or in which situations? How often?

• *Situational?* We'll want to see if the dysfluency is specific to a particular linguistic task, such as describing a picture, or to a specific setting (only at home), or is pervasive across tasks and situations.

• *Hesitations and pauses.* Fluency is perceived by a smoothness and ongoing connection between words that flows easily. When that flow is disjointed or stopped and started, it jars the listener and makes it hard to focus on the message itself.

Special Considerations:
Testing Infants and Preschoolers

Infants generally are evaluated through informal testing, which consists of observing and playing with them in different settings (with a parent, with toys, food, etc.) and noting what they do. Does your baby make any noise? Does she seem to anticipate the objects you present or even notice them? Does your baby look at you? The other important part of the evaluation is the interview with you, because you can answer questions about the baby's habits, development, and medical history. Watching your baby eat is another important part of the evaluation, because the examiner can watch how your baby's "talking muscles" work when she is eating.

Tests given to preschoolers are often a combination of formal and informal tests. The formal tests are designed to accommodate the shorter attention span and limited skills a young child possesses. You may be present in the room during the testing, but often a child responds better when the parent is close by but out of sight. Evaluators will let you know what their preferred practice is. The activities are often more "hands-on" and less clinical. As mentioned previously, to keep your child relaxed, avoid discussing the testing ahead of time or using the word *test* to describe what will happen. As far as your son or daughter needs to know, he or she is going to "play with" some new people.

A team, rather than an individual, often does the testing for this age group. This team assesses speech and language as well as other developmental skills, such as basic concepts, attention span, socialization skills, self-help skills, balance, coordination, and muscle tone. Members of the team should include a speech-language pathologist, an occupational therapist and/or a physical therapist, and a special education teacher. A psychologist can also add invaluable insight into diagnosis and program development. Because delays in infants and preschool children are often not isolated to speech and language problems, team assessment offers a host of benefits. The other specialists can observe deficits in areas in which the speech therapist is not properly trained. These delays are often difficult to detect and often go unnoticed by the parents as well.

Bilingual and Multicultural Populations

Testing children who come from homes where more than one language is spoken presents a challenge for SLPs. Ideally, the assessment should be administered in the child's primary language, but most SLPs in the United States only have access to standardized tests in English or Spanish. Sometimes when a child has a caregiver who speaks one language, parents who speak another language, and a school setting where yet one more language is spoken, it is very challenging to determine if the speech-language-auditory issues are due to the child's trying to learn and use different language systems or if it is a pervasive issue that would have occurred regardless. The SLP will want to know if the difficulties are observed in all languages, and the amount of time the child has been exposed to the language being tested. For example, let's suppose a girl was born in France and exposed to French for her first three years, but then moved to the United States. Now she is trying to learn English, and is going to an English-speaking preschool. The exposure to French is reduced to speaking it with her parents in the evenings and on weekends. If we test her nine months after arrival, we may find that her command of both languages is behind her peers'. That is a natural process as she transitions to a new language. For a child with a true language disorder, it is tricky business for SLPs who are trying to sort out whether a language "difference" is in fact a disorder, and sometimes it might be impossible to do that until more time has gone by.

It is especially important that the SLP is knowledgeable about the child's primary language. For example, if the child is struggling with verb tensing and pronoun use, are these grammatical features absent in the primary language? If so, difficulties using these forms in English could be due to a lack of exposure and practice.

Understanding a child's culture is also important. As we look at play behaviors, eye contact, asking questions, and body language comprehension, the SLP needs to be mindful that not all children are raised with the same cultural expectations. When conclusions are drawn regarding a child's social/pragmatic behaviors and "chattiness" with the examiner, it is essential that there is a solid understanding of the child's culture and what part that may play in the way the child interacts with others.

After the SLP's evaluation comes the report, filled with data and terminology you may have trouble interpreting. The next chapter will help translate the report for you. Chapter 4 will also help you plan the best treatment program for your daughter or son, in partnership with the appropriate professionals.

4

After the Evaluation

Understanding Report Jargon and the IEP

Once the speech-language pathologist has performed the actual evaluation, it will either be discussed with you at that time, or you will be asked to come in and discuss the results at a later date. In either case, the SLP should send a written report within a few weeks. If you are not given a written report detailing the results of the evaluation, however, request one. In this chapter, I will help you understand the jargon and numbers in the report.

The Numbers Used to Measure Performance

As we discussed in chapter 3, a speech-language therapist uses informal tasks (sometimes called informal tests) or formal tests (sometimes called standardized tests) to evaluate a child.

Standardized tests provide charts that indicate what is a typical or expected performance in various skill areas at each age. The therapist then indicates how a particular child performed in comparison to a typical child of the same age. These comparisons can be expressed in percentiles, standard scores, standard deviations, stanines, and age equivalents. Many tests have charts to supply information in several of these ways. It's no wonder parents find reports to be so confusing!

You don't need to become an expert in testing statistics to understand these numbers. Nearly all tests use percentiles and/or age equivalents as the primary measure of performance. The other numbers provide additional systems for interpreting the data. If you become familiar and comfortable with percentiles and age equivalents, you should be able to understand most reports.

Percentiles: What They Mean

Percentiles, also called *percentile ranks,* are sometimes abbreviated on reports as "%tile." Most achievement scores are provided as percentiles and are particularly helpful in comparing the performance of one child to that of others in the same age group (or sometimes the same grade). Percentiles range from 1 to 99 and usually can be interpreted as follows:

95–99	far superior to peers
75–94	high average/above average
25–74	average
7–24	below average
1–6	significantly behind peers

Schools and other institutions with speech-language programs establish their own criteria as to how far below average a child must be to qualify for services. California schools use the 7th percentile as their cutoff. This inconsistency among school districts and states can present a dilemma when a child moves from one school system to another. If a child scores low, but not low enough to qualify for public school services, the parents may need to pay for private therapy.

In looking at your child's percentiles, another thing to bear in mind is the culture and expectations of the school your child attends or the town in which you live. At some highly competitive schools, having language or auditory scores hovering across the board at the 7th to 25th percentiles will mean your child is much more likely to struggle within the academic environment, particularly when your child's peers are all top-performing. While technically speaking those scores may not qualify your child for special education services in the public school setting, I would advise getting intervention and support for your child in these situations.

It's important to note that the overwhelming majority of children will score between the 25th and 75th percentiles on any given standardized test. Percentiles are not the same as a *percentage* (the number you may remember scoring on a test as a child), which indicates the percentage of correct answers. Percentiles do not tell you how many questions were answered incorrectly.

For example, a 5-year-old child may only need to answer five of a given fifteen questions correctly to be considered within the "average" (or "normal") range, because the questions are difficult. If the same fifteen questions are asked of a 7-year-old, perhaps eight questions would need to be answered correctly for the child to be considered within normal limits. The number of "correct" answers increases with age. (If those responses were scored as traditional percentages, the 5-year-old would receive a score of 30 percent, which would sound like a failing score, whereas in reality, the percentile score translates to the 63rd percentile, which is well within the average range.)

The actual percentile number—65, for example—indicates that your child scored better than 65 percent of the children who took the same test. In essence, a score of 65 means your child's performance is in the top 35 percent of all the children who took the test. The speech-language pathologist is primarily concerned with your child's development in terms of what is normal for other children of the same age. That is why percentiles are an excellent tool to determine this comparison.

Age Equivalents

Though your child's actual *chronological age* may be 7–4 (seven years, four months), his performance, or *age equivalent* (sometimes abbreviated as AE), may be comparable to that of a younger, 5–3 (five years, three months) child on any given formal test. These scores are also given in years and months in the same way as a chronological age. The score means your child performed at the level of a child of the age given.

Standard Scores

Standard scores (sometimes abbreviated as SS) are based on a system in which 100 is the average score. Any score within 15 points on either side of 100 (85–115) is considered within the higher and lower ends of average. Scores lower than 85 are below average; scores above 115, above average. IQ tests are typically reported using standard scores, but language and auditory tests sometimes use this system as well.

Standard Deviation

Each test determines its own measure of what constitutes a *standard deviation (SD)*. The professional who administers the test has that information in the manual accompanying the test. Standard deviations measure how far from average (otherwise known as the "mean") a child scores. "One standard deviation below the mean," written as –1 SD, is below average.

But that does not necessarily mean it is low enough to qualify the child for a remedial program. Likewise, any standard deviations above the mean would be considered an above-average performance. For example, one standard deviation above the mean would be written as +1 SD.

Most specialists use two or more standard deviations below the mean as the criteria to qualify for remediation. This is typically written as –2 SD.

Stanines

Stanines are based on a system from 1 to 9. Five is considered average. A stanine rating of 1 or 2 indicates a below-average performance. A stanine rating of 8 or 9 indicates an above-average performance. If you multiply a stanine by ten it will give you a ballpark equivalent of a percentile.

After the Evaluation: Using Public School Services in the United States

If your child was evaluated through the U.S. public schools, a second meeting will usually be scheduled to discuss the results of the evaluation and to consider recommendations. A school administrator should be present at this meeting, as well as any teacher or professional who works with your child.

IDEA 2004 and What It Means to You

The original Individuals with Disabilities Education Act (IDEA) was reauthorized in 2004, and became effective on July 1, 2005. The new version included some clarifications of terminology, changes in procedure, and the implementation of a new process called "Response to Intervention" (RtI). With the RtI process, there is an emphasis on the schools' providing a wider range of services to a larger group of children, without necessarily doing formal testing or going through the special education process. Up until the 2005 implementation, many schools refused to provide any speech-language therapy services to a child unless he or she fell under the strict criteria imposed for special education services, which often meant that children with mild or moderate difficulties fell through the cracks. As a result of the 2004 IDEA, your child may receive intervention for speech and language difficulties, but not necessarily as part of a special education plan. There is more emphasis on using a

A Note about Your Child and Testing

These are some truths I have come to know after many years in the field:

1. Toddlers and preschoolers are notoriously poor standardized test takers. Sometimes they are "in the mood" to comply, and other times they are not. They may answer one way on Monday, but completely differently on Tuesday. With very young children, their behaviors can fluctuate tremendously. Are they hungry? Tired? Not used to the examiner? A good, comprehensive evaluation of a young child requires more than a one-hour snapshot. Observing the child in other settings and/or getting to know the child over several sessions is usually best. The examiner should ask you, "Is this how Susie would typically respond to that question?"
2. Some school-age children perform just great in the "real world" but are terrible test takers. They get nervous, don't always perform their best, and habitually get lower scores than you'd expect.
3. Then again, some school-age children perform quite poorly in the "real world" but do amazingly well on standardized tests. These are the tricky cases. Is it boredom? A short attention span? A conflict with the teacher? If your child is not doing well in school, the SLP's tests that were used may not be targeting the specific areas that are causing difficulties. I would dig deeper—maybe with additional testing, but sometimes the answer is not in standardized tests, but emotional/psychological/health reasons.
4. Some children perform in a "gray" zone—not low enough to definitively qualify for services, but low enough that they are struggling, especially in a competitive school. With these children, you may need to seek private services. The bad news is, the therapy may not be covered under your insurance if the issues are primarily educational and not medical, particularly if the scores are not especially low.
5. Don't forget that play and social and situational language use are often not captured on standardized tests. For some children, these are the biggest difficulties. If this is an area of concern, much of the assessment report may need to be descriptive, rather than filled with data.

regular education team and process to help troubleshoot difficulties with the school-age child, and to avoid formal testing and labeling unless all other interventions have been unsuccessful. For children with demonstrated disabilities (e.g., autism, Down syndrome) the child will stay in the IEP/Special Education process. In other words, there may be no IEP for your child with mild to moderate difficulties, but he may still get help for that pesky articulation problem.

The IEP and IFSP

If your child has moved from the regular education (RtI) process to the special education process, a plan called an *Individualized Educational Plan (IEP)* is developed by the team at the meeting following the evaluation. A signed IEP is a legally binding document, meaning the school system *must provide* the program it has promised. Parents are equal members of this planning team; they have the right to express opinions as to what service their child receives, how often, where it takes place, and what is learned. For children age 3 or younger, this plan is called an *Individualized Family Service Plan (IFSP). As the parent of the child, you hold many rights, and with them, the ultimate responsibility. If you do not grant written permission to begin therapy as specified on the IEP or IFSP, therapy cannot take place.*

The following are some questions that should be addressed at this meeting with the school team. If these areas are not discussed, be sure to ask.

- How do these speech and language deficits impact my child's academic performance?
- What modifications should be made in the classroom to minimize the impact of these deficits?
- Does my child need an assistive listening device?
- What is the most appropriate learning environment for my child?
- How can my child's communication skills be strengthened within the classroom?
- How can I foster these skills at home?
- How do these speech, language, or listening deficits affect my child socially and emotionally?

If all concerned look at the bigger picture, an educational program can be tailored to your child's individual needs as much as possible. It is important that your child is challenged to meet new, yet obtainable, educational goals.

The IEP and IFSP, by U.S. law, must include the following information:

- A description of your child's present level of functioning and diagnosis
- The goals of the therapy program
- How often therapy will take place
- Which professional(s) will carry out the program
- Where therapy will be provided (usually a regular classroom, a resource room, or a therapy room)
- Whether the therapy will be one-on-one or in a group
- What methods and materials will be used
- The criteria for being released from the program

In Canada, each province has complete autonomy when it comes to providing speech-language therapy and educational services. Unlike the United States, Canada does not have national laws that dictate how this is to be carried out. However, local school boards must provide appropriate programs for children with "exceptionalities." Speech and language are considered "communication exceptionalities." A report and program will be prepared for your child by the school or the speech pathologist. There is no national standard for what information this report must provide. The school may or may not choose to provide the services of a speech-language pathologist, since this is often considered a health issue. Some provinces provide financial incentives to local school boards to secure specialists such as speech-language pathologists or psychologists. As in the United States, if you disagree with the recommendations, you can appeal the program that has been recommended in this report.

Modifications in the Educational Program

Modifications are invaluable and are often necessary, because they allow a child to compensate for a particular weakness. Appropriate modifications can mean the difference between a child who functions at top potential and thus enjoys school, and a child with lowered self-esteem who dreads school because of certain deficits. No child deserves to be overwhelmed by the educational system on a day-to-day basis through no fault of her own. Modifications can be implemented through a regular education process or as part of an IEP.

For children with language disorders, teachers can do the following:

- Write directions and assignments on the board (for students with auditory memory problems)
- Speak at a slower rate (for students with auditory memory or language processing deficits)

- Give the child time to think and mentally organize before expecting a verbal response (for students with expressive language deficits such as word retrieval problems or sequencing difficulties)
- Provide written tests instead of oral tests (for students with auditory memory or processing deficits)
- Use multiple-choice or "word bank" test formats instead of fill-in-the-blank format (for students with word retrieval deficits or spelling deficits)
- Simplify, paraphrase, and prioritize oral and written information to be learned by the child (for students with receptive language deficits or language processing deficits)
- Exempt students from annual standardized tests or allow untimed tests (for students with a receptive or expressive language deficit whose skills are better evaluated individually)

Options for Speech and Language Therapy

It is important to know there are no hard-and-fast rules, professional or legal, as to how often a child receives therapy or in what manner. These issues are determined on a case-by-case basis, depending on the needs of your child, your wishes, and scheduling issues for your child and the professionals who will be providing assistance.

Individual or Group Therapy?

Individual therapy is beneficial in some cases, particularly when a child's problem is unique or severe or when an appointment simply cannot be scheduled at another time. However, in other cases, group therapy may be helpful and more productive. The trick with group therapy is to make sure the members of the group are compatible, although not necessarily working on the same skills. For example, a fifth-grade boy should not be scheduled with a group of kindergarteners and first-graders regardless of what skills he needs to work on. It simply would be degrading for him and awkward for the other students. Also, children in school need to be scheduled in a way that won't take them away from an important subject area, so this may limit scheduling and grouping options, thus resulting in small groups or individual sessions.

Speech-Language Therapy in the Classroom

Often parents worry their children will be ostracized for leaving the classroom to receive special help. Today it is not uncommon for children to leave the room throughout the day for a variety of programs and services. Lately, however, the trend has been toward trying to provide services of all kinds within the classroom walls, so the child's day and program are not too fragmented. This is particularly true and beneficial for preschool and early elementary age children receiving several different types of special help. You might consider the following issues when deciding what is best for your child.

Team Teaching

Some speech-language pathologists now go into the classroom and work with children by "team teaching" with the classroom teacher on a periodic basis. This shows the classroom teacher how to structure speech and language lessons in the most effective way and provides an opportunity for the child receiving therapy to reinforce in the classroom skills learned in therapy. In other team-teaching situations, the lessons are planned by both the classroom teacher and the speech-language pathologist and are carried out by both professionals. For example, after the classroom teacher introduces the lesson, the speech-language pathologist takes over the discussion portion of the lesson to maximize the involvement of those students who have specific speech and language goals. Team teaching involves the entire class, not just students with special needs.

Research has not been done to document whether this approach is more effective in addressing a child's speech and language needs than the traditional "pull-out" therapy program. For a child with a normal IQ demonstrating a specific moderate or severe deficit in speech or language, I would not recommend a team-teaching approach as the complete program unless the classroom teacher has some special training in this area and is able to teach and reinforce needed skills throughout the day.

On the other hand, children with Down syndrome and other intellectual disabilities often do well with a team-teaching approach, improving their speech and language by imitating the other typical children's speech with a minimal amount of direct therapy. Children with lower IQs benefit from this approach because they learn better in everyday, natural settings as opposed to in a clinical, "isolated" setting. If an intellectually disabled child has a specific speech or language problem, however, individual or group therapy also may be very appropriate, if not necessary.

For children with autism, many social language (pragmatic) goals are well suited for being introduced in the classroom setting rather than in isolation. Also, for children with listening disorders, team teaching can be a very effective way of addressing a variety of listening skill goals.

In general, my experience has shown that team teaching is appropriate (and often ideal) for students with mild problems or certain types of language or listening weaknesses. However, team teaching alone does not provide enough individualization or opportunities for responses from children with more serious or specific problems, particularly in the area of articulation. Also, the classroom teacher cannot be expected to substitute for a professionally trained speech-language pathologist or have time to provide speech therapy to several children in a class of twenty-five or more.

In-Class Therapy

With preschool and young elementary students, having the speech-language pathologist come into the classroom to provide therapy to individuals or small groups can be more easily accommodated, if not preferred, at times. Children with mild problems or who are working on integrating previously learned skills can benefit from in-class lessons. Children who have pragmatic language (social use of language) delays also benefit from working on these skills in the classroom setting. Classrooms with several children needing services provide an excellent opportunity for the speech-language pathologist to group students and utilize interactive games. When therapy is provided in the class, only those students who have identified speech, language, and listening problems typically receive direct services.

Conducting therapy sessions in the class, however, is limiting as far as the nature of the lessons conducted. For example, music and movement activities, which are helpful with younger children, would be distracting to the other students. Children who are working on certain listening skills may need a quiet room with minimal distractions, particularly in the early stages of their therapy program. Children who are working on speech skills also need to speak at a normal conversational level so that the speech pathologist can hear whether they are pronouncing the words correctly. When a teacher is trying to conduct a lesson, this can be distracting for the child, teacher, and class. Thus, in many cases, in-class therapy is simply not the most practical way to provide services.

Some parents prefer this in-class therapy so that their child does not have to feel awkward going for special help. However, with this arrangement, the rest of the child's classmates see the therapy taking place right in the classroom, which sometimes draws perhaps even more attention to the child. It is important to weigh all the issues when deciding where the therapy should take place. Most schools try to accommodate a parent's wishes in this regard if appropriate or feasible.

Therapy with Private Practitioners, Hospitals, and Clinics

If you take your child to see a private-practice speech-language pathologist or one in a hospital or a clinic, you can expect your child will be asked to attend sessions once or twice per week, for thirty to sixty minutes per session. This may be increased or reduced as needed and may be on an individual or small-group basis.

The therapist who works with your child should give you suggestions for ways to reinforce at home the skills taught in the sessions. Additionally, if your child is of school age, the child's teacher should be made aware that she is receiving this help. The therapist should be encouraged to communicate with the teacher, either through reports or telephone calls, about the nature of the therapy and in what way the teacher can help. It is also a good idea to inform the school's speech-language pathologist, so he or she knows the child's needs are being addressed.

Therapy in U.S. Public Schools

In the public school system, the services offered to children with speech and language problems vary as far as what therapy is provided, as well as where it is provided, according to the age of the child and the child's needs.

Public School Therapy Programs for Children under 5 Years Old

Young children's speech, language, and listening development can be addressed in a variety of ways, depending on their unique needs. Again, there is no one right way to provide therapy or help.

If your child is under the age of 2, a speech-language pathologist can be contacted through the school and typically will work with you in your home or have you bring your son or daughter to a location for therapy. Sometimes therapy may be done on a monthly basis. For this age, the SLP helps you and other caregivers in your family learn to provide stimulation to your infant to facilitate development. In special cases, such as hearing impairment (particularly with a cochlear-implanted child) or cleft palate, therapy may be more direct and frequent. Again, the child's needs have to be considered.

If your child is between the ages of 3 and 5, intervention is typically provided through actual therapy sessions at a local public school or as part of a preschool program. The therapist may go into the preschool classroom and work with your child or the whole class in order to address speech and language development skills. Many schools now set up their own preschool classes, several mornings or afternoons per week, for local children with special needs. Preschoolers with no learning problems are often included in these programs in many communities. This helps the special-needs students by allowing them to see children their own age setting good examples. Typical children benefit as well, because they are provided with a preschool program (sometimes at no cost) with much smaller classes and more teachers than a traditional preschool program. Many states are encouraging and funding such programs in response to recent changes in federal law and past successes.

Public School Therapy Programs for Elementary School Children

Once your child has reached kindergarten, speech and language therapy is provided in many different ways.

For mild speech and language problems, you might expect the following:

1. Individual or group therapy sessions, if needed at all, may be held once a week or even less frequently. Therapy may instead be concentrated in your child's classroom or in a "speech room." Another alternative is the team teaching or consultative approach described earlier in this chapter.
2. The therapist will communicate regularly with you and the classroom teacher.
3. Your child's progress in speech, language, and listening, as well as in other academic areas such as reading, will be monitored.

For moderate to severe speech and language problems, you might expect the following:

1. Individual or group therapy sessions may be held two or more times a week. This may take place in your child's classroom, in a therapy room, at a learning or resource center, or in a combination of places.
2. Team teaching when possible and/or joint planning sessions (called consultation) will be conducted with your child's classroom teacher and any other specialists working with your child, to plan lessons and strategies that would be beneficial for his speech and language development within the curriculum being taught. This may be nec-

essary on a weekly basis for some children and should be written right into the IEP if it is expected. As mentioned previously, however, many schools are suffering from shortages of speech-language pathologists and may have difficulty working weekly consultation times into the schedule.
3. The therapist will provide regular communication and, if appropriate, follow-up activities you can do at home to improve your son's or daughter's speech and language skills.

Public School Therapy Programs for the Adolescent

As your child enters middle school or junior high school, new issues arise. You, the speech therapist, and classroom teachers must weigh priorities and examine your child's progress in therapy. Is your child still improving? Does your child resist going to therapy or doing the recommended home activities? Is your child feeling overwhelmed with all the responsibilities and changes of middle school? These questions are valid to ask at any age, but they become particularly necessary once your child leaves elementary school. If your child still has a language or auditory disorder (it can be assumed to be a permanent problem if it has continued to this age), it should be discussed at a joint meeting with you, the speech pathologist, and all teachers involved. If changes (modifications) in the way teachers present lessons and/or tests are needed for your child to succeed, these should be discussed and written into the IEP, regardless of whether your child receives direct therapy.

The following are some reasons why therapy may *not* be appropriate at this age:

1. Adolescents may resist going for help, and therefore may be poor candidates for therapy.
2. Scheduling demands often create problems. A student may adamantly refuse to leave a class in which he does well in order to attend therapy sessions, although the student logically should miss that one rather than a class that is more challenging. With many teachers involved, there is less flexibility during the day.
3. Progress may have reached a "plateau." The fact is, there are some students who will always have a speech, language, or listening problem. Once compensation strategies have been taught, isolated exercises and therapy may be of little use by this age, particularly for children with language or listening disorders.
4. Students with other learning disabilities may need to focus their attention on succeeding in the classroom, which may leave little time

or energy for attending separate classes or completing separate homework assignments. Again, prioritizing your child's needs is the key.

Remember, there is no single right way to plan a student's speech, language, and listening program. Many adolescents continue to attend speech and language classes through high school and continue to improve. If your son or daughter continues to make steady progress and does not resist attending therapy or language classes, I recommend continuing your child in the program, even at the middle school or high school level. Many schools are trying to find innovative ways to involve the speech-language pathologist in the classroom and make the goals and activities more functional and meaningful for those students who need special help.

PART II

Speech, Language, and Listening Problems

5

Understanding Speech Problems

Speech (articulation) problems often trouble parents far more than children. If children can speak well enough to be understood, especially at a young age, they are usually satisfied. But as a parent, it can be unnerving to hear your child stutter or ask for a "wewwwow cwayon," like an old Elmer Fudd cartoon. "Oh, no," you may think. "I remember Jimmy Wesner talking like that in eleventh grade. People used to make fun of him. I don't want anyone to make fun of *my* child."

In your heart, you may know it's probably something that your child will outgrow in a few years. After reading the first few chapters of this book, you may be even more reassured. Always remember that a speech, language, or listening problem is only a very small part of who your child is. It does not define your child. And, with all of the resources available today, there is no reason to simply wait and hope. You can seek help and support your child's development, if help and support are needed.

Because of changing attitudes toward disabilities and differences of all kinds, children today are exposed to many people their age who are different from them. By the time they reach eleventh grade, seeing someone who looks, acts, or speaks differently should be far less unusual for your child than it was for earlier generations.

In this chapter I give you a crash course on the most common speech problems. I explain the nature of and treatment for stuttering, pronunciation problems, and voice problems. For each one, I describe the characteristics of the problem, how a child is affected, and what you as a parent can do to help your son or daughter.

It is not necessary for you to become an expert in the field, but by becoming better informed, you will have a greater understanding of your child and her unique needs.

Stuttering

M-M-Mom? C-C-Can I go over to-to-to Billy's house? I-I-I . . . I will be back after lunch. Wha-Wha-Whaaat are we having for lunch?
—Jamie, age 6

We've all had problems tripping over words before. If you pay close attention when you talk today, I bet you'll find yourself repeating words. In fact, "stuttering" is a normal part of everyday conversation. Speech requires quite a bit of coordination involving the mouth, the vocal cords, and the brain. Sometimes one is moving a little faster than the other, and-uh-and we stutter. But what makes our normal, everyday repetitions of words different from those of a person with a true stuttering problem? In this section you will learn how to recognize and understand a child with Jamie's problem and what can be done for children like him.

When children learn to talk, they go through a normal "phase" in which they repeat words or phrases. For example, "Mommy, Mommy, look at-look at that!" It sounds and looks a lot like stuttering. This usually happens between the ages of about 2 and 5. Sometimes the child does this for a few days; other times it lasts for months or even a few years, even though the child does not have a stuttering problem. The key to distinguishing between a normal phase and a true stuttering problem is how often the child stutters and in what way.

Diagnosis and Causes of Stuttering

A child who stutters is said to be *disfluent*. Although diagnosing the difference between a normal stuttering phase and a true disfluent speech pattern is tricky in the preschool years, there are some specific indicators that a speech-language pathologist will examine. For example, stutterers like Jamie tend to get stuck on the first sound of a word, often the first word in a sentence. They may repeat the first sound or syllable several times, instead of just once or twice. Once they get the word out, stutterers tend to speak very quickly, as though in a mad rush to finish before getting stuck again. Jamie knows what he wants to say. The hesitancy in his speech happens when the word gets stuck in his throat, not because he needs time to collect his thoughts.

Stuttering usually begins gradually, by the time the child is about age 5. But sometimes the only way to be sure that a child has a stuttering problem is to watch what happens over time to see if it gets better or worse.

To diagnose stuttering, the therapist observes the child talking in a number of situations and takes careful notes as to how many times the child exhibits stuttering behaviors; the therapist also notes whether the child shows frustration. Some behaviors that show frustration are stamping feet, clenching fists, blinking eyes, and grimacing. Standardized tests and informal methods for diagnosing and rating stuttering exist as well. Typically, a combination of both is used to diagnose a disfluent child.

Another type of disfluent speech is called *cluttering*. Children with a cluttering speech pattern often speak quickly, in a roundabout way, stopping and starting their words. Their articulation is sometimes imprecise, and word retrieval problems may contribute to their difficulty organizing their thoughts in a cohesive manner.

What causes stuttering? Quite simply, there is currently no clear answer. In years past, stuttering was thought to be primarily a psychological problem. Although we do know that anxiety can make stuttering worse, we now also know that there is much more to the story. Some researchers theorize that stuttering has a physiological basis or that a child is genetically predisposed toward stuttering, but we really do not know why it happens in some children and not in others. It is entirely possible that stuttering has multiple causes.

While we don't know why stuttering occurs, we do know that there are some risk factors that are associated with it. We know that almost half the children who stutter have a close family member who also stutters or stuttered, that boys are more likely to stutter than are girls, and that the older the child is when the stuttering first appears (3½ years or older), the more likely it is to be more than just a passing phase. If a child has other articulation difficulties besides stuttering, there is a greater likelihood the stuttering will persist. Last, if a preschool child's disfluent phase has not abated after about twelve months, it would suggest a higher risk for stuttering.

Characteristics of Children with Stuttering Problems

Children with stuttering problems might do the following:

- Repeat the initial sound in a word ("Sh-Sh-She is nice.")
- Repeat parts of words ("Mis-Mis-Mister Jones is here.")

- Prolong the initial sound in a word ("M————ommy's home.")
- Say "I can't say it!" or "I can't get it out!"
- Hesitate before talking, although they appear to be ready to say something (". . . I want some juice.")
- Get stuck on the first word in a thought or a phrase
- Rush the rest of the sentence once a word that was stuck is spoken
- Open their mouths with no sound coming out when trying to talk
- Grimace when trying unsuccessfully to talk
- Show frustration by blinking, stamping feet, or clenching fists

How Does Stuttering Affect a Child?

A stuttering problem can be very frustrating for a child. But as with every speech, language, and listening problem, each child will respond to the frustration in his or her own way. Some may cope by avoiding speaking situations and becoming "shy." Sometimes children who are unresponsive to speech therapy have other anxieties or issues unrelated to the stuttering that "fuel the fire" of stuttering. For those children, dealing with the underlying causes of stress through a type of counseling called cognitive-behavioral therapy (CBT) may help them benefit from speech therapy. Any kind of stress or excitement may aggravate a stuttering problem, which is why holidays, birthdays, and beginning a new school year are particularly difficult times for a child who stutters. Likewise, certain situations, such as talking on the telephone or speaking in front of an audience, can sometimes be troublesome for children who stutter. They may avoid talking in those situations because of associations with past stuttering incidents. Sometimes certain words trigger a fear of stuttering for the same reason, and the child may find creative ways to avoid using those words. Because fear can propel a child who stutters into a more pronounced stuttering episode, the child will avoid situations or words that induce fear. The speech pathologist will help the child gain confidence in nonthreatening speaking situations before approaching the child's personal fear-inducing words or situations.

In my experience, however, children who stutter are frequently not overly self-conscious or inhibited about speaking, especially at a younger age. This is particularly true if their parents are relaxed and tolerant of the stuttering. Sometimes adults are so conscious of how they look and act around other people that they assume a child will feel the same way. But many children who stutter have learned to accept their differences and express themselves quite openly and readily. Children who feel their message is valued will tend to want to talk more and not let the stuttering stop them.

As far as how stuttering affects a child's academic performance, there is no research that indicates any relationship between the two.

Therapy for a Child Who Stutters

There are many philosophies regarding stuttering therapy. Previously, most therapists took a "wait and see" attitude with preschool stutterers and deferred formal therapy until a child was of elementary school age. Today, however, more therapists initiate intervention at an earlier age and find success. Usually a child is monitored for a period of time, perhaps six months, to see whether a sporadic or recent problem becomes a more consistent, long-term problem. For example, before beginning formal speech therapy, the speech pathologist may give the parent some suggestions for facilitating a conducive speaking environment for the child at home. If the stuttering behaviors do not change, or if they worsen, formal therapy may be initiated, even in the preschool years.

Do children "grow out" of the problem if nothing is done? Perhaps some will. In fact, as many as 80 percent of stutterers eventually stop stuttering without help. The reasons for this are as mysterious as what causes stuttering.

Speech therapy is designed to improve a child's fluency. For a severe stutterer, intensive therapy several times a week may be helpful, particularly in the beginning. As the child gains more confidence and control in speaking situations, the frequency of the sessions can be reduced. Although some children completely stop stuttering after attending therapy, speech therapy is not a cure. Rather, it gives the child strategies to minimize the stuttering blocks and teaches special breathing and relaxation techniques to keep speech flowing more fluently. For many stutterers, this requires constant conscious thought when speaking—that is, they cannot always talk freely without focusing on these strategies. For many others, however, these strategies become second nature. There also are stutterers who, for some reason, do not respond to speech therapy despite their best efforts.

What Can Parents Do to Help a Child Who Stutters?

Your child's speech pathologist will undoubtedly have specific activities for you to regularly practice and "play" with your child. How often you should practice and which activities you should do will depend on the age of your child, the nature and degree of the stuttering problem, and the therapy method being used. However, some general guidelines are applicable to all children who stutter. Here are some ways to help if your child has been diagnosed with a stuttering problem:

- Speak to your child in a calm, slow, relaxed voice.
- Keep stress and conflict in the home to a minimum.
- Let your child finish speaking, no matter how long it takes, without interrupting.
- After your child speaks, pause before you respond.
- Avoid drawing attention to your child's stuttering.
- Do not insist that your child repeat mispronounced words or grammatically incorrect sentences. Instead, simply rephrase what your child said using correct grammar and pronunciation; for example, if the child says, "Jenny not g-g-going," you can say, "That's right. Jenny *isn't* going."
- Avoid putting your child on the spot by making him answer questions or talk in front of an audience of relatives or friends.
- If your child is reporting frustration with this speech, acknowledge it, give some comfort, and let your child know it's okay.

Case Study: Jenna

Jenna transferred into second grade in January. Her mother called the SLP right away to let her know that Jenna had been receiving speech therapy in her previous school system. "She was doing pretty well for the last year or so," she told her. "We even thought about discontinuing speech therapy. But the last few weeks have been pretty rough. Jenna can hardly get a word out without a struggle. I hope we haven't made a big mistake with this move. What should we do?"

The SLP spoke with Jenna's teacher, who also was concerned about her stuttering. She worked out a therapy schedule at Jenna's IEP (Individualized Educational Plan) meeting. Jenna would begin with speech therapy two times a week to help get her back on track, then once a week when she was speaking fluently 85 percent of the time. The decision regarding when to reduce Jenna's speech time would be made at a later meeting with Jenna's mother, teacher, and SLP.

The SLP assured Jenna's mother that this was probably just a short-term setback for her and was not unexpected under the circumstances. Although the move might have aggravated Jenna's stuttering for the moment, Jenna's mother and father certainly could not be blamed for her stuttering problem. The SLP pointed out that Jenna would have other sources of stress throughout her life and might have future lapses as well.

They would work together to help Jenna get control of her fluency again.

In about three months, Jenna began gradually to speak with more fluency. The SLP spoke with her therapist from her previous school, who was happy to share with her strategies she had tried with success, as well as those that were not helpful. Jenna's therapy focused on her breathing and speech patterns. They tackled troublesome words and situations gradually, after meeting success with easier words and phrases, By the end of Jenna's second-grade year, she was speaking with 80 to 85 percent fluency. When she was excited or upset, her speech would be less fluent.

Jenna is now in eighth grade and was phased out of speech therapy in sixth grade. Her mother reports that she is usually fluent but does have moments of struggling from time to time. When that happens, Jenna uses the strategies she learned in speech therapy to help her work through the block.

Common Pronunciation Problems

Most of the time I can figure out what Ben wants from us. We've developed a "code," if you will. For example, I know when he says, "Gogga" he wants me to take him somewhere in the car. I feel bad when other people don't understand him, but we've learned to be good translators. It's not a problem for us, so why bother subjecting him to speech therapy? I wouldn't want him to feel like he's different from the other kids. Besides, I heard that most kids outgrow this stuff. If he doesn't, they can work with him when he gets to kindergarten.

—Father of Ben, age 4

Unfortunately, Ben is probably painfully aware of how different his speech sounds from that of his friends. He is most likely frustrated at his inability to be understood and may resent the need for Mom and Dad to act as interpreters. His speech is a problem. When a child's speech is a problem, adults must reach out and get the help needed. Though time does do wonders for most children, for some it just adds up to prolonged frustration and embarrassment.

Knowing which problem your child will grow out of and which will continue to be a problem may be impossible for you to determine, even after reading this and other books. There are still many gray areas for professionals on this subject, so don't feel frustrated if it does not seem perfectly clear to you. It's not always an easy call for us either.

A problem pronouncing words may be classified in a number of ways. Problems pronouncing words are called *articulation delays* (also *articulation deficits* or *articulation disorders*). The degree and extent of the problem is characterized as *slight, mild, moderate,* or *severe.* By understanding the nature and degree of the pronunciation problem, the speech pathologist can better determine which therapy approach will be most effective. By understanding these differences, you can better understand why your child is having difficulty pronouncing words and why therapy often involves tasks other than practicing saying words.

At What Ages Are Certain Sounds Learned?

Over the years, quite a bit of research has been done on this topic. As a result, there are many different charts that show particular ages at which children master certain sounds to varying degrees, such as 80 percent or 90 percent of a given age group. While there is some overlap on all these charts, there are also considerable areas of disagreement. The reality is there is no single progression that we all follow, save for the typical *m, b,* and *d* sounds newly talking babies often jabber away with, which is why first words may often start with those sounds (*ball, Mama, more, boat,* or *dada*).

Babies make lots of cooing and vowel sounds in the first few months, and move to babbling with repetitive syllables ("Bah-bah-BUH-buh") while changing up the intonation and stress. They should be really noisy between 6 and 12 months of age, amusing themselves—and you—with vocal play, making raspberries (those motorboat noises with their lips that can be kind of wet), using their lips to drink from a cup and take soft food from a spoon. This kind of "lip play" and noisemaking helps your child learn how to control his voice and oral muscles in preparation for making real, "made-on-purpose" kinds of words. Having someone mirror those sounds back in a playful way inspires a typical baby to do it again. Thus your first "speech lessons" with your child!

Imitation refers to when the child copies what you say or do. Babies should have a natural desire to imitate you, and the sounds and words you make. By 12 to 15 months, if not sooner, there should be some success. For example, if you say "bee" there should be some kind of attempt to imitate you, such as "buh" or "ee" or "nee" or "pee." We call these attempts *approximations.* Approximations are when the child is trying to shape the word you are modeling, even if it doesn't sound exactly right. With babies, approximations start out a bit simplified, and over time become closer and closer to adults' productions. Jargoning is not the same because random noises are being produced, usually for the baby's enjoyment or self-exploration. If your baby doesn't pay attention to the sounds and words you make or try to copy them, it's time to check in with your physician.

The phonetic composition of our "first words" is often surprising. At a conference I attended, an audience of speech pathologists was informally surveyed regarding our own children's first words (or ours, if we knew it). As we went around the room, words such as *okay, Sammy, chicken, Nana,* and *cow* were reported, in addition to the usual ones such as *mama.* Since sounds such as *s, ch, k, n,* and *r* are not usually shown on developmental charts to be developing at the earliest stages, our experiences showed that the sound progression in each of us is somewhat unique and not necessarily predictable. That said, I did include a sampling of the usual patterns in chapter 1 so you are at least familiar with some broad guidelines, and there is information in this chapter as to the typical sounds that are misproduced and when.

How Are Sounds Produced?

There are attributes of sounds that we have organized into neat little categories. You will often see these descriptions or references in your child's articulation reports. When we look at your child's speech, we look at the sound the child is supposed to be making, and the sound that is being produced in its place, if at all. When we see patterns, it helps us define the underlying problem, and thus the quickest way to fix it. Here is how we organize sounds:

• *Sounds can be voiced or unvoiced.* When a sound is voiced, the vocal cords are used during its production. Vowels are all voiced. If you say "ahhhhhhh" and put your hand to your throat, you will feel it vibrate. Other sounds are identically produced, except for the fact that one sound is voiced and the other is not. Try this. Make a *z* sound. It is voiced. Now turn it into an *s* sound and keep your hand on your throat. Voilà! You changed nothing, except for the voicing. *S* and *z* are *cognates* (voiceless and voiced pairs that are differentiated only by their voicing). Other pairs are *p* and *b, t* and *d, f* and *v, k* and *g, ch* and *j,* and voiceless *th* (as in *bath*) and voiced *th* (as in *bathe*). If a child has difficulty pronouncing one member of a cognate pair, there is often difficulty with the other, but not always.

• *Sounds are made in different parts of the mouth,* sometimes using both lips (called *bilabials,* such as *m, p, w,* and *b*); the teeth and the lower lip (called labiodentals, such as *f, v*); the rear of the tongue against the soft palate (called *velars,* which are *k, g*); or the tongue tip making contact with the gum ridge behind the top teeth on the spot we call the *alveolar ridge* (such as for *n, t, d, s, z,* and *l*) or a little farther back (called *palatal sounds*, which include *sh, ch,* and *j*). Vowels are made primarily by moving the jaw up and down, retracting or rounding the lips, and moving the tongue. If you move your jaw from *uh* up to *ee* you will notice the change in your jaw position. The tongue and lips are relaxed for *uh* and tensed and retracted for a sound such as *ee.*

* *Some vowels are actually two vowels put together!* Did you know that *I* is actually *ah* plus *ee*? Yes, it's two quick movements! We call those *diphthongs.* For children with childhood apraxia of speech (CAS), these kinds of vowels can be particularly troublesome.

* *The way sounds are produced can be categorized as well.* Sounds that are made by quick, explosive movements (such as *p, b, t, d, g,* and *k*) are called *stop consonants* or *plosives.* Sounds that are made by blow-

---

Sound (Phoneme) Symbols

You may find that curious little lines and squiggles are used in some speech pathology reports in the articulation sections. We use a system called the International Phonetic Alphabet (IPA) to note the sounds produced more accurately on paper rather than traditional letters. I'm including the common ones below so you can translate them if you see them in a report. When we use phonetic symbols, we place a slash on both sides of the phonetic transcription. We write words how they sound, so sometimes a word is spelled with one letter, but transcribed with another. For example *rose* would phonetically be written as /roz/ since the *s* is voiced and comes out closer to a *z* sound. We don't hear the silent *e* at all, so nothing is written for it. The word *bottle* would be written /bɑdl/ since the *t* sound in the middle is generally closer to a voiced sound (*d*) than a *t*, which is the unvoiced cognate.

These sounds are just like they appear: /b/ /p/ /f/ /v/ /s/ /z/ /t/ /d/ /k/ /g/ /m/ /n/ /r/ /l/

These sounds are different:

/ ð /	voiced *th*
/ θ /	voiceless *th*
/ j /	the *y* sound, as in *yes*
/ ʃ /	the *sh* sound

ing the airstream and modifying the airstream are called *fricatives* (*f, v, s, z, sh,* and *th*). Sounds that are made with little direct contact with the tongue are called *liquids* (*r, l*).

Articulation Problems in the Toddler and the Preschooler

Speech-language pathologists tend to be less concerned about mild articulation difficulties in the very young child. Why? Because typically the child will outgrow the problem without any extra effort or attention at all. We call those kinds of speech differences *developmental articulation patterns*. The examining SLP might say, "Oh, don't worry, it's just developmental." That said, there are times when it makes sense to intervene and give our little ones a bit of a jump-start with their articulation. Because the brain is elastic at this age (due to "neuroplasticity") and

/ tʃ /	the *ch* sound
/ ʒ /	the *zh* sound, as in *beige*
/ dʒ /	the *j* sound, as in *juice*
/ ɚ /	the *er* sound, as in *her*
/ æ /	the *a* sound, as in *apple*
/ ei /	the *ay* sound, as in *pay*
/ i /	the *ee* sound, as in *keep*
/ ɛ /	the *eh* sound, as in *yes*
/ɑi /	the *I* sound, as in *side*
/ I /	the *ih* sound, as in *pig*
/ o /	the *oh* sound, as in *rope*
/ ou /	the *oh* sound, as in *slow* (a little longer, with an *oo* sound at the end)
/ ɑ /	the *o* sound, as in *hot*
/ u /	the *oo* sound, as in *too*
/ ʌ /	the accented *uh* sound, as in *luck*
/ ə /	the unaccented *uh*, as in *about*
/ ʊ /	the *u* sound, as in *put*
/ æ u /	the *ow* sound, as in *how*
/ ɔi /	the *oy* sound, as in *toy*

Can you guess what this says? /mɑI neim Iz pædi/. (My name is Patti.)

receptive to changes, supporting good articulation and sound awareness can also help your child prepare for later reading, spelling, and listening skills. By the age of 3, your child should be understandable much of the time, and by the time they are 4 to 5 years old, most of their sounds and words should be nice and clear, with perhaps a pesky *r*, *l*, or *th* still hanging on. Aside from having specific difficulties with sounds, children at this age have a delightful way of mixing up multisyllabic words. You get surgery at a "hopspital" or see "amimals" at the zoo. That's perfectly fine and normal.

I should also add here that when a child is evaluated for articulation problems, there is some subjectivity from SLP to SLP. Some of us are more conservative and like to take a "wait-and-see" approach, and some are much more proactive, and will nearly always recommend therapy, just to be on the safe side. I tend to be somewhere in the middle. There is no hard and fast timetable where at 28 months one kind of error is within normal limits and magically at 29 months, it is not. It's a bit more fluid than that, and since most articulation tests only look at word production rather than at connected speech, there is often an element of clinical judgment that enters into our decision-making. We have broad ranges that we look at, and if your child is just on the edge, it can sometimes go either way. That is why it's not unusual to have two SLPs see the same child and have different recommendations regarding when to initiate treatment, and if so, how frequently.

An unintelligible child is saying *something*, but you only catch words you recognize here and there, or maybe not at all. If you have some familiarity with the context, it's easier to guess what the child is trying to say. The word *intelligibility* means how easy or hard it is to understand your child. It is not related to intelligence. Sometimes the child has a particular pattern that you come to know, and that makes understanding him easier. In speech pathology lingo, we call those patterns *phonological processes*. While these are usually associated with preschool speech patterns, in children with more complex disorders, developmental disabilities, and hearing loss, these difficulties can persist into the elementary school years or even later.

Unraveling Multiple Articulation Errors: A Phonological Processes Primer

These are the most common errors associated with phonological processes. SLPs often reference them in reports, so it's helpful for you to become familiar with what they mean.

- *Voicing errors.* This is when sounds are produced with voicing, even when they shouldn't be. So a word such as *puppy* might be produced as "bubby." Children who are new talkers often do this because turning your vocal cords off and on requires delicate, fine control. It takes practice, and a more developed ear for the subtle differences. Babies often do this up until around 24 months. Other examples would be saying "doo" for *two*.
- *Fronting errors.* This is when sounds that are normally produced in the middle or back of the mouth are instead produced up front. Often a *d* or *t* sound is used in these cases so that a word like *car* is produced as "tar" and *shake* is pronounced as "tate." This is another frequent early speech pattern in babies who are just learning to talk, but it should gradually be reducing by about age 24 to 36 months, with an occasional lingering *k* or *g* sound error persisting a little bit longer.
- *Final consonant deletion.* This occurs when the last consonant sound in a word is left off altogether. For example, a word such as *boat* would be pronounced as "boa" or *five* is produced as "fie." Because many words are differentiated by the last sound, a child who drops the final consonant consistently can be hard to understand. This speech pattern is typical for babies and new talkers but should be gradually improving and disappearing for the most part by about 24 months. In some cases, final consonant deletion is a feature of African American Vernacular English (AAVE), which would be considered a dialectal difference as opposed to a speech disorder. Because final consonant deletion is associated with possible hearing loss, it's always a good idea to rule out any hearing difficulties just to be on the safe side.
- *Consonant cluster reduction.* When two consonants are put together, they form a consonant blend (in phonics lingo) or a *consonant cluster* (in speech pathology terminology). A word such as *spoon* may be produced as "poon" (leaving off the *s*) or "soon" (leaving out the *p*). The word *jump* could be reduced to "jupp." This pattern is universal in babies and toddlers. Putting those sounds together is tricky! Usually by age 4, it has largely diminished.
- *Syllabic reductions.* Children who are just learning to talk often take a longer, multisyllabic word (such as *telephone*) and reduce it by taking out the unaccented syllable. In this case, a typical mispronunciation would be "teh-phone." With three- and four-syllable words, that's common. However, two-syllable words should not be reduced to a one-syllable word, even in babies. There should be some kind of "marking" for that syllable, even if it is a vowel. For example, *tummy* should not be reduced to "tuh" or "me," which are single syllables, particularly after the age of about 18 months.

- *Stopping*. Sounds that should be continued (such as fricatives *s*, *f*, etc.) are sometimes stopped instead. For example, the word *soap* would be produced as "toap." The tongue and mouth are in the right place. There is no voicing, which is perfect since *s* is not voiced. The problem is the manner of production. The airway is stopped instead of continued. This is another common problem in toddlers and pre-schoolers. It's often an easy one for us to fix because once the child understands the pattern, it can be applied across numerous sound groups. This kind of pattern should resolve itself or be significantly improved by 36 months or sooner if it's in combination with other speech errors.

How Would an SLP Correct Multiple Articulation Errors?

The SLP may work on one phonological process at a time, or rotate specific sounds or specific words (or even phrases) that are targeted, all at the same time. We used to nearly always start with sounds that were produced earlier on the developmental charts (*b*, *m*, vowels) and progress along the same timetable that most sounds were thought to occur. However, newer research and philosophy finds that this isn't necessarily the best or only way to go about remediating children's articulation disorders. The variables that go into our decision-making when we jump in and tackle a child with multiple speech errors include:

- Is there a word the child needs to say and use on a regular basis that might be motivating?
- How well can the child imitate the target sound? If she can do that fairly easily, we say the sound is *stimulable*—easy to elicit. We often target sounds that are stimulable so the child can feel some success and form positive associations with the speech therapy process.
- Which sounds are particularly problematic for this child in terms of her being understood? Although *s* lisps are often left alone until kindergarten or first or second grade, if your child's substitutions are peculiar ("hope" for *soap*) or the *s* is omitted altogether ("The 'un is yellow") we will want to address it sooner. The *s* sound carries much linguistic weight because it is needed for plurals, possessives, and contracted verbs. Therefore, if it's missing, the child's grammar is also affected.
- In general, omitted sound patterns (final consonant deletions, initial consonant deletions, omitted syllables) and distorted vowels cause some of the most challenging speech patterns and will be targeted quickly.

Therapy for children should be playful, motivating, and fun, but make no mistake: for a child who struggles with speech production, it is still often hard! When a child struggles to learn a new sound, it can be very frustrating. Even the most talented SLP cannot wave a magic wand and instantly change a speech pattern without some amount of effort from the child. However, the entire session shouldn't be frustrating, and when that happens, the SLP should pull back and weave in easy/intermediate tasks so your child doesn't want to give up. It's all about finding the right balance. The types of activities and strategies the SLP would employ with a child with multiple articulation errors might include:

- *Phonemic simplification.* For very young children, we may not be able to teach a name such as Gwendolyn right away. It may be too difficult. So we can find a way to break it down into simpler productions that will "do" for now. Let's pretend your daughter is named Gwendolyn, but pronounces it as "Neh" or "Neh-win." A good approximation for Gwendolyn might be "Wennah-win" at first. (Matching the number of syllables is key if at all possible, as is using sounds that are easy to produce.) As the child gets more sophisticated in speaking, we can add more sounds: "Wendo-lin," which can later morph into "Gwenda-lin" by simply tacking on the initial *g*. We use this strategy as a transitional tool when the word is just too complex.

- *Minimal pairs.* When a child leaves off the initial/final sounds or leaves out sounds in a consonant blend, minimal pairs is a great strategy. For example, if the difficulty was final sound deletion, we might present the child with a bow—the kind that goes on a gift—and a boat. We could ask the child to find the *bow* and then to find the *boat.* Simple enough. Now it's the child's turn to ask us to find them. "Hmm, you're asking me to find the 'bow,' so here it is. But gee, now you're asking me to find it again." (Not really; he wants you to point to the boat, but he pronounced them both the same way: "boa.") By helping the child become alert to the fact that these are two different words, we can teach him to tack on those final sounds. Other great matches for final consonant deletion include *bee/bean, bee/beak, bee/bees, bow/bone, bow/bowl, bow/bows.*

- *Phonemic awareness.* If you have a kindergartener, you've probably heard this term before. It involves different activities to help children learn how sounds are put together to make words or change words. It is a building block for learning and storing words and for processing language, and it lays the auditory groundwork for later reading and spelling skills. In addition, having a good working phonemic knowledge is great for supporting articulation development. Some basic phonemic awareness activities include identifying the first/last sounds in a word, rhyming skills, counting or clapping out syllables, and blending sounds (*b-a-t* = ?). We can start some basic phonemic skills around age 4. In the meantime, reading Dr. Seuss books and nursery rhymes with lots of emphasis and animation are great ways to get started.

• *Touch cues, gestures, and other reminders.* When we want to remind (or "cue," in the speech therapy world) a child to make a sound in a word that we've been practicing, we try to stop short of modeling it (showing how to say it so the child can copy it). Why? Because we know that the new sound pattern will "stick" much better if we ask the child to create it herself, rather than be a copycat. To remind a child, we can associate it with an action. We often choose the cue to correct the nature of the error. For example, here are some common cues:

- If the child stops an *s* sound and produces a *t* instead, the SLP might wave her fingers to cue for the sound to keep going.
- If the child produces a *t* instead of a *k* sound, the SLP might tap under her throat—or the child's—to remind the child to place the sound in the back of the throat.
- If the child's lips are barely making contact and the word *boat* sounds more like "hoat," the SLP will probably take two fingers and tap the lips.
- If the child isn't retracting her lips for the *ee* sound, the SLP might smile and point to it.
- If the child doesn't finish words (final consonant deletion), the SLP might keep her hand open during the production of the word and then close her fingers together to cue the child to "close" the word at the end.

• *Providing sensory feedback.* The SLP will want to use everything possible to help the child hear the correct sound (plastic amplifying headphones, tape recorders, looping devices, special software), see the way the sound is produced (videotaping, mirrors), and feel how the articulators are supposed to be placed during the production of a speech sound. Sometimes this involves using creativity, including popping bubbles on the lips (to prompt the lips to stay together, such as for *m* sounds), rounding the lips to blow a horn (to help position the lips for the *oo* sound), or holding a Cheerio up behind the top teeth on the alveolar ridge with the tongue (to help find the "spot" for *t, d, n, l, s, z*). These kinds of oral-motor placement techniques can be quite handy if done for the right reasons, by a skilled SLP. Performing random oral-motor exercises for strengthening or for a "workout" is typically not recommended unless there is a specific condition that requires it, such as dysarthria, hypotonia, or cerebral palsy.

Common Speech Patterns

At times, a speech pattern might sound almost like gibberish. Children who are very hard to understand have many different kinds of difficulties. Here are a few of the more common ones. Which speech pattern sounds like your child?

• "Eee-ee-uh-oo." (The child is showing you a balloon, trying to tell you "Mimi's balloon.") In this case, there are only vowels in this child's speech pattern, but fortunately they match up with what the child is trying say. It's also good that there is at least a two-word utterance here. If your child is talking in mostly vowels and is over the age of 18 months or so, get it checked out sooner rather than later. The child either isn't hearing the consonants (they are higher frequencies than the vowels) or may have some difficulty with moving the tongue and lips. With this kind of speech pattern, the only thing that seems to be moving is the jaw (up and down) and the lips (which are tensing, relaxing, then protruding). What's going on with the tongue? Is your child also having difficulty chewing and swallowing? Is the tongue "tied"? The tip of the tongue should be able to stick out, without bowing like a heart in the front. It should be rounded and able to point up to the roof of the mouth, without restriction.

• "Dah!" (Car!) This is a typical misproduction when a baby is first learning to talk. If this same child came to my office at the age of 24 months or older and was communicating in one-word phrases (or just pointing or gesturing), the parent might be concerned about the status of his articulation. After all, he isn't saying his *c* sound correctly, and the *r* was totally left off. That's true, yes, but whenever a child's language is delayed and there isn't much chattering or usage going on, you will find that these immature articulation patterns will persist longer. The SLP will be far more concerned about the amount and use of language (not to mention the comprehension) than about the pronunciation. This sometimes irritates parents, but speech clarity is always secondary to speech development. At the very least, we need to have something for the child to say before we worry about how it sounds.

• "Duh-duh nunny . . . dah-doo boat!" (Your child is pointing and showing something to you, but you have no clue what he's saying. He jabbers rapidly like this a bit, without much frustration or effort.) This probably sounds like not a whole lot to you, but an SLP will look at this much differently. First, I'd be really happy your child wants to show you something and is making some effort at talking. Yay! The other good news is that there appears to be some kind of sentence structure—the words are differentiated, and he even is putting two syllables together. Once we fill in the actual words, your child will probably have the makings of a reasonable sentence. Intent and connecting words are a great start. The difficulty in this case is that the child is overgeneralizing sounds by making them in the front of the mouth, such as that *d*, as well as the *n* sound (remember the phonological process called "fronting"?), and it's hard to understand him. There are other things going on with this pattern, but since we don't know what he is actually trying to say, it's hard to connect the dots and identify all the processes that might be involved. We see this a lot. If he's under the age of 22 months, I'd probably hold off and see if things improve unless he's getting frustrated or inhibited. Definitely get his hearing checked to make sure there is no residual fluid or hearing loss interfering. If there's no change in a few months, spring into action. In general, this kind of articulation difficulty is called a "delay," meaning it might be developmental (he'll grow out of it) but might not. Insurance companies generally will not cover speech therapy for anything that is developmental, so you might see a fancier diagnosis if you are going for private therapy, perhaps "phonological processing disorder" or "other speech disturbance," which indicates a pervasive and systematic difficulty with the articulation pattern. Don't fret. We have such fun working with these kinds of cases. Progress is usually quick, and the child is far less frustrated and will be less inhibited socializing with peers once people know what he's saying!

- "Ah . . . fwuh-ppy . . . dah . . . dah-mah . . . dah-puh." (Your child gestures to show you that his toy puppy is jumping. He is groping and moving his mouth laboriously. The sentence he is trying to say is "The puppy is jumping," but he shakes his head and tries to correct himself on the second attempt at the word *jumping*.) In this case, the slowness of the productions, the extreme effort, and the difficulty with vowels would signal a possible *childhood apraxia* ("uh-PRAX-ee-uh") *of speech* (CAS) condition. Notice how the child substituted *fw* for *p* at the beginning of the word *puppy* even though he clearly can make the *p* sound just fine in other words. These are not the kinds of difficulties a child will "grow out of." Assuming this child is at least 22 months, you should take action soon as possible. As always, get the hearing checked. Is your child having other motor difficulties? How is his walking, running, and jumping? Are there feeding difficulties or trouble with holding utensils? Children with apraxia usually have other systemic motor difficulties. For more detailed information about apraxia, read further in this chapter.

• "Gih me duh gee boa!" (Give me the green boat!) So what's going on here? As you know, we SLPs love to find patterns. The phonological process pattern here is final consonant deletion. Sometimes children develop this pattern for no particular reason. Other times, it signals a possible hearing loss, since we know that final sounds are produced with less volume. If the child doesn't *hear* those sounds, they won't be pronounced. Get the hearing checked to be sure. If that's fine, try some of the suggestions later in the chapter to facilitate better speech. If there is no improvement in a few months, get it checked out, certainly no later than about age 36 months.

• "I gah a ih ah ee bah." (I got a fish and three balls.) In this child's case, there is yet another interesting pattern. Sounds are completely omitted—not distorted or replaced with others, but absent altogether. Sounds that are not voiced (e.g., *t, k, s, f, p, sh*) happen to be the group of sounds that are missing. Is it a coincidence? Probably not. This kind of speech pattern would be suggestive of a high-frequency hearing loss. All the omitted sounds are high-frequency sounds. That is the pattern. It could be that the child had ongoing middle ear infections that have since cleared up (thanks to medications or tubes) but now the problem has been habituated, and in some cases, the child has not had enough auditory input at the critical learning time to pay attention to those sounds. This child needs a good hearing evaluation and should get speech therapy and auditory training, especially if older than 20 to 22 months.

• "Duh . . . [breath] pah . . . [breath] pee . . . [breath] wah reh." (The puppy was red.) In this case, there is a distinct choppiness and extra breaths, followed by final consonant deletions. In a 12- to 18-month-old, not so unusual, but as age 2 approaches, we should see phrases connecting with fewer pauses and breaths. When children are taking too many breaths, it is suggestive of a lack of adequate breath support. This could be due to an obstructive breathing pattern, but more likely is due to a lack of diaphragmatic breath muscle strength and overall low muscle tone. Is there drooling? Is the child a messy eater? Is she having other motor issues? As always, hearing problems should be ruled out. The final consonant deletions on *was* and *red* might have more to do with the child's running out of air than having actual difficulty pronouncing those missing sounds. Children with Down syndrome and cerebral palsy (ataxic) often have speaking patterns like this, which can be described as "dysarthric." Later in this chapter there is more information on this speech condition.

• "Thuthie ith thopping for a threth." (Susie is shopping for a dress.) Technically, the *s* sound and consonant blends such as *dr* and *sh* are not always learned in a 2- or 3-year-old. Yet . . . in this case the child is protruding the tongue consistently for nearly all the consonants, causing them all to be *th* sounds instead. The jaw is probably dropped open more often than not. It can become habituated very quickly and be hard to undo. If it were just the *s* sound, I'd say leave it alone at this age, but if it affects numerous sounds and makes it hard for your child to be understood, I'd get it checked out after about 3½ to 4 years old. Let the SLP help your child get that tongue in there! You also would want to rule out any physiological issues, such as enlarged tonsils, that could be causing your child to breathe through the mouth, which would exacerbate the problem. Is your child drooling? Is there additional evidence of a lack of muscle tone in the posture? The other issue here would be whether or not your child is still using a pacifier or sucking his thumb. Sometimes that can really breed these kinds of speech patterns, and if that's the case, the SLP will want to work with you to phase them out right away.

• "We're goin' shoppin' tomorrow with my uncle Feh-Feh." (We're going shopping tomorrow with my uncle Fred.) In this case, the parent was concerned because try as she might to have her child call Fred by his actual name, her 3-year-old persisted in using "Feh-Feh." This is pretty typical with toddlers and preschoolers. In the early stages of speech development, children often develop baby names for things (such as blankets or stuffed animals), pets, and people they have emotional attachments to. Once they've given them the label, they may resist "upgrading" the name once their articulation skills become a bit more sophisticated. In this child's case, we can see there is clarity in all the other words, with even a big word like *tomorrow* sprinkled in there. The best thing you can do is to continue to model the correct production and not reinforce the incorrect, "baby" version of the word your child clings to, but don't be punitive or get into a power struggle. He will eventually accept the grown-up word.

• "Mmagunng?" Let's call this one "the mumbler." In these cases, there are times you can figure out what the child is saying, but other times—particularly when he is speaking very quickly—the words get mushy and so indistinct as to not resemble anything one could write. Moderate to severe mumblers should be checked out after age 2 or so. A little mumbling is okay. Rule out hearing loss or middle ear fluid as soon as possible. Let a speech pathologist check out the mouth and make sure the oral muscles are up to par. How is your child's chewing and swallowing? He may need help learning where one word starts and another stops (word boundaries), or simply increasing awareness of how his speech sounds to others. ("I don't know if I have a 'mmagunng.'What's that?")

Of course there are many other variations of early speech difficulties, but these are the more common ones. Many times, we see a child with an assortment of issues, not just one.

Articulation Delays in Children with Hearing Issues

Does your child have frequent colds and allergies? Sometimes the ears don't bounce back, and a sneaky fluid buildup can occur, even without a fever or obvious pain. The fluid can, over time, make listening and learning speech more difficult. Ears that are overly "waxy" can get clogged and need a good cleaning. Keep your child's hearing in tip-top shape. While family physicians and pediatricians are expert at diagnosing actual infections, remember that an audiologist is the specialist who can best look at the function of the ears and the quality of hearing.

These days, physicians have become much less proactive in treating multiple ear infections due to the overuse of antibiotics in the past. While this is understandable, a young child who is in the critical stages of language and speech acquisition needs to be able to hear clearly. If your child is struggling with speech development and articulation, I would highly recommend getting aggressive with treatment for persistent ear infections, including the use of pressure equalization (PE) tubes. PE tubes are tiny tubes that are placed in the eardrum to allow drainage of chronic fluid impacting the function of the eardrum. I have seen countless children significantly improve their articulation difficulties within a few weeks of getting tubes. The other advantage is that the child will have the necessary clear auditory input to develop the auditory skills and listening habits that are the foundation to learning.

If your child has a mild hearing loss, it needs to be monitored closely by an audiologist. Go for the frequent checkups recommended and keep an eye on it. You will need to take steps to ensure that your child's listening and speech are developing on schedule. Even a slight or mild hearing loss can impact this process. In some cases, when there is an unknown origin, the hearing loss can be progressive over time. If your child is losing speech and language or her articulation pattern is becoming more "mumbly" you should suspect there is a change in hearing, and have it checked right away.

If your audiologist has recommended a hearing aid for your child, please, please make absolutely sure it is worn and turned on at all times, aside from while bathing and sleeping. At every moment, your child needs to learn how to perceive and process sound, attend to listening tasks, and hear and learn new words. Hearing that is compromised can result in speech delays, inattentive listening, and unclear speech.

If your child's hearing loss is significant enough that a cochlear implant is advised, please know that the technology today is amazing. It's not unusual to see a child speak just beautifully, despite being deaf without the implant. "The younger the better" is true, but remember that intensive auditory and speech intervention needs to go hand in hand with the implant. That means a bit of homework for you, no matter how often your child goes to see a speech pathologist or an auditory-verbal therapist (a therapist trained in special techniques for children with hearing loss, also called an AV therapist). Listening and learning language needs to be facilitated all day long.

Children with Articulation Delays: The Mouth

When the SLP does an evaluation, I mentioned previously that we like to check out your child's mouth. There are a number of things we look for, because good "working parts" help ensure that your child will be able to talk as clearly as possible. Here are some of the issues that come up:

- *Teeth.* We actually don't use our teeth for talking very much. The *f* sound is one of the few that can't get by without them. That said, we do care about the state of your child's bite and alignment. The bottom jaw should be fairly well aligned with the top so that the top teeth are just slightly overlapping the bottom teeth. If the jaw is jutting forward or sliding around, it causes the tongue (which is rooted in that lower jaw) to move with it. The other thing we are looking for is something called an "open bite." An open bite refers to the fact that the child is biting down, but there is a hole between the top and bottom teeth in the front. This is often caused by missing teeth, but if it persists, it could also be from a "tongue thrust," which is when the tongue pushes forward when swallowing, instead of retracting. Another cause is thumb-sucking and pacifiers. A tongue that is pushing forward will be less easy to tame and pull in if there is a lisp.
- *Lips.* The child's lips should be able to retract for the *ee* sound,

("Watch me; can you say this?"), come together for the *m* sound, and protrude for the *oo* sound, particularly by the time your child is 18 to 24 months, if not a bit younger. Can your child drink from a cup without a sippy top? Using a regular cup as often as possible after 15 months or so helps, even if there is a little spilling. Children who drool a bit often have difficulty with lip closure or swallowing. They may also have a decreased ability to feel the drool on their lips and chin due to a lack of sensation. If they are struggling to make speech sounds that use the lips (such as *p, b, m,* and *w*) we will want to see if they can take soft food, such as yogurt, from a spoon to eat.

• *Tongue.* Your child's tongue goes through stages. Some children really enjoy getting sensory input by wagging the tongue outside the mouth a bit, often while they are focusing on something else. That's pretty harmless, and usually doesn't persist much beyond the preschool and early elementary school years. The tongue does need to have enough mobility to retract, lift, and lateralize. While *ankyloglossia* ("tongue tie") is fairly uncommon, it does happen, and it can limit the tongue's ability to move as it needs to for swallowing and speech. In those cases, we can try stretching exercises if possible or alternative ways to produce the sounds. If those are unsuccessful, a quick laser treatment by a knowledgeable dentist or oral surgeon will do the trick, followed by exercises to promote tongue elevation. A tongue that is consistently forward or protruded, whether the child is talking or not, can set the stage for a lisp. We will check the tonsils and nasal passages to make sure nose breathing is possible. Continued use of a pacifier (after 18 months or so) can also contribute to a child's pushing the tongue forward.

• *Sensory awareness.* Children who have a decreased awareness or perception of the muscles around the mouth area are said to be *hyposensitive.* With these children, it is not uncommon to find excessive drooling or food stuck to their face long after a meal (*What sauce?*). The child may not react to it or be bothered by it. When eating crackers, he may "stuff" the crackers into his mouth because he doesn't sense when his oral cavity is adequately filled. Sometimes these children seek strong tastes, such as pickles and spicy flavors. Other children are overly sensitive to oral inputs. We say they are *hypersensitive.* They resist having their face washed or their teeth brushed. They may be very, very neat eaters and become upset if there is something on their face. They may prefer milder, blander tastes such as pasta, rice, potatoes, and bread. How oral sensory issues impact articulation directly is unclear, and so the extent that speech therapy should spend to normalize a child's oral perceptions often varies among SLPs who treat young children.

When children have oral sensory differences, there are often more per-vasive sensory issues present. Does the child seem unusually irritable or uncomfortable in noisy situations, perhaps putting her hands over her ears at parties? Does she resist wearing clothes with long sleeves or long pants, preferring to run around in her underwear long after most chil-dren do? Is bathing an ordeal? In these cases, a referral to an occupa-tional therapist for a sensory integration disorder screening would be appropriate.

Simple Articulation Problems

When a child has a problem pronouncing a particular sound or a few sounds, it is called an articulation problem. Typically, the child has con-sistent trouble saying that sound, or sounds, in every word in which the sound occurs. A "simple" articulation problem means it is usually just one or two sounds, and there are no other physical issues that would pre-clude normal speech development.

A child who is learning to speak the English language after living in another country or being raised by non-English-speaking parents will obviously have some pronunciation differences. This is called an *accent* and is not considered a speech disorder. Pronunciation of Eng-lish will naturally improve in time if a child speaks English daily and is exposed to other children speaking English. Public schools do not have programs to change a child's accent. Adults may choose to work with a private speech pathologist, who can help with accent reduction.

As discussed in chapters 1 and 2, it is normal for infants and toddlers to have problems pronouncing words. But by the time children reach first to second grade or so, all sounds should be pronounced clearly. Exactly when to recommend a child receive speech therapy to "correct" a mispronounced sound is somewhat subjective and can depend on which developmental chart the speech pathologist is using. Many school systems have policies using the age of the child and the sever-ity of the problem as criteria to determine whether the child's speech is normal.

An articulation problem can be diagnosed using standardized tests that ask the child to name or describe certain pictures. But a speech pathologist can often diagnose simple problems by observing the child speaking in conversation. The speech pathologist looks at how the child pronounces words and examines the mouth to see whether a phys-ical problem is interfering with the child's speech. Articulation may be just one of many areas examined when a child is experiencing other language or listening problems. Many children with articulation problems do, in fact, have other language and listening problems, but many do not.

Children with hearing impairments, cleft palate, cerebral palsy, traumatic brain injury, or developmental disabilities tend to have unique articulation problems. These are discussed in chapter 8 in greater detail.

Therapy for a Child with a Simple Articulation Problem

Therapy for a single sound difficulty can often completely correct a child's mispronunciation within months if done intensively. Some sounds (such as *r*), however, are a little more challenging and may take a year or more to correct. Much of a child's success depends on the child's motivation, the parents' support, the amount of regular practice that takes place at *home*, physical conditions (such as cerebral palsy) that prohibit normal articulation, and the presence of other speech, language, and listening problems that may take precedence over an articulation problem. The other variable, of course, is the training and skills of the SLP. Some are great with articulation, but some—truthfully—are not, and this is often why some simple articulation errors take much longer than they should to be corrected. Following is some information about the most common articulation problems.

Problems with the K and G Sounds

We often see children who mispronounce the *k* and *g* sounds, usually during the preschool years ("I saw titty tat" for "I saw a kitty cat"). These sounds are grouped together because, as you learned earlier in this chapter, the *k* and *g* are voiceless and voiced cognates, or pairs. If a child has difficulty with one of these sounds, chances are the mate will also be affected. These sounds are produced in the back of the mouth, with the rear part of the tongue rising up and making contact with the soft palate. What we will want to see is whether or not these sounds are misproduced consistently or primarily in words or phrases that include *t* or *d* sounds, such as shown above. If your child says *key*, *eek*, *go*, or *bug* correctly, chances are the *k/g* sound errors are occurring in anticipation of the other sounds in the word. That is why some children say "gog" for *dog* even though they have no trouble saying a *d* sound in the beginning of other words, such as *Daddy*. The influence of the other sounds in the word is called *coarticulation*. The *k* and *g* sounds in particular are more challenging in words with *t* or *d* (*duck, kite, cut, take, tick-tock, cute,* etc.) because producing them requires a quick movement from the back of the mouth to the front or vice versa. Sounds with lips (*p, b, m, w*) or open syllables (just the *k/g* along with a vowel, such as *coo*) are much easier to pair with the *k* and *g* (*pig, bag, cap, make, pack,* etc.), and so we usually will start to elicit them in words like these first. When these sounds are omitted completely, we want to see if there are any patterns, such as initial or final consonant deletion. In those cases, we'd focus more on the pattern than on the individual sound.

The speech pathologist may elect to wait and see if there is some spontaneous improvement over time, usually up until around age 3½ to 4. If the sound is stimulable (able to be produced correctly with just a little coaching), the SLP may try to get it fixed up a bit earlier, particularly if the child is already getting speech therapy for other issues. If the *k* and the *g* are the only speech errors, though, chances are most SLPs will wait it out until the child is around age 4. In order to correct a *k* and *g* sound problem, an SLP would have the child do the following:

- *Recognize the sound.* As with all articulation errors, we usually want to start with helping the child learn to auditorily recognize the target sound, and to attend to it. Remember that we are talking about sounds here and not letters. We know that the *k/g* sound can be spelled in various combinations, but we are only concerned with recognizing the sounds. Sometimes we jump to the next step and then go back and introduce the sound after it's elicited ("Guess what sound we just made?"). Using some kind of cue (touching the throat) or label ("Let's practice our throat sounds") to connect the sound and how it's made helps your child associate the place of articulatory contact with the *k/g*. We will have you emphasize the new sound in your speech so the child really starts noticing it. ("The *k*ing said, '*C*an I have some *c*orn?' Hey, did you notice? I heard some of our *k* sounds in some of those words! Did you?")
- *Make the sound.* Some SLPs find it helpful to elicit it from a coughing sound or by tipping the child's head back while he is lying on the floor and gently tapping under the throat. Another strategy is to hold down the tongue tip with a tongue depressor or a spoon so the back of the tongue can hump up for the contact with the soft palate.
- *Practice the sound.* Once a word has been elicited, the SLP will work on practicing it several times in a row (five to ten), moving to phrases and sentences in play and conversational context. We have lots of card games and board games with *k/g* pictures to make practicing fun. If all goes well and there are no complicating physical or intellectual vari-

ables, it can take a matter of weeks to several months for the sound to become habituated and used during conversation.

The S and Z Lisp

You have probably heard the term *lisp* before and have some idea of what it is. A lisp is regarded as a distortion of the *s* and *z* sounds. They are cognates produced in an identical manner, with the *z* being "voiced" by the vocal cords. To understand this better, make an *s* sound. While holding on to the *s* sound, try to make a *z* sound. The only thing you had to do was turn on your vocal cords. Your tongue never moved, and the air kept flowing, didn't it? Say the word *business*. The first *s* is produced more like a *z* than like an *s*. The last *s* in the word is a true *s*. We produce *z* sounds more often than you think!

The *s* and *z* are usually made by elevating the tongue tip on the gum behind the top or bottom teeth and blowing out with the top and bottom teeth nearly touching. Many SLPs report making contact with the sides of their tongue and molars for an *s*. Sometimes we have to experiment to find the placement that is most comfortable and clear for your child. To produce these sounds correctly, the tongue should not push on or between the teeth. If the tongue pushes forward, an *s* or a *z* may sound more like a *th* sound, and the child is said to have a *frontal lisp* or a *lingual protrusion*. If the *s* or the *z* sounds "slushy," it is called a *lateral lisp*. Speech pathologists may refer to both of these patterns as lisps.

One of the most common reasons why children lisp is a condition called a tongue thrust, also known as a reverse swallow. With this condition, the tongue pushes between the front teeth during swallowing and often when talking. You may notice the tongue sticking out, with the mouth slightly open, when the child is watching television, writing, or listening. Tongue thrusts, an imbalance of the tongue, lip, and other facial muscles, can cause or aggravate other speech or orthodontic problems. A speech pathologist may want to address this underlying cause first, with some specific muscle exercises and retraining, before working on the *s* and the *z*. Often once the child's oral "posture" is improved the *s* and the *z* almost will correct themselves. A specialist in this area is called an oral-myofunctional therapist or orofacial myologist. School-based SLPs often are not trained in this area or are counseled not to address the swallowing component, since it is not considered part of an education speech therapy program. For this reason, if the problem persists beyond a year or so, you may want to seek a private specialist in this area.

Another contributor to the development of lisps (and tongue thrusts) is thumb-sucking. When a child puts a thumb in her mouth, it puts pressure on the top teeth and the upper gum ridge, flattening the tongue under the thumb. Since the tongue needs to lift up for the *s* and the *z*, this encourages the opposite tongue position. Thumb-sucking is especially troublesome if the child is sucking all night, which means half the child's time is spent with the tongue, lips, and jaw muscles in an unnatural position. If your child is a thumb-sucker, work on eliminating or minimizing this habit to help your child's speech and reduce the risk for further orthodontic problems. For ideas on helping your child break this habit, see pages 252 to 253.

Is a lisp a problem? It depends on the child's age. Most children seem to outgrow lisps by the age of 6 or 7. Speech problems that are typically outgrown are referred to as *developmental* speech problems.

Once your child is 6 or 7, and there has been no improvement in clarity, other issues need to be considered:

- Does your child have a tongue thrust when swallowing? If so, you will probably need to address that as well as the lisp to make headway with the speech problem. If the tongue muscles are going the wrong way each time your child swallows, it will be difficult for him to retract the tongue properly when speaking. The speech pathologist or a dentist can tell you whether your child has a tongue thrust.
- Are you as a parent willing to devote the daily practice time required to successfully remediate this type of problem? Will your child be receptive to working on the activities? If the lisp does not bother your child or if your child is resistant to the whole idea, speech therapy may be ineffective.
- Does your child's school provide therapy for lisps? If the lisp is not adversely affecting your child's educational or emotional well-being, the public school may choose not to offer formal speech therapy. Private therapy may be quite costly.

There is no one universal way to correct a lisp, and the methods an SLP uses often depend on the child's current way of producing it. That said, the following is the more traditional way of fixing the *s/z* lisp.

- *Auditory discrimination.* Since there are two different types of lisps (frontal protrusion and lateral lisp) there are also different techniques for correcting them. In the case of a substitution of a *th* sound for an *s/z*, the SLP will first start with increasing the auditory discrimination and awareness of the *th* versus *s*. "If I say *thumb*, what sound do you hear at the beginning? How about *some*?" Once the child can hear the difference between the two (without looking at your mouth) it's helpful to move toward distinguishing a clear *s* from a fuzzy or distorted *s*. "Which one is the clear *s* that we want to reproduce?" The child needs to have a good ear for recognizing it so when it is finally produced, it can be readily replicated. As with other sounds that are targeted, we will want you to emphasize the sound we are targeting throughout the week. ("*So,* should we *see* the movie on *Saturday?* Hey, I heard some of your *s* sounds in there! Did you?")

• *Get the sound clear.* A good *s* can sometimes be easily elicited on the first try with a minimal amount of coaching. ("Watch me. Do it this way.") We love that! One trick is to have the child make a *t* sound and hold it out. Don't even mention *s* or the child will jump back into his old way of saying it. Sometimes it's easier to start with it at the end of a word such as *bat* ("battttsss") just to get the sound out clearly. You can isolate it and work from there. We often need to cue children to get those teeth a bit closer (almost biting down) so the tongue isn't popping out. And in case you are wondering, it is a bit trickier doing this with a child who has her top front teeth out. Sometimes we do wait for them to come in, but other times we can elicit the sound just fine anyhow. If the tongue pushes through, the jaw slides, and the *s* sounds fuzzy or slushy, a good SLP will know how to facilitate a clear production by helping the tongue and jaw work together in harmony so the sound is perfect. When children produce a variety of sounds between the teeth that are normally produced on the alveolar ridge—the gum behind the top teeth—*t, d, n,* and *l* in addition to the *s/z* lisp—it often makes sense to work on the production of all these sounds at the same time so the child gets into the habit of retracting the tongue during speech and resting it on the alveolar ridge. We also want to encourage the child to keep those lips together and breathe through the nose throughout the day so the tongue can pull in and the muscle gets trained to retract.

• *Practice, practice, practice.* With speech homework, the trick is to not have the child practice a fuzzy or poor production. Practicing the wrong way is not at all helpful and will discourage the child from continuing to work on fixing the lisp. The SLP should put the practice activities in a notebook or a folder and explain how to do them. There should be some fun games to play, pictures to color, or puzzles to solve. Exercises to help train the tongue and jaw position are helpful if there is an associated tongue thrust. However, the bottom line is that many repetitions are needed to undo the speech habits that have developed. In the beginning, your child may think the new *s* sounds "funny" and feels "weird." Daily practice (10 to 20 minutes) is important, but the child's motivation to change his speech pattern is essential. Without it, it is very hard to make the transition to a new sound production, no matter how good your child's speech pathologist is. Fixing up an *s*/*z* lisp can be quick (a few months), but it also can be long and laborious if the child is reluctant to integrate the new production into his speech pattern unless prompted. It's helpful to practice the *s*/*z* in words and then try to get the child to begin using the new *s*/*z* in controlled sentences, structured speaking tasks, and then eventually in conversation. Speed drills help the mouth become more adept at quickly producing the word, which aids in carryover into other speaking situations. Make a big fuss whenever the new, correct sound is used without your reminders. ("Wow, that word *stop* was perfect! What a great *s* you made, and I didn't even remind you!") At this stage, you may need to provide some kind of tangible reward to get over the hump. In the beginning, using the new sound requires so much concentration that children resist doing so because they don't like paying attention to how they talk. Usually I find that if a child can be motivated to use the new *s*/*z* in conversation—with occasional subtle reminders and coaching from you—for three solid weeks nearly all the time, by the fourth week it usually has become habituated. However, you need to wait until the child has progressed enough and is ready for that stage in the process. If in doubt, ask the SLP.

Problems with R

Aside from the *s* and *z* sounds, the *r* sound is probably the most commonly mispronounced and the most challenging to fix. You may have the following questions:

- *Is it an accent?* Many times, people think their child has an "accent." That might be true if you live in Boston or New York, but even then, there are differences between an accent and a typical *r* distortion. How can you tell the difference? Typically, the *r* sound at the beginning of words is not affected with accents, while the *r* at the beginning of words for a child with an *r* problem may be. Sometimes it is not a complete substitution of *w* in place of the *r*, but rather another sound somewhere in between a *w* and a true *r*. With an accent, we might find it is dropped off or substituted with *uh* (as in *us*) so that *hammer* becomes "hammuh." In cases where the child has an *r* problem, the *er* sound becomes distorted, often sounding more like *oo* (as in *moo*: "hammoo"), *u* (as in *put* or *hook*: "hammuu"), or *aw* (as in *awful*: "hammaw"). If you're not sure, have your child say "hammer" and hold out the last sound as long as possible so you can really hear it.
- *Will my child outgrow it?* When we evaluate the probability of a

child's outgrowing the distorted *r*, we might listen every few months and note if the child is stimulable (able to copy it with some coaching) or not, or if the *er* is a bit closer to being correct than before. If there is some change over time, chances are better that it would resolve itself. If there is no spontaneous improvement, chances are it won't happen naturally. Have your child say "wing ring." The two words should sound different, and the lips on the word *ring* should not be rounded and pulled out, but tensed with only a little bit of flat protrusion. The other difference is the *er* sound at the end of words. Producing the *r* sound at the beginning of words (or in words such as *carrot* or *kangaroo*) involves tensing the lips, with just a bit of tongue tension at the same time. Consonant blends with *r* sounds (as in *br*own and *fr*ee) use similar movements and are often addressed once the *r* at the beginning of words is fairly consistent. The *r* at the end of words is actually produced a little bit differently. We call it the "vowel-controlled *r*" sound, and it is often the trickiest kind of *r* sound to make. There are several variations on what the tongue specifically does, but usually children are coached to curl the tongue back, keeping contact along the molars with the edges of the tongue, but not touching the roof of the mouth. Vowel-controlled *r* sounds include *ar, air, our, ear, ire*, and the dreaded *or*, which can be the most challenging of them all. We often need to tackle these one at a time since the position of the vowel that precedes the *r* will influence the oral movements. Having an SLP who can really hear the subtle differences in the various *r* attempts and provide appropriate feedback is important. To correct an *r* problem, the SLP will have your child focus on the following:

- *Auditory discrimination.* When children have difficulties producing the *r* sound clearly, we often find confusions in their spelling patterns as well. In order to change their production, they need to really hear and memorize what the correct target is supposed to sound like. The SLP might produce a word with *r* at the beginning such as *rabbit* with slight distortions ("ewwabbit"), big distortions ("wwwabbit"), and everything in between until the perfect *r* is produced ("rrrabbit!"). Can the child jump in and tell you when the perfect *r* is produced? That discrimination is key. When *r* is produced in the various *r*-controlled words, hearing the *er* is essential because the other vowel-controlled *r* sounds include it. For example, *air* is actually *ay* plus *er*, *ear* is *ee* plus *er*, and so on. If the *er* is distorted or the child can't hear it, all the *r*-controlled vowels will be distorted. Producing words that have both *r* and *l* (*world, girl, roller coaster*) is typically extremely challenging, as is producing words with two *r* sounds (*farmer, hamburger, warmer*), so these should be saved until the child is a bit more confident.

- *Making the* R. The SLP will work hard to shape the *r* sound so it is clear. This can be challenging and may involve breaking it down into smaller steps, such as working on the position of the lips or the tongue. It is often easier to start with *r* at the beginning of words and in consonant blends, but each case is different. The key here is not to have the child practice saying word lists at home if the production itself is still flawed. Practicing should focus on clarity. After the *r* is clear, repetitions and speed can be introduced, with the new sound integrated into familiar phrases ("How are you?") and conversation, with lots of cueing and support. Feedback here is critical, with the child becoming more adept at recognizing his own errors and fixing them. Using a mirror, videotape, and articulation software are just a few ways children can monitor how they are producing the sound. The jaw is sometimes sliding or dropped too low, the tongue may be too flat, and the lips may be too rounded, so the SLP will have to give pointers to get all these parts working together in perfect harmony. The SLP and the parent will want to have some common language related to the *r* sounds; often referring to it as "the new *r*" gives it an identity. Avoid judgmental terms such as "your bad *r* sound" or "the baby way of saying *r*."
- *Integrating the* R *into conversation.* Children often struggle to transition out of their old habits with *r* and integrate the new sound into their daily conversation (carryover). It's often a laborious process trying to remember to use it; it can feel "weird"; and at first it might sound more effortful and awkward than their usual way of saying *r* sounds. Hang in there! Remember, the key is to promote not carryover of a flawed or "halfway there" production, but the correct one. Because using a new *r* sound is so challenging, consider giving your child a little treat for reaching some key benchmarks. In the beginning, you might have to start with just using the sound in a "safe" environment, such as at home, after school. In time, you can expand it to other settings. Develop some kind of mutual signal to remind your child to say it right, but don't go overboard—reminding him two or three times a day is plenty. It's more important to praise the attempts and effort when it's done right. Make the rewards for longer-term goals, such as using the sound for a whole week, at least 50 percent of the time. Each week, set the bar a little higher, and before you know it, your child will forget how to say it the old way.

Problems with L

Difficulties pronouncing *l* are pretty common. Often, children who have difficulty with *r* sounds also struggle with *l*. In very young children, we often see the word *yellow* produced as "weh-wo" or "yeh-yo" or "yeh-wo." The reason this particular word is so difficult is that producing the *y* and the *l* back-to-back is a tricky oral movement. Often, the child has no difficulty with a word such as *love* or *lap*. Another combination that is challenging is when an *l* sound and an *r* sound are in the same word, such as *girl*. When your child has trouble with *l*, but only in these situations, it will usually resolve itself in time without direct therapy. But if the *l* is consistently misproduced or omitted in words, or if your child is having trouble spelling words because of the speech problem, is frustrated or self-conscious, or is at least 6 years old, it's probably time to work more directly on it with speech therapy. Here's how we might go about fixing that *l* sound:

- *Recognize the sound.* In order to help change the way a child produces the *l*, it's important that the child be able to identify the target sound. "Does *lion* start with the rrrr sound? The 'yuh' sound? The 'wuh'?" Remember, we aren't talking about letters and spelling patterns here, just the sound that is heard. An isolated *l* sound is hard to make (just like *w* and *y*), but it's important that it's not made as "ill"—the back of the tongue needs to be lower, more like "ull." When the SLP says *lion* correctly with an *l*, does the child recognize it? We'll want the parent to emphasize the *l* throughout the week so the child can start noticing which words have it. ("*L*ook, there's no cerea*l l*eft in your bow*l*.")

- *Use the sound in words and phrases.* The *l* sound is going to be elicited right away in syllables, words, and then sentences. It should be produced with the tongue tip up on the gum right behind the top teeth. The top and bottom teeth should be fairly close together so the mouth isn't open too far. While the *l* sound can be made acoustically pretty clearly by sticking the tongue out between the teeth, this production should be discouraged because frankly it looks funny and is considered to be a more immature speech pattern. We normally wouldn't initiate speech therapy just for that reason, but tongue tip up and inside the mouth is the way to go. Once the production is clear, speed drills and daily practice will help the mouth habituate the new pattern.

- *Carryover.* As with all articulation difficulties, reminding and rewarding a child for attempting to use the new *l* sound is helpful, but don't overdo it. Two to three reminders a day, done discreetly and with silent signals, is often the best plan. More than that, praising and acknowledging attempts at using the new sound is best. ("Wow, I just heard the most fantastic *l* sound when you said 'clown'!")

Problems with TH

Many children have difficulty producing *th* sounds before they reach the end of first grade or so. They typically produce these words with an *f* sound, which is a convenient and appropriate substitution because the two sounds are quite similar. If a child says, "I have a loose too*f*," everyone knows the word is *tooth*. This kind of speech problem really isn't a problem at all for a young child, but by the time a child reaches first grade, there may be some confusion when trying to spell words. Even without associated spelling issues, by second grade, it may sound "babyish" and fixing it is definitely in order. In these cases, working directly on recognizing and producing the *th* is the first step. The SLP will show the child with a mirror how the *th* is produced with the tongue just a little bit between the top and bottom teeth, while gently blowing out. ("You get to stick your tongue out at me!") It's a fairly easy and straightforward sound to teach, and is usually mastered within weeks or a few months in most cases.

Common Motor-Speech Disorders

One of the most important parts of an articulation evaluation is examining the child's *oral-motor* function. If you think of the word *oral* as pertaining to the mouth area and *motor* as pertaining to how it moves, it will give you an idea of what this means.

Dysarthria

The speech-language pathologist should check for oral muscle weakness, known as *hypotonia* ("hi-po-TOE-nee-uh"). By having your child eat a variety of foods with different textures, we can take a look and see what happens. Does your child drool? Do crumbs slip out? When the child is drinking, does liquid leak out due to a weak lip seal on the cup? If so, this may indicate a weakness with the lips, which are important for the pronunciation of many sounds. The jaw may be dropped a bit due to lax muscles connecting the mandible and the jaw, causing the child to breathe through the mouth, with the tongue protruded, even when the child is not talking. The speech pattern of a child with hypotonia is usually a bit mumbly or slurred, with the tongue and the lips making very light contact or sometimes no contact. The voice itself will typically be softer and sometimes hard to hear, although there can certainly be short bursts of loud speech as well. In most cases, there is corresponding muscle weakness in the trunk and diaphragm, causing breath support to be reduced. The connected speech may be choppy and distracting due to the insertion of breaths, pauses, and unusual stress and emphasis. ("I [breath] HAVE a [breath] ball-that-has [breath] a stripe on [breath] IT.") This type of speech pattern is called *dysarthria* ("dis-AR-three-uh"). In general, dysarthric speech patterns are associated with neurological or physical conditions that cause it, although sometimes doctors are not able to pinpoint anything in particular as a cause. Some of the associated conditions are cerebral palsy, Down syndrome, brain injury, or developmental disabilities. Children who exhibit dysarthric speech patterns should have a neurological evaluation and typically require occupational and/or physical therapy for associated difficulties in strength and coordination throughout the body.

Because there is a physical cause that underlies the dysarthric speech pattern, there are limits to how much change speech therapy can make. Usually, we are not expecting the child's speech to ever be completely "normal" just from practicing exercises. The amount of progress will differ from child to child. Children with normal to above-normal intelligence are generally more able to internalize and apply the strategies that are taught. Likewise, the more severe and involved the physical and cognitive problems, the less likely it is that the dysarthria will respond to treatment. However, it is indeed possible to make progress in many cases, and it's worth pursuing. Because children with dysarthria are often participating in multiple therapies for long periods of time, they sometimes need breaks from it. With a renewed energy, perhaps a new SLP or a new approach and some maturity, it's possible that you can go back and forge ahead. Some typical types of activities include:

• *Improving breath support and coordination with speech.* A good, ongoing airstream is the "fuel" we need to produce speech. Children with dysarthric speech patterns often struggle to coordinate the exhalation phase of speaking with the onset of their speech, losing valuable air and limiting the number of words that can be spoken on that breath. Sometimes they take short little breaths and need to learn to take bigger ones. Using horns (focusing on making the sound loud and in one continuous blow) and games (such as blowing a Ping-Pong ball across a table in one breath), the child can work toward repeating a certain word with multiple repetitions on one single breath. For example: "[Breath] six-six-six-six [Breath]."

• *Strengthening the muscles for speech and feeding.* The tongue, lips, and masseters (those rubber band–like muscles by your cheeks that connect the bottom jaw to the mandible) all need to have sufficient strength to do their jobs. Exercises and supportive feeding strategies (such as using certain cups, spoon-feeding, selecting foods that promote chewing), as well as emphasizing practicing with a strong, loud voice to promote the need for more pressure on the articulators, is helpful.

• *Pacing, pitch, intonation, and emphasis.* We call those subtle characteristics of speech production *suprasegmentals.* Suprasegmentals are the glue that holds words and sentences together. We often don't even notice them until something is different about the way someone speaks. Dysarthric speech patterns often benefit from some direct work on these skills. There are some great software programs out now that SLPs can utilize to help a child "see" how their voice can rise and fall. Visual feedback of some kind (showing a line going up and down) and pacing (tapping on a drum to show each word) as well as strategies to increase self-monitoring (videotaping) can be used.

Childhood Apraxia of Speech (CAS)

Some children may have adequate strength in their oral muscles but lack the ability to move them with the necessary control to initiate, plan, and produce speech clearly and quickly. This condition is also called *dyspraxia* and *apraxia*, but recently it has been defined by the American Speech-Language-Hearing Association in children as Childhood Apraxia of Speech (CAS). A child with apraxia ("uh-PRAXY-uh") often pronounces individual sounds quite well, but when they are combined into words, has difficulty sequencing the movements necessary to put the words together. It is most noticeable in longer words. The speech errors are usually inconsistent and highly dependent upon the sounds and words that come before and after them and the length of the utterance itself. For example, the child may be able to say these words separately: *Mommy, has, a piece, of, apple,* and *pie.* However, when asked to repeat them together in a sentence, they may sound more like this: "Mompee pee bappuh bie." If asked to repeat the sentence, the child may say it in an entirely different way. Often you can see that the child is groping to form the words. One of the hallmarks of children with apraxia is a distinct gap between their receptive language skills (comprehension) and their expressive language, with receptive language being a bit higher. Difficulties with sentence structure and morphology are common. Other motor skills, such as fine motor (holding a pencil) and gross motor (climbing, riding a bike) may also be impacted. When a child pronounces words differently from situation to situation, distorts vowels, and gropes and struggles to form the word correctly, CAS is a usual suspect. CAS families are fortunate in that there is a strong parent support network (www.apraxia-kids.org) through the Childhood Apraxia of Speech

Association of North America (CASANA). If you think your child may have CAS or if she has been diagnosed with it, check out the comprehensive information, conference schedule, and message boards on CASANA's Web site. It is helpful for both parents and professionals.

How early can we recognize CAS? We know that children with apraxia are often reported as being quiet infants, with little noisy babbling. They may be slow to say their first words, or perhaps not. If your child is 18 months old and only saying a word or two, you may wonder if it is due to apraxia. Unfortunately, that's really hard to say at this point in your child's development. Maybe, maybe not. Without more speech to analyze, we can't see if there are inconsistent errors or a loss of speech clarity as the length of the utterance increases, let alone observe groping behaviors if the child isn't attempting to talk. Without the child's attempts at copying what we want him to say, it is difficult to know if it is a just a garden-variety speech delay, a lack of volitional control, disinterest, or any number of other causes. Sometime after the child has reached the age of 2, the SLP may make a tentative diagnosis of CAS or perhaps say that your child will be monitored for CAS, pending his response to therapy and further analysis of the speech patterns that emerge. Therefore, it may take some time before a definitive diagnosis of apraxia is conclusive.

Therapy for apraxia requires much intensive drill and practice, aside from the speech therapy services. The selection of sounds and syllables to work on in therapy is not necessarily the same as an SLP might choose with a more traditional articulation approach. Your child's SLP should have some extra training in this area so that the therapy methods used are most effective for your child. These methods include the following:

- *Intensity and frequency of service.* Children with CAS benefit most from frequent sessions. Once a week is not going to suffice, until the articulation errors are largely resolved. For children who are highly unintelligible, three sessions a week is usually appropriate, even if for only thirty minutes at a time. Because the work is so strenuous, hourlong sessions held less frequently may not be as desirable.
- *Focus away from single sound productions.* Because motor planning difficulties are heavily influenced by the context of the sound combinations and movements within a particular word, or phrase, emphasis should move toward integrating target sounds at the syllable, word, and phrase level as soon as possible.
- *Multiple repetitions.* Because the nature of CAS is rooted in a deficit

in motor planning skills, children with CAS need many repetitions of a new speech-sound combination in order for it to "stick" and for the motor plans to form. Exercises should include games that require your child to say a particular syllable, word, phrase, or sentence multiple times, with consistency of production across these attempts being a key goal. While there is no magic number, ten repetitions seems to be the norm.

• *Word shells and approximations.* Words with many syllables are typically quite difficult for children with CAS. Therefore the speech pathologist may help your child form a word with a simplified structure until the child is later able to pronounce it normally. A word such as *dinosaur* may be taught as "di-o-suh," but for children with severe difficulties, may be reduced even further, to "di-so" or even "i-o" or "di" depending on the child. The child adds sounds to the word over time. This helps the child have a consistent, recognizable label until the mouth is physically able to produce a word with more complexity. These close-sounding words are called "approximations" or "word shells." This is an approach developed by Nancy Kaufman. (See her excellent articles on the CASANA Web site: apraxia-kids.org.)

• *Multisensory cues.* To help your child "feel" how to move his mouth from sound to sound, the SLP may press or tap places around the face (such as on the lips or under the neck) as the child is attempting to produce the word. These are called "tactile prompts" and are very effective for CAS therapy. One such method that utilizes these types of cues is the PROMPT system, developed by Deborah Hayden, which is a very systematic approach for using tactile prompts. (See "Childhood Apraxia of Speech" in appendix A.) Visual cues that help a child associate a given sound with its manner of production or place of production are helpful.

• *Sequencing and sentence structure.* Because sequencing is a big challenge for children with CAS, there is often difficulty sequencing words in a grammatical way to put sentences together. Therefore, therapy might also need to address how to combine words ("Did + you + see + the + boy?") in the right order. To facilitate this, the speech-language pathologist may use visual cueing, such as sign language, to help your child "see" and feel the word order. The SLP might also use picture icons arranged in order on a board.

• *Troubleshooting related issues.* Children with CAS may also have sensory integration issues and fine/gross motor planning difficulties, which would benefit from occupational therapy. Additional support in using new speech patterns in social situations without an adult to interpret for them may be helpful if their speech difficulties are severe enough. Troubleshooting and role-playing these scenarios so the child has a rehearsed response can reduce his apprehension about social situations. ("I'm sorry. That's hard for me to say.") For children who are really struggling to initiate and use language independently outside the home or the therapy situation due to anxiety, cognitive-behavioral therapy (CBT) taught by a licensed psychologist may be effective.

• *Alternative and augmentative language systems*. For children who have severe speech problems due to CAS, it may make sense (especially in the beginning) to incorporate a kind of alternative language system so your child has some way to communicate until her speech is more developed. This may be as simple as a picture board, which requires your child to point to what she wants, or as sophisticated as an electronic computer with synthesized speech. These are called AAC (augmentative and alternative communication) devices. (See "For Information about Augmentative and Alternative Language Technology" in appendix A.)

How Do Pronunciation Problems Affect a Child?

For some children, a slight or mild speech problem such as a lisp has little or no direct effect on them at all. In fact, it is often more distracting or annoying to the person who is listening to them. Often these children have grown so accustomed to the way they speak that they are largely unaware that anything is unusual. Friends may never have mentioned, or ridiculed, the way the child speaks. Mild speech differences are easy to get used to, and rarely, if ever, cause any kind of learning difficulty in school. However, a tongue thrust left unchecked can lead to later orthodontic problems.

For children with moderate pronunciation problems, the effects are more clear. Studies have shown that adults and other children draw conclusions about a person by the way that person speaks. When a child has obvious pronunciation problems, others may assume the child is stupid. The older the child is, the more stigmatizing the speech problem can be. Adolescents are sometimes cruel and insensitive toward a peer and can seriously hurt that person's feelings.

When a child's speech is very difficult to understand, social development can sometimes be affected. Because the child has problems speaking clearly, others may need to have certain words repeated or explained if they are confused about what the child has said. After a while the child may become frustrated and refuse to repeat the words, saying, "Never mind, it wasn't important," rather than face the humiliation of mispronouncing the word yet again. Such a child may also participate very little in class discussions and become a passive observer in school. When a child feels uncomfortable participating in class, school can be a boring and awkward place.

As discussed earlier, some speech problems are associated with reading and spelling problems. A child who enters kindergarten with a moderate speech problem will be at a distinct disadvantage when trying to learn letters and sounds. For example, when asked to look at a picture of a kite and tell what the first sound or letter is, children often will write the sound they make when saying the word. So for a child who pronounces *kite* as "tite," the answer is *t*.

Speech problems also can cause tension at home. Parents sometimes can be overzealous about trying to help children improve their speech. In an effort to remind a child to say words correctly, a parent can overdo it. Instead of being helped, the child may become resentful and resist speaking as the parent wishes. The child may also not be physically ready to incorporate the new skills into conversation and feel frustrated at letting the parent down. Communication with your child's therapist is important for this reason.

Some children resent the extra work at home that is essential to overcoming the speech problem and may resist at times. For a child with other learning or emotional problems, this added burden can indeed be troublesome and a source of conflict between parent and child.

A child with a severe speech problem who does not improve by first or second grade may also become quite self-conscious and experience lowered self-esteem and increased frustration. Feeling this way can certainly affect a child's behavior and even the way a child's personality develops. Some children react by being aggressive, rude, or temperamental; others become shy and say very little. Children with severe speech problems will need help coping and need to be motivated to keep working on improving their speech.

What Can Parents Do to Help a Child with a Pronunciation Problem?

If you have a child with a pronunciation problem, remember these points:

- Don't try to help by making the child repeat mispronounced words correctly, unless a professional suggests you do so. As discussed earlier in the chapter, there are sometimes complex reasons for your child's pronunciation problems. Perhaps your child's muscles are not ready to say those sounds, or maybe your child has not processed speech "rules" yet. You can make it worse by frustrating or embarrassing the child.

- If a speech sound is missing or distorted, try to reframe what was said with extra emphasis on the target sound. For example, if your child says, "I have a ha [pointing to a hat]," you can reframe it as "Oh, you have a ha*t*" with extra emphasis on the *t* sound. Don't ask your child to repeat it, as tempting as it may be.

- If you can't understand your child, try to ask questions about what was said. Ask your child to say it again, but don't insist it be said your way. Sometimes I will say, "I'm sorry. I can't hear too well sometimes. Can you tell me that again?" Deep down, I think children know this game, but it takes the embarrassment off them and puts it on me.

- Listen carefully to what your child says. Respond to the message and not to the way it is said. *Never* say, "You sound like a baby" (or a "sissy," or any other negative label). Insulting your child into "speaking right" never works. Your child is not mispronouncing words on purpose. Young children, in particular, are not "lazy" talkers.

- Help your child's speech improve by following the speech pathologist's directions and performing any recommended activities as often as suggested. A few speech therapy sessions a week or less will have little impact and will take much longer to work if there is no consistent follow-through at home. I often tell parents that 90 percent of speech therapy should take place at home; the therapist merely introduces skills and strategies. Consider a child who takes a piano lesson every week yet never practices. That child will never master the piano. Similarly, the child who does not practice speech exercises (recommended by a therapist) will not improve. Consider a special treat for practicing speech exercises so your child stays motivated.

- Be patient. Improvement takes time. It may take years of hard work for a child to overcome a speech problem. Don't hound your child weeks or months after beginning therapy to start speaking correctly. Sometimes improvement comes in small steps. If you feel your child is not improving after a few months of therapy, talk to the therapist. Ask if the therapist has seen progress, and if so, in what way. Sometimes when you are so close to someone, you can miss those small, day-to-day changes. It may take an aunt who visits at the holidays to comment on the improvement in your child's speech for you to notice or believe it.

Case Study: Paul

Paul's mother called me when he was 4½. She was concerned about the way Paul was pronouncing words. She thought he would have "grown out of it" by now, but he hadn't. As I always do, I asked Paul's mother to bring him in to see me. As far as Paul knew, he was meeting a new "friend" at the school.

At this first meeting, the screening, Paul and I played with puppets and some plastic animals. We made them talk to each other. We looked at some picture books and made the characters pop up by pulling on a flap. We talked about those, too, and finished by playing with a plastic airport.

As a result of this visit, I could tell that Paul needed a more in-depth evaluation. His speech was very, very difficult to understand. He called an airplane a "pay," a tiger a "guh," and a giraffe a "rah." Many words were unidentifiable.

I reviewed Paul's medical and birth history, and events such as when he began talking, with his mother. Nothing stood out about his birth or his early developing years. There was no history of frequent ear infections. All his other skills, such as walking, happened at the normal time. He was going to preschool three days a week and interacted well with the other children. His mother also commented on how well Paul was doing with prekindergarten skills, such as counting and reciting the ABC's. In fact, he was already writing his name with little help.

With his mother's permission, I scheduled an evaluation, to begin a week later. Paul had a good attention span during the testing, was cooperative, and answered all my questions thoughtfully. We took breaks so he wouldn't become too drained. I evaluated Paul's receptive language (what he understood) as well as expressive language (what he could say), in addition to his obvious pronunciation problems. The school nurse also checked his hearing and found it to be normal.

The results of the tests showed that Paul had severe articulation problems. He could be described as having a phonological disorder due to the nature of his mispronunciations.

On the receptive language tasks, Paul showed a strong understanding of many language concepts such as "behind" and "few." His understanding of vocabulary was also appropriate for his age. However, he did show some difficulty on the listening part of the test. Paul would easily forget directions if they were long, and he could not repeat a series of words back to me. If Paul had difficulty remembering what people said, it made sense that he would have difficulty remembering what the words were supposed to sound like when he tried to say them in conversation.

Paul began speech and auditory (listening) therapy soon thereafter. He came twice a week for a half hour. He and his parents worked diligently on the speech and listening activities sent home. Paul was sometimes resistant to practicing the activities, so we tailored a program based on football-oriented games, which was Paul's passion. For example, he practiced pronouncing the names of the players on his favorite team and used a paper football that he kicked with his finger to words on the "field."

By the time Paul finished kindergarten, he could be understood much of the time. As he felt more successful and confident, he was increasingly willing to try new, more difficult sounds. By the time he finished first grade, he was understood most of the time. His listening skills had also improved. By the time he finished third grade, he had difficulty pronouncing only r and l sounds and was reduced to one weekly therapy session. As a reward for using his corrected speech in conversation at home and in school, he was allowed to come once a month for "maintenance" in fourth grade. By the time he entered fifth grade, Paul spoke normally and was phased out of speech therapy.

Common Voice Problems

Johnnie has always sounded like he's getting over a case of laryngitis. I figured it was just the way he talked, so it never seemed like a "problem" to me. He coughs a lot from allergies, so I'm sure that's not helping. Some days he's "squeakier" than others, but nobody has trouble understanding what he says. He's always yelling over his three brothers, I'll tell you that! I don't have any reason to worry, do I?

—Mother of Johnnie, age 6

Maybe, maybe not. Although Johnnie is usually understood easily, he is straining every time he talks. A number of things can happen when we put constant stress on the vocal cords. Some are serious; others are simply annoying.

Speaking requires the cooperation of several body parts. Your vocal cords alone do not dictate how your voice sounds. Your lungs and chest muscles are very important parts of the speaking process. Nerves in the brain control the vocal cords and their ability to work properly. The tissues in the back of your throat and in your nose help give your voice its unique sound quality. So when we talk about the "voice," remember that many parts of the body play a part in how the voice sounds.

The voice is a highly sensitive instrument and is our own personal "signature." The way we sound when we speak can say a lot about us. Think of famous actors and actresses such as Scarlett Johansson, Marlon Brando, Adam Sandler, Morgan Freeman, and Rosie O'Donnell. Their voices have set the tone for the types of characters they have played and established their images.

Fortunately, Johnnie doesn't have to worry about an image. He's only 6 years old. But he does have one of the more common types of voice problems that we'll discuss in this section. (Voice problems related to cerebral palsy, Down syndrome, hearing impairment, cleft palate, and traumatic brain injury are discussed in chapter 8.)

Diagnosis and Causes of Voice Problems

In a common case of laryngitis, some vocal strain is expected and should be gone in a week or two. However, when your child's voice sounds "froggy," "squeaky," or "hoarse" on a regular basis or for weeks or months at a time, it should be checked out. You may ask a speech pathologist to listen to your child speak if you are not sure there is truly enough hoarseness for you to be concerned. However, no speech pathologist will or should attempt any kind of therapy or intervention until a medical doctor has examined the child and given the green light to do so.

The doctor who examines the vocal cords is called an *otolaryngologist*, also known as an ear, nose, and throat doctor, or an ENT. The doctor needs to see the vocal cords to find out what is causing the hoarseness. The vocal cords may be better examined with fiber optics, which are wire-thin tubes called endoscopes that are typically fed through the nose to the vocal cord area. This allows the doctor to watch the vocal cords move as the child is asked to make certain sounds. It is a slightly uncomfortable procedure but not painful. A local anesthetic can be sprayed to make it more comfortable. The camera can take pictures, which is helpful for later comparison after treatment. A stroboscopic exam takes a movie of the vocal cord movement during speech, allowing the doctor to freeze a picture and examine the vocal cords as they vibrate, which is impossible to do with the naked eye.

So what should the doctor see? The vocal cords are shaped like a small V in the middle. They sit in the windpipe (pharynx). The air you breathe goes through the opening in the V. The inside edges have very thin membranes that need to move back and forth without interference in order to produce sound. When you speak, they vibrate many times as the air passes through from the lungs. When one side has a growth or is thicker than the other, the vocal cords (*vocal folds*) will not be synchronized properly when they vibrate. This results in a gravelly sounding, or hoarse, voice.

Both physical and medical conditions can cause a child's voice to sound hoarse or strained. The most common causes are vocal polyps or vocal nodules, which can be a result of the child's using the vocal cords incorrectly.

Vocal Polyps

Vocal polyps are fluid-filled sacs that can form on the lining of the vocal cords. Usually only one side of the vocal cords has a polyp. It can be caused initially by straining the voice on just one occasion, such as singing during a long, loud concert. If the child continues to overuse his voice, the strained cord is further irritated and the polyp will grow. A child with a polyp may sound breathy or hoarse and may feel like clearing his throat because it feels like something is "down there." Unfortunately, clearing the throat can make the problem worse, because it irritates the polyp.

Vocal Nodules

Vocal nodules are small, callous growths that can start on one side of the vocal cords. As the irritated side bangs against the other vocal cord when vibrating, its hardness irritates the other side of the vocal cords, so it is fairly common to see two vocal nodules, one on each side, in a child with a long-term hoarseness problem. Nodules are typically caused by a long-term source of irritation, such as cheerleading, yelling, or speaking loudly too often; chronic coughing; or singing or speaking with stress or strain (another example of vocal abuse). Nodules are more common in boys and more common than vocal polyps. The child with vocal nodules will tend to get "tired of talking" and become more hoarse as the day wears on. It may be difficult for the child to speak loudly or yell without discomfort.

If a vocal polyp or nodule is left untreated, the child may continue to work even harder to speak, causing the problem to become more and more noticeable until he can hardly speak above a throaty whisper. If you wait too long, surgery may sometimes become the only option.

Papilloma

Papilloma is a wartlike growth that can occur in the vocal cord area of children. The majority of papilloma cases occur in children under the age of 6. When speaking, the child may sound as though she has vocal polyps or vocal nodules. The papilloma can eventually block the child's airway, causing difficulty breathing. This, along with other, less common medical problems, is one of the most important reasons why hoarseness in a child should not be taken lightly and should be assessed by a physician. The treatment for papilloma is strictly medical. It is not caused or aggravated by how a child speaks. Surgery involving lasers, followed by voice rest, may be necessary to remove the papilloma.

Other medical problems can also cause a hoarse voice. Hemangiomas, granulomas, and laryngeal "webbing" are not common but do occur. Intubation during a surgical procedure or a blow to the windpipe, as well as infection or disease, can set these in motion. These problems are not caused by misuse of the voice, and they require medical attention. Again, simply listening to a voice is not enough to make an accurate diagnosis. A medical examination that looks directly at the vocal cords is necessary to rule out these problems.

Many times children with hoarse or breathy voices do not exhibit any medical problem with their vocal cords during an exam. It is usually advisable in this case to help the child change the *vocal abuse* pattern (speaking or using the voice in an unhealthy way) that is causing the hoarseness, because continued strain can eventually (but does not always) lead to growths such as nodules, and then, sometimes, surgery. Young boys and teenage girls are high-risk groups for vocal abuse behavior. In addition, children who are "high-strung" may put undue stress on their voices.

Characteristics of Children with Voice Problems

Children with voice problems might do the following:

- Make "squeaking" sounds when speaking
- Run out of air before finishing a normal sentence
- Not speak loudly enough to be heard across a room
- Sound hoarse, harsh, "husky," or "gravelly" for more than ten days at a time or have frequent bouts of "laryngitis" throughout a single year
- Clear their throats frequently
- Sound more "throaty" by the end of the day than in the morning
- Open their mouths and have nothing come out for a second or so
- Sound like two people are talking at the same time, but with different pitches

- Have their voice crack while talking
- Sound strained and "throaty" when laughing or crying

How Do Voice Problems Affect a Child?

Vocal hoarseness may not cause much of a problem for some children, especially in the early stages. Aside from medically related problems, vocal hoarseness may be more of a nuisance than anything else. The problem, of course, is the long-term effect on the strength and quality of the child's voice, and the possibility of surgery if the hoarseness gets worse. I have known children who have gone through twelve years of school with a mildly hoarse voice, which, for the most part, has gotten neither worse nor better. For them and their parents it wasn't a problem worth fretting about. This is especially true when a child, like Johnnie, has always talked this way.

For other children, however, vocal hoarseness has more serious effects. In addition to the possible long-term effects previously mentioned, if left untreated, vocal hoarseness can seriously impact some children's ability to communicate and participate effectively in class.

Why Treat a Voice Problem with Speech Therapy?

When a vocal polyp or nodule is found, the doctor may ask a speech pathologist to try some therapy and behavior changes for a few months to see whether the growth decreases. If it does not, surgery may be necessary to remove the growth, followed by voice rest, which means total silence (not even whispering) for a week or more. After the vocal cord has healed, speech therapy will again be important, because the problem will recur if the child continues the old vocal abuse pattern. Correcting the problem with speech therapy rather than surgery alone is important. Repeated surgeries take a toll on the vocal cords, because a layer of membrane is literally stripped away. Scar tissue from repeated surgeries may cause further irritation, making more surgery ineffective. By changing the way he speaks, the child can break this vicious circle.

Voice therapy is a bit of a niche in the speech pathology field. One of the big pioneers in our field in children's voice issues is Dr. Daniel Boone in Tucson, Arizona. Many of our most popular texts and programs were developed by him. Most pediatric SLPs get very little hands-on experience treating voice cases and as a result often feel uneasy treating them. My experience has been that typically the most skilled SLPs for voice disorders can be found in a hospital setting or in private practice. They also have more sophisticated software and feedback devices, which aid in helping the child monitor his vocal use. Here are some strategies they would likely employ:

- *Treating causative issues.* Treating voice problems caused by vocal abuse focuses on changing the behaviors that strained the vocal cords. A child like Johnnie with allergies should have them treated promptly. Every time he coughs, clears his throat, or sneezes, he is causing his vocal cords to slam together in a very stressful way.

- *Changing vocal behaviors.* If a child likes to make loud car noises or animal noises with his throat or grunt when playing with toy action figures, his condition will worsen. His mother may need to organize "quiet talking time" in the house so he doesn't need to shout over siblings to be heard. Setting up a reward system to help him increase his awareness and control over these habits will also be necessary.

- *Adjusting the resonance.* Sometimes children keep their tongue too far forward or too far back in the mouth when talking, instead of in a neutral position. This results in excessive tension, but with proper training, the tongue can be repositioned to improve the sound of the voice.

- *Vocal relaxation.* When children have restricted range of motion with their jaw while talking, they can almost look like ventriloquists. Children who have too much tension in their jaw and tongue can also place that tension in the laryngeal area, which can further exacerbate vocal pathologies. To work on this, your SLP may introduce exercises for chewing and talking, as well as yawning and sighing.

- *Softer onset.* Children with vocal pathologies will often have a harsh onset to their word, also known as a "hard glottal attack." The SLP will seek to change the way your child starts words so the voice is softer and more relaxed.

What Can Parents Do to Help a Child with a Voice Problem?

If your child demonstrates any of the characteristic behaviors of a voice problem for more than a few weeks, have a doctor check it out. An ear, nose, and throat doctor is preferable. The most important step you can take is to ensure that there is not a serious medical problem causing the voice change. If the doctor feels it is appropriate, a referral to a speech therapist may be made. Once a diagnosis has been made, keep these thoughts in mind:

- Try to help your child change speaking habits by following the speech therapist's recommendations carefully.
- Keep a quiet home. Make sure your child doesn't have to be heard over loud music or noisy dishwashers.

- If voice rest is recommended, it is imperative that your child make no sound at all in order for this treatment to have the desired effect. This means no laughing, crying, or whispering, although this is often difficult to control in a child.
- Make sure all allergies and respiratory and sinus problems are addressed so that your child does not have to cough, sneeze, or clear his throat frequently.
- Keep the radio off in the car so your child doesn't have to shout over it to be heard.
- Help your child get in the habit of walking over to the person she wants to speak to, instead of yelling across the room or down the stairs.
- Monitor the condition of your child's voice carefully to prevent future relapses.

Case Study: Frank

Frank's mother called me after a visit to her son's ear, nose, and throat doctor. Frank, a bright and active 8-year-old, had been to the doctor for an examination of his ears, which seemed to have yet another infection. The doctor noticed Frank's unusually raspy-sounding voice. His mother commented that his voice had been gradually getting more and more hoarse over the past six months. It was so gradual that she hardly noticed it until the doctor mentioned it.

As the doctor examined Frank's vocal cords and asked him to imitate certain sounds, he noticed the beginning of a vocal nodule on Frank's left vocal cord. He suggested Frank receive speech therapy to prevent any further growth or resulting irritation on the right vocal cord. If the therapy was successful, the present growth might subside completely.

When I met with Frank's mother, we discussed his speaking habits as well as other behaviors that might aggravate the vocal nodule. She reported that he had a postnasal drip from his allergies, which caused him to cough and clear his throat frequently. We discussed why it would be helpful to have this medically managed so that Frank didn't need to strain his voice. Because Frank was having problems hearing, he was speaking more loudly than a typical child. His doctor found residual fluid lingering in Frank's middle ear as a result of frequent ear infections. When antibiotics and antihistamines were unsuccessful in eliminating the fluid, tubes were inserted, which immediately improved Frank's hearing to within normal limits. As a result, his voice volume returned to a more normal level.

At Frank's house, his teenage brother apparently liked to blast the stereo. Thus Frank often yelled up the basement steps from the playroom to his mother in the kitchen to be heard over the din of the stereo. We discussed how he would need to walk up the steps instead of yelling, and how the stereo would have to be turned down when Frank wanted to talk. Frank also had a habit of making a loud grunting noise whenever he threw a basketball toward the hoop on his driveway. Since he played basketball every afternoon, that was a lot of grunting!

We agreed to work on these and other changes to help improve Frank's voice habits. We then discussed these changes, and the reasons for them, with Frank. I saw Frank every week for six weeks after this meeting to monitor his progress. I began to notice some improvement in his voice quality. Unfortunately, because voice cases are not widespread, my school (like most) did not have sophisticated instruments, as some hospitals do, to objectively measure the changes in Frank's voice. However, a good ear and careful notes sufficed.

By the end of three months, Frank's voice sounded relatively normal. I asked his mother to have his doctor reexamine him. We were pleased to learn that all evidence of the vocal nodule was gone. We never did need to initiate formal voice therapy with Frank. The problem was caught fairly early and responded well to some behavior changes.

Frank's mother tells me that he occasionally slips back into his old habits and does need some reminding. If she notices the hoarseness returning, she immediately helps Frank work extra hard to be "nice" to his voice. He has never had his vocal nodule return.

6

Understanding
Language Problems

"Your child has an expressive language delay." Just what does this mean? *Language* is a very broad term. As we discussed in chapter 1, language is divided into receptive and expressive components. If your child is diagnosed with an expressive language delay, you will want to find out exactly what *kind* of expressive (or receptive) language weakness he or she is exhibiting.

In this chapter I describe the symptoms of and typical intervention for the most common language problems. I also explain how a child is affected by each problem and what you as a parent can do to help. Some of the early language problems of infants, toddlers, and preschoolers discussed in this chapter include developmental delays (sometimes called "maturational" problems), sensory integration deficits, and fluctuating hearing loss.

As children get older, they may have trouble understanding words (receptive vocabulary problems) and/or using words (expressive vocabulary problems). They may also have difficulty with morphology (word forms), syntax (grammar), word retrieval, and using language to express what they mean. All of these problems are covered in this chapter.

A speech-language pathologist examines many aspects of a child's use of language to see if he or she is developing language normally. Some of the activities that are analyzed include the following:

- Developing first words (language development)
- Speaking and communicating in social settings (pragmatics)

- Putting a sentence together (syntax)
- Using words (semantics)
- Retelling the plot to a story (sequencing)
- Changing word endings, depending on the context (morphology)
- Learning word meanings (vocabulary)
- Remembering words learned before (word retrieval)

Some children have a weakness in only one particular area, such as those described above, and are sometimes referred to as having a *specific language impairment* (SLI). It is a bit of a generic label that essentially describes the fact that some facet of language development (receptive, expressive, or both) is below age-level expectations, in the absence of any other etiology. Additionally, researchers and professors also use the term *language-learning disabled* (LLD) to describe these children, which can include those with associated reading or writing disorders. These are not terms that are usually included on IEP forms, and so school-based SLPs may not choose to use them. Private practice and hospital-based SLPs typically need to use terms that are included in the insurance company's list, which are associated with certain codes they must write on their receipts. These terms are not included on the list, and as a result you'd more typically see a diagnostic label such as "receptive/expressive language disorder" on reports instead. But for most children with expressive language problems, several of these language areas are affected at one time.

Language problems are not something you can easily "cure." Just as some children will never be adept at math or the long jump, some children will always be weak conversationalists. Learn to accept your child as a unique individual and emphasize the things he or she does well. Try not to make the language problem bigger than it is. Yes, it is a shame to be burdened with these difficulties, but with the right help, language problems need not be an obstacle to a successful and happy life.

Your Baby's First Words

As we discussed in the first chapter, speech development is really about two things: what we understand (receptive language) and what we can say (expressive language). If your child has been paying attention to what everyone has been saying for the first twelve months, and has been able to accurately hear the words you say, there should now be a fairly good storage of concepts just waiting and ready to come out. All we need is for the mouth to figure out how to do it!

Around the age of 12 months, your baby should be quite "chatty" and noisy. The sounds should resemble the phonemic sounds of your language, and be a combination of vowels and consonants, not just vowels, mumbling, or one particular syllable (such as "dah!"). There should be a good mix. By about 12 months, your child should be ready to figure out how to make the words start to come out of his mouth—on purpose! And with meaning! Those are what *real words* are. Random sounds that also happen to sound like real words don't count; (e.g., "Mamamamama" while the child is banging a spoon and looking at the pot doesn't count for *Mama.*) Once that happens and your baby sees how excited you get, more are sure to follow. First words can be just about anything, from *Mama* to *sock,* but are generally common nouns. Progress should be on the whole a steady affair, with more words added, and eventually little two-word phrases with pauses ("Daddy . . . car!"), which we excitedly applaud and try to decipher. Well, that's what's supposed to happen. But you may be reading this book because for some reason, in your child's case, it isn't happening. If your baby is not producing any first "real" words by age 15 to 18 months, ask yourself the following questions:

1. *Is there a hearing problem?* Go to a pediatric audiologist and have a thorough hearing evaluation performed to find out if her hearing is adequate for speech and to ensure that there is no middle ear fluid. That's your first job.
2. *Are there risk factors to consider?* Is there a family history of speech delay? Was your child a bit premature? Do you have another child with a diagnosed condition, such as autism? If so, you may want to be more proactive in having it followed up since we generally find that in many children there is a genetic link to speech delays, and thus the likelihood of its resolving on its own may be less.
3. *Is there enough language "inputting" happening?* In order for language to come out, it needs to be programmed "in" first. To do that, someone needs to be carefully, routinely, and intensively feeding that language to your child. How do you do that? Talk to your child about everything you do. ("Look, Mommy's washing her hands now. Wash, wash, wash!") Repeat key words. Speak clearly and distinctly, not softly or under your breath. Look at your child and make eye contact. Read lots of baby books to your child. If your child is in day care, is there enough individual attention to ensure that this is happening?
4. *Are you making a big fuss and encouraging speech?* Sometimes parents tell me they don't want to "pressure" their child to speak and so

just wait for it to happen on its own. Ah, but you must communicate to your child that this is what you want her to do! Even if your child babbles back and forth with you nonsensically, it is "communication" in some form. Get excited and cheer her on! Respond to her attempts. ("You want your 'bah'? Here's your bottle!") Play games where she copies your simple sounds; *ee, ah, oo,* and *mmmm* are good ones to start with.

5. *Is your child interested in you?* Since a child is typically motivated to form words to show off to you and get a positive reaction—and to interact with you, what happens when your child is indifferent to your emotions, doesn't look at you for any length of time, or is not interested in interacting? Children who exhibit these symptoms should be checked by a specialist in autism spectrum disorders. There is more about this topic later in this chapter. Children who are disinterested in other people are far less apt to be motivated to talk, even if their mouth is ready.

6. *Is your child's mouth physically ready to talk?* Children who have trouble feeding, chewing solids or crunchy foods, or drinking from a cup should be checked. Lots of choking and gagging? It could be something called *dysphagia* ("dis-FAH-zhuh"), which is a difficulty with the swallowing process. Speech delay, coupled with feeding issues, needs to be checked out sooner than later.

7. *Have there been other major health issues?* Babies who are fighting major illnesses or are hospitalized may be on a slightly different timetable. Medications can cause sedation, irritability, and trouble sleeping. It's hard to focus on learning language if you are in pain, hooked up to tubes, or struggling to breathe. Take care of the physical issues, keep "inputting" that language, and wait until your child is a little healthier before following up on the speech delay.

Toddlers and Preschoolers with Delayed Speech or Language

Jessica is a very bright child, so I know there can't be anything wrong with her. Besides, we've given her so much stimulation from the time she was in the womb! Still, my sister keeps telling me that maybe she should be saying more than a few words at 2½ years old. My pediatrician doesn't seem concerned, so I guess I'll just wait a few years and see if she outgrows it.

—Mother of Jessica, age 2½

Just because Jessica is having a "slow start" with her speech and language development, it does not necessarily mean she is mentally "slow" or will struggle with a lifelong problem. That is why, in most cases, difficulties at this age are called "delays" as opposed to "disorders." It doesn't mean her mother and father haven't done a wonderful job stimulating her. And, although pediatricians can be quite helpful, they are not trained speech-language pathologists. If you continue to be concerned despite a physician's reassurance, you should have your child's speech checked.

Chapters 1 and 2 showed you that a child exhibiting Jessica's speech pattern is not progressing as expected. In this section you'll discover what kind of problem a child like Jessica may be having and what her parents can do to help her.

Although nature has a hand in how a child develops, don't underestimate the power of a nurturing parent. In this section you will also learn just how significant that role is and how you can make the most of the time you have with your child at this important age.

Children under the age of 5 have special considerations when it comes to speech and language development. Because there is a wide range of what is considered normal language development at this time, many delays are just that: delays. At times, however, a child's language development needs special attention.

Delays in Speech or Language Only

Jessica, described on page 128, seemed to be developing normally in every way except for her speech. Sometimes this happens. In many cases we really don't know why. A *developmental delay* (also called a *maturational* problem) simply means the child is not developing in one area as expected. It is a descriptive term, making no judgment as to whether the problem is permanent. In a case such as Jessica's, her parents should seek an evaluation. The speech-language pathologist may choose to make home visits because of Jessica's young age and work with Jessica's parents to help stimulate her interest in talking and communicating using informal activities. Activities to develop her listening skills will also be included if needed.

In most cases, after about six months, the therapist will evaluate how the child is progressing. Sometimes children like Jessica make rapid progress and will need to come in only for periodic checkups to monitor their speech and language development. If progress is slower than expected, a more aggressive approach should be considered. Formal speech-language therapy sessions may be scheduled, often at a public school site. Therapy sessions are play-oriented and are usually fun for the child.

In many cases a child like Jessica may be speaking and comprehending normally (or near normally) by the time kindergarten comes and may experience no difficulty in school. In more involved cases, the child will continue to need help. When a child has a significant delay in speaking or listening, there is some risk that academic problems may surface later, even if the speech or language problem itself is corrected. However, mild pronunciation problems are not usually a sign of later difficulties.

Research does not yet tell us which children will have problems later. However, if a child begins school already identified as having a speech or language delay, the staff will monitor progress closely and implement special teaching strategies if academic problems start to develop.

Autism Spectrum Disorders (ASD)

When young children are identified as having significant delays in several skill areas (talking, listening, playing with peers, and attention span), the speech pathologist or physician probably will refer the parent to a diagnostic team. The team will want to see if these behaviors are symptomatic of an *autism spectrum disorder*. ASD is a group of disorders that affect a child's development, primarily in the areas of communication and social interaction. Symptoms may be present at birth, but in many cases the child starts out developing normally, with delays growing more noticeable over time. Having a delay in these areas does not necessarily indicate an ASD, as there are other reasons why children exhibit delays. Rather, it is the nature of the delays, as well as the areas of strength, that the team will examine. If your child does have an ASD, it is important to identify it early, because the treatment for it is somewhat different from therapy for more routine developmental delays. For a more complete description of autism spectrum disorders, see page 255.

Sensory Integration Problems

An infant learns about the world by tasting, touching, smelling, hearing, and seeing. When the brain fails to process these sensations correctly, the child is often unable to make sense of the world. Listening and speaking delays can occur along with *sensory integration (SI) disorder.*

Noisy places such as malls and parties normally overstimulate infants because the sights and sounds overwhelm them. Bathtime and dressing can cause major meltdowns. This often results in crankiness or screaming (which are ways of expressing discomfort) or sleepiness (which is a way of withdrawing). As infants grow into 3- or 4-year-olds, their neurological systems are better able to process these sights, sounds, and tactile sensations. For children with sensory integration problems, however, the sights, sounds, and textures are too much to handle at once, even at 3 or 4 years of age. Crying outbursts and irritability are typical ways these children cope when their circuits overload.

Often the child with a sensory integration weakness displays difficulties in other areas, particularly with physical coordination and/or balance, as well as attention span. If these symptoms are present, you should consult an occupational therapist (an OT) specially trained in sensory integration. In rural areas this may be easier said than done. Some schools contract with occupational therapists who come in to provide services to students who need them. These specialists should be utilized to assist in a thorough evaluation and treatment plan.

To address the communication needs of children with sensory integration problems, a speech-language pathologist should work closely with other professionals involved with your child's care. This intervention may be in the form of formal therapy sessions or as part of a team within a special preschool classroom. Often these children respond best when speech and language therapy is integrated into a more natural setting, such as the home or when the SLP and the OT coordinate treatment at the same time, in the same physical space.

Many sensory integration deficits improve significantly with appropriate therapeutic intervention and time. As the children mature, it may be difficult for an untrained eye to notice any problem at all. In other cases, the problems persist. Many children have sensory integration weaknesses in addition to other diagnosed disabilities, such as autism.

Congenital Conditions

Babies born with diagnosed conditions such as Down syndrome, Hunter syndrome, cerebral palsy, deafness, or cleft palate typically have speech delays. In most cases, doctors can diagnose congenital problems at birth. In some cases, however, particularly with progressive hearing loss, a problem may not become apparent until the child does not develop in some way as expected. Congenital problems are usually diagnosed in the first year or two by your child's pediatrician.

A child with a congenital problem will need more stimulation than the typical child and often will need a specialized educational program. Hospitals assist with setting up these programs at birth. Insurance companies sometimes cover the cost of speech or physical therapy services. U.S. public schools are now being asked to provide services from birth for children with handicapping conditions, typically through a regional agency.

In many cases, speech-language therapy is provided directly in the home until a child is 3 years old. The typical focus of therapy is to develop muscles in the mouth used for feeding as well as speaking. Also, parents and caregivers are instructed in ways to facilitate the child's speech and language skills in daily situations.

As the child approaches the 3-year mark, therapy may take the form of a preschool program run by the local school system. In this kind of program, therapists work with the preschool teacher to plan activities that help the child develop needed skills. In recent years many programs combine children with special needs with a typical preschool population. As mentioned previously, this allows the children with special needs to imitate the speech and behavior of peers who can set a good example. Typical children also benefit from the program because it is free, has a low teacher-pupil ratio, and allows the children to get used to learning side by side with children with learning differences.

For children with significant speech and language delays, particularly those with deafness and cleft palate, aggressive speech-language therapy is usually necessary.

Middle Ear Fluid and Your Child's Language

When babies are born, their eustachian tubes are tiny. They are not terribly efficient for draining residual fluid that may accumulate from an event such as a cold or allergies. Sometimes it happens spontaneously with no apparent trigger. Sometimes an initial acute ear infection, called *acute otitis media* (AOM), will set off a chain of events that breeds more fluid that lingers long after the pain and fever of the initial infection have passed. The good news is that in 75 to 90 percent of AOM, the residual fluid will disappear within three months. It is more common in the winter months and studies have shown that children in day care have a higher probability of having middle ear fluid. The eustachian tubes tend to lie somewhat horizontally in babies, but over time get better at their draining function, usually when children are between the ages of 6 months and 4 years. That's why most children (90 percent, in fact, according to the American Academy of Pediatrics) will have some kind of middle ear infection or fluid prior to starting school. Middle ear fluid without an active infection is known as *otitis media with effusion* (OME).

How Is Middle Ear Fluid Detected?

Physicians are now urged to use a pneumatic type of otoscope for this purpose. Just shining a light and looking into an ear canal with a traditional otoscope is not enough. By using a more sophisticated instrument that sends a small puff of air into the ear canal, the doctor can check how the eardrum responds and thus detect OME with fairly good accuracy.

Another way to check for OME is by the use of an instrument called a *tympanometer*. A rubber-tipped probe is inserted into the child's outer ear. This is usually only slightly uncomfortable for the child, if not painless. The tympanometer sends sound waves through the ear canal and measures how they travel. While an SLP, a nurse, or a physician can perform this test, usually an audiologist will follow up and interpret its findings, in particular how it impacts the child's hearing.

What Are the Symptoms of Middle Ear Fluid?

Children with chronic middle ear fluid might display the following symptoms:

- Talk later than expected
- Have speech or language skills deteriorate instead of progress as expected
- Ignore you when you call their name, particularly if there is ambient noise in the background such as a TV
- Say "What?" or "Huh?" often
- Leave off endings of words frequently; for example "I saw fie [five] cat on the gra [grass]."
- Often breathe through the mouth because the nose is too congested
- Have a short attention span for conversation or stories unless there are pictures to see
- Have difficulty with balance and coordination; be clumsy
- Have periodic acute infections, with residual fluid not fully disappearing between infections

How Does Middle Ear Fluid Affect Speech?

When eustachian tubes don't drain well or there is an excess of middle ear fluid, the fluid backs up and causes the tympanic membrane (the eardrum) to be a bit soggy. We know that musical drums need to be bouncy and have a little snap to them. It's hard to be a good drum if the covering is mushy and wet, and your eardrum is no different. So when sound waves bounce off the eardrum during episodes of OME, the resulting sound is a bit mushy. To get an idea of what I mean, take your right hand and cover your mouth. Say, "Hi. How are you doing?" You can certainly hear the words, but they are muffled and indistinct. That's often how a child "hears" when there is chronic OME.

There has been research that shows that for some children, persistent middle ear fluid and frequent ear infections are associated with later problems in school, but other research has not borne this out. However, we know that hearing speech clearly is necessary not only so the child can reproduce the words clearly, but also so the information can be stored and phonemic awareness skills can be developed, which are the foundations of listening, speaking, reading, and writing. What is less clear is exactly how many episodes of OME need to occur in order for the OME to cause difficulties and for how long the OME needs to be present in order for this to occur.

How Do Physicians Treat OME?

In 2004, the American Academy of Pediatrics, in a collaborative effort with the American Academy of Family Physicians and the American Academy of Otolaryngology—Head and Neck Surgery, worked with the Agency for Healthcare Research and Quality and other related professionals in order to arrive at a consensus for the identification and treatment of OME. These updated guidelines urged physicians to differentiate acute otitis media episodes from residual otitis media with effusion. Another significant recommendation regarded differentiating those children who are "at risk" for speech, language, listening, and academic problems from typically developing children who are otherwise functioning as expected. The guidelines recognize that children in these risk categories do not tolerate even a minimal degradation of their hearing acuity, and thus should be treated more aggressively than the typically developing child. Some of these risk categories include children with the following conditions: cleft palate, Down syndrome, autism, cerebral palsy, developmental disabilities, hearing loss, speech or language delay, attention span or behavioral difficulties, and other structural or cognitive anomalies.

For children who do not seem to fall into the at-risk categories above, the guidelines urge the physician to exercise "watchful waiting" and recheck in three months. Antihistamines and decongestants are now not advised, nor are long-term low doses of antibiotics to treat or prevent middle ear fluid. For persistent cases of OME after three months, follow-up hearing and speech-language testing is recommended in order to determine the impact of the OME on the child's development. Should the child present as having other risk factors or structural changes within the ear itself as a result of the OME, the surgical implantation of PE (pressure equalization) tubes may be considered. If the ear remains healthy and no other risk factors are observed, the physician may opt to continue monitoring the middle ear fluid (and resulting risk factors) every few months until it eventually resolves itself. In other words, if the middle ear fluid is not causing a noticeable problem or exacerbating an existing one, the risk, discomfort, and cost of surgery is probably not worth it.

There were no recommendations for homeopathic or chiropractic interventions, and treatment for allergies as an intervention for OME was not supported at this time due to a lack of conclusive research showing a direct correlation with OME. If enlarged adenoids or tonsils contribute to a persistence of the OME after the insertion of PE tubes, they may be removed when the next set of PE tubes is placed.

If your child does need tubes, the surgical procedure itself is extremely quick. Your child is put to sleep on an outpatient basis, and before you can read a few magazine articles, it's over. The surgical opening of the eardrum is called a myringotomy ("meer-in-GOTTA-me"). Once the opening is made, a tiny pressure equalization tube is placed there, which will eventually fall out all by itself, usually in a year or two. With the pressure in your child's middle ear equalized, the eardrum will be less likely to be retracted, or to have permanent scarring or other dysfunction due to the frequent infections. But most important, your child will be able to hear better. Recovery usually involves a lazy afternoon, and within a day or so, your child should be feeling good as new.

How Do Early Language Delays Affect a Child?

Children who have difficulty communicating have even more opportunities for temper tantrums than do typical children. For example, if a child like Jessica wants a glass of a particular kind of juice, she may grab her mother's hand, bring her to the refrigerator, and point to what she wants. If there are many things in the refrigerator, her mother may have to ask her a number of questions before she picks up the item Jessica wants. "Do you want some milk?" Jessica's response to this question is most likely a shake of her head to indicate no. "Do you want some grapes?" At this point, Jessica's response is likely to be a whiny cry. Because she is only 2½, Jessica doesn't understand why her mother cannot literally read her mind. When her mother does not pick up the juice she wants, her reaction is frustration. Most children under the age of 5 display frustration by crying, stamping their feet, whining, or falling to the floor. And in many cases, unfortunately, a child exhibits all of these behaviors. The good news is that, in my experience, the frequency of these kinds of behaviors is reduced dramatically once a child is able to communicate more successfully.

Other children, particularly those with accompanying brain damage, may cope with their language delays by being passive. They sit patiently and wait for others to initiate interaction. Because they are unable to communicate their feelings, they may give up trying and sometimes retreat into their own little world. These children can sit in front of a TV for hours at a time and never fuss. Although these passive children are easier to manage behaviorally, as a therapist, I am more hopeful when parents tell me how frustrated and whiny their language-delayed child is. Even though it is more taxing for you, it is an important sign that your child *wants* to communicate, which is the first critical step toward learning to speak.

It is hard to determine how early language delays affect children socially. Because they can't tell us how they feel, we have to draw conclusions from what we see. Some language-delayed children do become shy and uneasy with other children; others are undaunted and will tumble, run, and play blocks with the gang as any other child would. Several factors seem to affect how a language-delayed child interacts with other children.

- *Does the child have any other handicapping condition?* For example, if the child is having trouble hearing or walking, many activities may be more difficult to join. For these children, creative play solutions with your child's therapist may be in order.
- *Does the child have a naturally shy personality?* For this child, the added burden of a language delay will certainly make playing with other children more challenging.
- *Does the child have opportunities to meet other children?* For a language-delayed child, physical activities such as tumbling, karate, or arts and crafts can provide a nonthreatening social environment where what they can do is more important than what they can say.

As for the future, a child with an early language delay may eventually catch up and have no further learning problems, it there are no other areas of delay. Even a child with no other delays, however, is at risk for *possibly* developing learning disabilities later if language development is slow. If a specific problem accompanies the language delay, such as neurological impairment, retardation, hearing impairment, or autism, the prognosis is difficult to generalize because each child's progress is unique.

What Parents Can Do to Help Develop Early Language Skills—Some General Guidelines

Parents often ask me what they can do to help develop their child's speech, language, and listening skills. In some cases, parents want to help a child with delayed speech or listening skills catch up; other parents want to maximize a child's potential by building a solid foundation before anything goes wrong. The following are some keys to help your child achieve his or her potential:

- *Eliminate pacifiers.* Children who have a pacifier in their mouth have less opportunity to talk. In addition, it helps to create an unhealthy environment for the mouth by positioning the tongue and the lips in an unfavorable position. More and more experts also believe pacifier use helps create an unhealthy environment for the ear, contributing to middle ear infections and fluid. While infants often have a physical need to suck, it is best to get rid of the pacifier after your child's first birthday.
- *Listen to your child with enthusiasm and interest.* If you want your child to talk, you must show interest in what the child is saying. Stop what you are doing and look at your child as you look at an adult when listening. Children *do* know when you are half listening as you watch TV or read the newspaper. Though the bug outside may not be so exciting to you, your 3-year-old is eager to share the news with you. Try your best to respond with some enthusiasm and interest, no matter how mundane a child's discovery seems to you. Ask questions about it. Share information about the subject the child is talking about. Children who feel that what they say is of no importance are less likely to keep trying to communicate in a desirable way. In other words, they may try to get your attention with aggressive or whiny behavior instead.
- *Read to your child every day.* I can't overstate the importance of reading to your child. Simple books (usually cardboard and with few pages) that are designed to teach word names right from birth are avail-

able. Establish a routine and comfort with books. It is also a nice way to have private mother-child or father-child time. Go to the library every week, and as children reach the age of 2 or 3, let them pick out books that interest them. Read your child's favorite books over and over, ten times a day if your child wants! Talk about the stories and the picture names. Let your child "read" them to you. If he wants to change the story, let him be creative. Show interest in his ideas. If the story your child selects is too long or wordy, shorten and simplify it as you go along. Young children have a very short attention span, so you may not want to spend too long on one page. As your child gets older, you can incorporate more and more of the actual words on the page.

Remember to work on having your child let *you* hold the book and, by 15–18 months, you should read to him at least half the time, without him grabbing the book or flipping the pages. Remember that we want the experience to build language; if your child is merely looking at pictures and flipping pages, it becomes a visual experience and not one that supports language development. The other thing to bear in mind is that if your child gravitates toward books with concepts only (colors, letters, vocabulary pictures, for example) you will be missing the boat. You need to read simple stories with characters and plot, certainly by age 24–30 months, even if you are simplifying it and narrating only a single sentence on a page.

• *Resist talking like your child or encouraging baby talk.* Some parents imitate a child's infantile way of saying a word, thinking it is cute or helpful to the child. For example, if Arden calls a blanket a "boo-boo," Mom may get in the habit of asking Arden to get his "boo-boo." If only a few words are involved, that's fine. Just don't overdo it! However, if Mom or Dad begin incorporating baby talk more and more into their own vocabulary, the child may lose the incentive and the opportunity to learn the correct way of saying words. By imitating your child's pronunciation, you are giving him the impression that this is the right way to say it. By talking like an adult, you afford your child the opportunity to hear and attempt the correct way to speak.

• *Avoid letting older siblings speak for your child.* Sometimes we observe children whose older siblings try to help by speaking for their younger brother or sister when the younger one is asked a question. Unfortunately, their dominance can often lead a younger child to be less verbal and less comfortable initiating conversations. If you find an older sibling doing the talking for a younger child, encourage the child to speak for herself.

• *Praise any attempt at speaking—perfection is not the goal.* Some parents, in their zeal to foster good speaking skills, push for perfection when their child is learning to talk. This kind of pressure is not helpful. Your child can read criticism in your tone of voice, facial expression, or persistent request to "say it again the right way." A child picks up on this disapproval and may react by feeling inhibited and less willing to attempt to speak. Learning to speak requires practice, practice, and more practice! If a child feels comfortable in failing, she will be more apt to try again, probably in another situation and time, without being forced.

You can help in this regard by showing enthusiasm for *any* attempt at speaking and putting words together. A smile and repetition of what the child said (in corrected form) shows the child you understand *and* approve of what was said. The following conversation is an example of a positive exchange between a parent and a child:

Mom: What would you like for lunch, Jessie?
Jessie: How 'bou andith [sandwich]?
Mom: A sandwich? Okay, what kind of sandwich?
Jessie: Peanut buttoo and delly.
Mom: I think we have peanut butter and jelly.

• *Talk with your child about everything—being together is not enough.* Some parents, when reviewing test results with me, will show surprise when I tell them their child was unable to name a goat, a necklace, or other object. Consider 5-year-old Gina's mother and father, for instance. "Gee," her mother said, "little Gina sees those all the time. We're so careful about bringing her to see things, like the animals on the farm. How can she not know their names?"

On further discussion, Gina's parents reconstructed the visits to the farm and museum and realized that they were accompanied by some of Gina's cousins, Aunt Amy Jo, and Uncle Ben. Who were Mom and Dad talking to during this visit? Actually, the adults talked about business, the weather, politics, you name it. The children ran around and fed some of the animals with little or no interaction from the parents except to tell the children to get down from the fence, stop running, or tie their shoes.

The kind of visit just described is strictly recreational. But it could be an educational experience if the parents interacted directly with the children. It does not need to be a formal lecture or lesson. Make comments out loud while the children feed the animals. Ask the children thoughtful questions. This will help reinforce the names of the animals as well as develop other related vocabulary. The following exchange is an example of a meaningful and educational conversation at a farm:

Mom:	Look, Gina. That black goat is eating grass. He looks hungry. What are those things on top of the goat's head?
Gina:	They're sharp!
Mom:	That's right! Those sharp things are called horns. Horns are sharp. Do all these goats have horns?
Gina:	No. Those little ones don't have them.
Mom:	That's right. The little goats are baby goats called "kids." Kids don't have horns. Sometimes we call children "kids," too, don't we?
Gina:	Yeah, I'm a kid!
Mom:	You don't have horns, do you?
Gina:	(laughing) No! I'm not a goat; I'm a different kind of kid! I like the little brown one. Which goat do you like best, Mom?

Talking about what you see with your child while you see it is important. Simply exposing your child to places and experiences is only the first step in developing a well-rounded child. A parent must show personal interest in the event and provide the vocabulary necessary to describe and explain what you both are experiencing. Getting verbal feedback from your son or daughter not only shows that you have information to give to your child but also shows that you are interested in your child's opinion, feelings, and observations. A conversation should always be a two-way discussion, not a lecture.

If visiting places such as a zoo or an aquarium is financially or geographically out of the question, your local library can supply enough books to make you and your child feel like you've been there. Most libraries also lend videos, which can provide another good source for learning about everything from sharks to dinosaurs.

• *Answer questions completely.* Often a child will ask a question about how something operates, what the parts are, or why it does something. Even at the ages of 2 to 3 years, children can absorb surprising amounts of information. By teaching them specific words such as *van*, *station wagon*, and *jeep* instead of just calling all vehicles cars, you can expand their vocabulary. Try to answer your child's questions in a straightforward manner, using vocabulary that is always a little ahead of the vocabulary the child now uses.

This is *not* a helpful exchange:

Child (age 3½):	Dad, where does a horse live?
Father:	Oh, a horse lives in a place with other animals on a farm.
Child:	Where on the farm?
Father:	Inside, with other horses.

This father mistakenly assumed that since the child was familiar only with the word *farm*, it would be best to answer in words the child already knew and could understand.

This is a more helpful exchange:

Child: Dad, where does a horse live?
Father: Most horses live on farms. On a farm, there are big build-
            ings called *barns*. Remember when we fed the cows near
            Aunt Sue's house? That big red building on the farm was
            a barn. The horses live inside the barn with other animals
            in a stall.
Child: Do they have kitchens and bathrooms?

Well, as you know, one good question often leads to several more! This father knew that his child would be able to process the information better if he could associate it with something familiar. If the child hadn't ever seen a barn, the father could draw one or find a picture of one. Understanding the new terms *barn* and *stall* then becomes much easier.

The next step is to manipulate the conversation to give the child the opportunity to say the new word *barn* as often as possible. Dad can say, "So the farmer puts the horses in a . . . what is that big building called?" Encourage the child to use the word over and over so it eventually feels comfortable.

• *Talk about what you are doing.* Another helpful way to incorporate new words into your child's vocabulary is through "self-talk." Most parents do this when their child is very young but give it up as the child learns to talk. Self-talk means you narrate your own actions. Children with expressive vocabulary deficits not only need to hear the words used over and over by you but also need practice and encouragement to use the words themselves.

Following is an example of a self-talk exchange:

Parent: Brian, I'm measuring this flour to see if I have the right
            amount. Would you like to measure with me? The flour has
            to go all the way up to this line.
Brian: Okay.
Parent: (Puts in less than needed) Hmm . . . did I measure this cor-
            rectly? Did it go all the way up to the line?
Brian: No, it's not enough.
Parent: You're right. I didn't measure it right, did I? Do you know
            what kind of cup this is? See, it has these lines on it so I can
            tell how much flour, sugar, or whatever I'm measuring

there is. It's a measuring cup. Do you remember what kind
of cup this is?

Brian: A measuring cup.

Parent: Great! That's right. It's a measuring cup, and it's used for
m——— ?

Brian: Measuring.

Parent: What are some other things we could measure in this cup?

Notice how the parent continued to repeat the new word (*measure*) and
elicited the use of the word from the child.

• *Help your prekindergartener learn about words and sounds.* A
good way to facilitate language awareness in prekindergarten children
is to help them begin to notice rhyming words and patterns. Dr. Seuss
books such as *Green Eggs and Ham* and *The Cat in the Hat,* and A. A.
Milne's *Now We Are Six* are great for this. Your local librarian can help
you find other appropriate books. Make up silly words that rhyme; for
example, "We're having 'bancake-pancakes.'" Make rhymes with the
names of the people in your family.

Help your child begin to observe initial sound patterns. "Does *horse*
start the same way as *hat* or *boy?* Let's find some other things around
the house that start like *horse.* What sound [it's not necessarily important to identify the letter *h* at this point] do we hear at the beginning of
horse?"

An excellent book about developing your child's early language
skills is *It Takes Two to Talk.* It is written in an easy-to-read format and is
available in many languages. It is published by the Hanen Centre, a nonprofit agency. Call (416) 921-1073 or access it at http://www.hanen.org.

Case Study: Jake and Hutch

*I recently visited the homes of two toddlers. One child, Hutch, is at 2$^{1}/_{2}$ a
very verbal and inquisitive child. He delights in experiencing new things
and is filled with questions and observations that belie his tender age. He
even makes up his own knock-knock jokes. Though his sentences and pronunciation are still evolving, what he is saying is clearly quite advanced
for his age.*

*The other child, whom I'll call Jake, is slightly older. Jake is within nor-
mal limits for his age, but Jake doesn't have much to say. The questions
he asks are more functional, such as "Can I have lunch now?" He doesn't
show much interest in or enthusiasm for books or new people. He spends
most of his time playing on swings and slides. He seems disinterested in*

his surroundings and elaborates very little when answering questions. His vocabulary is noticeably less developed than Hutch's.

Were Hutch and Jake born with these traits, or were they the result of nurturing? Most experts agree that we are born with a certain amount of potential. Genes, prenatal care, and birth complications play a part in what a child has to work with from the start. If the right kind of stimulation does not occur, however, that potential shrinks over time. Jake and Hutch might have been born with the same potential, but even at their young ages, I could see that Hutch already had an edge over Jake.

What could be happening to cause the differences in Jake and Hutch? Certainly any parent will tell you that each child has a distinct personality from birth. Some children are just not talkative and never will be! Personalities aside, language and learning behaviors are greatly influenced by a child's environment.

Hutch's mother has a family membership to the zoo and the aquarium, which they visit regularly. They go to the library each week. Hutch's father shows an interest in what Hutch says. Hutch's parents patiently respond to his questions with appropriate, complete answers. They all read books together; Hutch knows some by heart from hearing them so often. In addition to reading stories, Mom and Dad talk enthusiastically about them with Hutch. When they go somewhere, they explain where they are going, what they see, and why, why, why! It's no wonder Hutch has found it productive to talk. Someone he cares about, more than anyone, listens to him and values what he says. He has learned that it is fun to say new words and to understand why.

Jake's mother finds it easier to let him play independently or with the other neighborhood children, because it keeps him busy. Jake and his brothers watch cartoon videos at home in rainy weather. Mom gives short, perfunctory answers to Jake's questions and lets him know with her tone of voice and facial expressions that he is bothering her with his trivial queries. After all, she has wash to do. It's important to keep his clothes clean, she tells me. They also go to the library, but Mom doesn't look at what Jake selects. She hastily takes the books for checkout and leaves them on his dresser at home. She figures he can look at them if he chooses. Sometimes she will quickly read one at night, but she grows impatient when Jake wants to hear it again or asks questions. There's too much to do, and his questions are fatiguing. Jake has figured this out, because he rarely asks them anymore, his mother says with a sigh of relief. At the dinner table, the children are urged to be quiet and eat.

Both sets of parents are doing what they think is best for their children. Jake and Hutch are each loved and adored by their parents. Both mothers are even able to stay at home full-time with their children. While Jake's house and clothes may be a slight bit more tidy, his intellectual development is not being stimulated as it could be. Jake may do okay once in school, but he could do much better if stimulated now.

It is important sometimes to let certain tasks go in order to take time with a child—time to talk, to explore, and to be good nurturers. Learning and language development is crucial in the first five to seven years. You can't, and shouldn't, wait for teachers in school to open up your child's mind to the world.

Whether this stimulation comes from a parent or a caretaker, it must come from someone. And it must happen on an ongoing, day-in, day-out basis. A good day-care placement in a nurturing environment can be just as stimulating for language development as a parent. In Jake's case, he may have more opportunities for stimulation in a day-care situation because the babysitter or caretaker would not be as a distracted with household chores.

Language and learning can occur during even the simplest of daily activities, such as mealtimes, shopping, and while watching TV. But only if someone facilitates it. Bringing a child to a zoo is not teaching a child about a zoo if there is no exchange of information or parental enthusiasm about the adventure. If all your time is spent silently watching animals or catching up on news with adult friends, your child has gained little from the experience.

Reading a story about a funny monkey may not be exciting for you. Seeing an elephant eat hay or hearing a horse neigh is probably "old hat" for us grown-ups, too. But a child experiences these things with wonder and delight. When a parent shows interest and enthusiasm in these things, it tells the child, "I enjoy doing this with you. Learning about new things is fun. Asking questions is good." When a parent is disinterested and does not value learning, a child is being set up for a lifetime of mediocrity.

When Learning New Words Comes Slowly: Vocabulary Problems

Sometimes I don't understand what Miss Rodriguez is talking about. I've heard the words before, but I forget what they mean. When I have to write my spelling words in sentences, I hate it! I kinda know what they mean, but not exactly. When I read stories, I don't understand what's going on. And when I take tests in class, I forget everything. All the names and places start to sound the same. Maybe my teacher is right: if I really tried, I could do better.

—Janet, age 10

Probably the most common trait found in children with language problems is the inability to understand or use words correctly. Our *vocabulary* represents the bank of words we use and whose meanings we understand. Janet is an example of a typical child with a language delay or disorder. She may have had difficulty learning to speak or putting sentences together as a toddler, or perhaps she did not show any sign of a language problem at all.

Understanding and using words is an important part of language development. Many children with language problems have difficulty learning or comprehending words, which is why it is usually one of the first areas a speech-language pathologist evaluates when testing.

Children like Janet are easy to miss. Typically, the brighter the student, the less likely it is someone will think there is a problem. Also, if the student is older, a parent or a teacher is apt to think that someone would have found the problem, if there was one, by this age. Janet's speech probably sounds normal, and she may be a very bright girl. However, something is getting in the way of her learning and classwork. In this section you will learn how to recognize and understand a child with Janet's problem and what can be done for children like her.

Difficulty Understanding Words: A Receptive Vocabulary Problem

Receptive vocabulary refers to all the words a child understands. Whether the child ever uses the words is a different matter. Receptive vocabulary is probably one of the most important language skill areas assessed. After all, children won't speak or write with words they don't understand. They can't accurately follow directions, written or verbal, if they don't know what the words mean. They can't understand what they are reading if the words don't make sense. If a child has this problem, we call it a *receptive vocabulary deficit*, a *receptive vocabulary delay,* or a *receptive vocabulary weakness.*

Difficulty with receptive vocabulary can have a serious impact on a child's academic achievement and should not be taken lightly. It is also probably one of the most critical areas in which a parent needs to take an active and aggressive role daily.

When a baby is acquiring a receptive vocabulary, parents often play verbal games with picture books, asking questions such as "Can you show me the boat?" and "Where's the cow?" These are helpful and fun games, but they also let you know that your child is making the important connection between a word and the object it represents. Children usually can do this before they can name the picture itself. In fact, asking children to point to the picture is a good way to prepare them to say the word later.

If you refer your child for a language evaluation, you can expect that the child will be given a receptive vocabulary test. To find out which words your child understands, the speech-language pathologist probably will ask the child to point to a particular picture with a set of four pictures to choose from. Often children with receptive vocabulary difficulties know *something* about the word, but they don't know it very well. For example, a 6-year-old boy may know that a goat is a farm animal, but when a picture of a goat is shown next to a sheep or a ram, he becomes confused. He vaguely knows *goat,* but he doesn't know it specifically. A 10-year-old girl may know that a fossil has something to do with age and rocks, so she may assume that all old rocks are fossils. She knows *fossil* vaguely, but she doesn't know it exactly. The age at which a child is expected to really know a given word has been determined by researchers studying thousands of children.

Receptive vocabulary encompasses all types of words, not just the names of objects. These are the word groups typically examined:

- Nouns: words identifying a person, place, or thing, such as *table*
- Adjectives: words used to describe nouns, such as *tall*
- Verbs: action words, such as *jumping*
- Prepositions: positional words, such as *below*
- Adverbs: words telling how something is done, such as *quickly*

When a child has difficulty *using* words, a speech-language pathologist will first want to know if that child is *comprehending* the meaning of words with accuracy. Receptive vocabulary weaknesses (deficits) are often at the heart of expressive vocabulary problems. You can't say or use words you don't fully understand, can you?

How Does a Receptive Vocabulary Deficit Affect a Toddler and a Preschooler?

Detecting and improving receptive vocabulary weaknesses is a critical part of the evaluation and treatment process. It is the backbone of communication. In your children we might notice the following signs:

- *Delayed speech.* Has your child started talking yet? If she hasn't, we will want to know how much she is understanding the words we use. If there is weak comprehension, talking will be limited. Comprehension of word meanings is a necessary ingredient in the "fuel" we need for talking. That is why your child's speech pathologist will be emphasizing the development of receptive language *first*.
- *Difficulty attending, listening, and following directions.* Is she struggling with following directions? Attending to what you say? Able to point to things you describe? When you read books and ask questions, pointing to pictures you describe might be challenging for her.

How Does a Receptive Vocabulary Deficit Affect a School-Age Child?

Difficulty in understanding or remembering the meaning of words can make a person feel isolated and confused. Imagine waking up in a foreign country with only a minimal knowledge of the language. People speak to you, perhaps ask questions or make requests, but you're not sure what all the words mean. You may try to follow along or guess the meaning because everyone expects you to know what they are talking about. Consider this exchange in the classroom from the point of view of Heather, a student with a receptive vocabulary deficit:

Teacher: Class, today, since our bordet of sool is harvent, I would like all of you to plen and let the others jess. Now, Heather, what is the barnish there?

Heather: Uh, I'm not sure.

Teacher: Were you listening? Hmm . . . maybe someone can help Heather out. . . . Allison?

Think of how exhausting it would be to follow a discussion with so many bits and pieces missing! Here are some ways a vocabulary weakness can impact a child at school:

- *Social style.* Eventually a child may tune out or cover up confusion by making a joke out of it. Since social conversations are sometimes confusing, the child may avoid them. The child may prefer other ways of making friends, such as through sports. On a soccer field, most communication is nonverbal and thus is much easier to understand. It feels great for any child to be "one of the gang."
- *Taking tests.* In the course of an everyday conversation, the problems may not be apparent for a child with a mild problem, but in the classroom, new vocabulary terms are introduced every day. Most tests are structured to see how many terms a child understands. Think of a typical

science or social studies test. They are filled with matching columns, fill-in-the-blanks, and true/false. What does a child do when all the words become a blur when presented side by side? Typically such children perform poorly on tests and lose the incentive to study, which, in turn, is blamed as the source of the problem. Whenever students tell me they study but can't pass the tests, I make sure their vocabulary skills are evaluated thoroughly.

• *Reading comprehension.* Receptive vocabulary weaknesses also affect reading comprehension, requiring the child to rely on pictures and context clues to discern the meaning of the words. This often suffices in the early grades but eventually may be overwhelming due to the amount of reading involved in social studies, science, and other subject areas in later grades.

• *Attention to instruction.* Attention span during oral discussions is often affected because the child has to piece together the meanings of so many words that it is all but impossible to follow along for long periods of time.

• *Following directions.* Because a teacher may use words that are confusing in explaining how to do homework or a project, your child may do it completely wrong. Make a *collage*? *Sketch* yourself at the bottom of the poem? Describe the character's *motivation*? How frustrating! You may find he needs to call a fellow student or review the instructions for projects with you so he's clear on what he needs to do.

• *Long-term issues.* Children who continue to be two years or more behind their peers in receptive vocabulary skills by middle school or high school will surely struggle in college. As an adult, understanding what people say is also important for understanding news events discussed on TV, social conversations, and work-related tasks. Someone who continues to have low receptive vocabulary skills as an adult will probably have better success in occupations that require less intense conversation, such as computer programming, plumbing, carpentry, and other hands-on fields.

Difficulty Using Words: An Expressive Vocabulary Problem

If a child has difficulty finding or knowing the most appropriate words to use when speaking, we call this an *expressive vocabulary deficit.* It can also be called an *expressive vocabulary weakness* or an *expressive vocabulary delay.* This can be observed when the child is unable to name an object or a picture, express emotions with clarity, retell a story, or describe someone or something. An expressive vocabulary weakness is typically part of a larger expressive language weakness or disorder.

How Does an Expressive Vocabulary Deficit Affect a Toddler and a Preschooler?

When a toddler or a preschooler has a weak expressive vocabulary, it causes a significant difficulty because individual word use creates the building blocks for putting together sentences. Here are a few ways we'd see this impact a child's language:

- *Uses fewer words and less language.* Children with weak expressive vocabulary may talk and initiate language interactions less often. They may be less verbal during play and do less "chattering" to themselves in that early stage of language development (12 months to 24 months). There may be a smaller variety of words, and the rate at which they learn new words may be slower.
- *Uses a word only in specific contexts.* Part of learning a word is the generalization of that word into other situations and representations. In other words, if your child can name "goat" when he sees it in his favorite storybook, but fails to connect the dots by recognizing the "goatness" of the goats he sees in the form of a goat puppet, a photo of a goat, or a toy goat, there is no generalization. These are often the children who do poorly on standardized tests. You may think your child could easily name "drum" but find there is little association if the drum in the picture doesn't have stripes on it like the one at home.
- *Holds onto babytalk.* While young children often use pet words for favorite objects or people, children with expressive vocabulary difficulties struggle to transition to the real words.
- *Overgeneralizes words.* For example, a child may refer to all flowers as "roses" or all drinks as "juice" well past age 2, where specific words should have been developed to differentiate juice from milk or water.
- *Speaks in telegraphic sentences.* Sentences that are primarily made up of nouns ("Dog . . . bone . . . dirt!") often are exacerbated by weak expressive vocabulary for verbs, prepositions, and early descriptors. That is why the SLP will often target teaching the meaning of those words and then transitioning to expressive tasks so your child will be motivated to use them.
- *Experiences language "shutdowns" under stress.* When a child has a limited pool of words in his "inventory" we often find that gaining access to that storage is particularly challenging when an emotional, thrilling, scary, or stressful situation is occurring. For example, let's pretend your daughter comes to you and is crying, holding her hand. You say, "What happened?" but that may only bring more tears or random

words. Telling her to "use her words" is generally not helpful. The words at this point might be locked up, and the key is nowhere to be found. That won't help her find them. Soothe your child, and let her calm down. You may need to ask specific questions to find out what happened. Provide some possibilities. ("Did you hurt your hand? Were you by yourself?")

- *Relies on gestures and noises.* Sam has an expressive vocabulary delay. He wants to tell you all about the new toy he has, and how he loves crashing it off the couch. Your encounter might go like this: "Mom . . . zhooom [shows his hand zooming] a car . . . a couch!" Because Sam can't readily find the words—especially when he's excited—he will naturally use everything he can in his arsenal to get his point across to you. Children like Sam are often very theatrical and expressive, just not with words. In fact, this compensation is one of the key differences between children with autism spectrum disorders (who generally do not use these compensations) and children who are simply expressively delayed.

How Does an Expressive Vocabulary Deficit Affect a School-Age Child?

Older children with expressive vocabulary problems often exhibit the following symptoms:

- *Vanilla vocabulary.* A child with an expressive vocabulary problem often uses general or vague terms instead of specific words. For example, when asked to describe a boy sledding in a blizzard, a fifth-grade student with an expressive vocabulary problem might say, "It's a boy riding down the hill. He has winter clothes on. It's bad outside."

This description may be appropriate at the kindergarten or first-grade level, but by fifth grade, most children have acquired a *working,* active vocabulary to more accurately describe that scene. In most cases the child may indeed understand or recognize the concepts in question. ("Is there a blizzard in this picture?" "Yes.") The difference is that the words have not become incorporated into the child's everyday language at the age one would expect, and tend to sound bland, without color. I sometimes informally refer to this as having a "vanilla vocabulary." Other symptoms include:

- *Stalling.* If the words are punctuated by a lot of pauses, "ums," "uhs," "whatchamacallits," and "like—you knows" there may be a word retrieval problem contributing to the vocabulary deficit as well. Later in this chapter, word retrieval problems are discussed in greater detail. If your child has been diagnosed with an expressive language deficit, a word retrieval problem may be part of the overall profile because it often goes hand in hand with expressive language delays.

- *Weak semantics.* As mentioned in chapter 3, semantics is how we use the words we know. For example, children often say, "I was bitten by a bee." It's not that children haven't heard or don't know the word *stung,* but the subtle differences in meanings are still not clear. They may say a building is *big* when they really mean *tall,* or they may say their bug bite is *scratchy* instead of *itchy.* These misuses of words are a normal part of development for children. However, in time a child should be able to use the correct forms more readily. When a child has vocabulary deficits and/or word retrieval problems, semantic skills are compromised. For example, a child with weak expressive vocabulary might make up words such as a train's "camoose" (caboose) or constantly mispronounce names or places that should be familiar.
- *A lack of higher-level vocabulary skills.* Some children are good at naming pictures in isolation but don't use the words in the correct context in conversation during certain language tasks, such as the following:

  - Using synonyms (words with similar meanings)
  - Using antonyms (opposites)
  - Using words with multiple meanings
  - Classifying words into categories
  - Using words in sentences

- *Repetitive sentences.* When a child with an expressive vocabulary deficit writes sentences or stories, the sentence structure may seem dull, repetitive, or short due to the limited pool of words the child draws from. For example, when asked to write these words in a sentence—*sun, seal, seat*—a child in second or third grade with an expressive vocabulary problem may write: *I see the sun. I see the seal. I have a seat.* It's not that the child doesn't know that the sun is yellow, is in the sky, and gives us light and warmth, it's just that using or thinking of the words is difficult.
- *Trouble defining words.* In reading activities, a child with an expressive vocabulary deficit may have no difficulty understanding the content or the vocabulary in the story. However, when asked to define new words or use them in isolation, the child may have problems. This difficulty carries over into social studies or science as well.

What Can Parents Do to Help a Child with a Vocabulary Weakness?

The good news is there is much you can do to improve your child's vocabulary. Individualized therapy in isolation has little impact on your child's receptive or expressive vocabulary unless constant and regular rein-forcement occurs at home. Remember that some children need to hear and use a word twenty times before it will "stick." Aside from rep-etition, how you introduce, teach, and help pull out the word in context can make this process more efficient. Using a camera is particularly help-ful, but for action words (verbs) a camcorder or a FLIP video works well (see below). Google Images is your go-to place for finding pictures of what you want, and many different representations. Verbs you want to target can often be found on YouTube (e.g., "Monkey climbing") but make sure you preview them first! Unfortunately, there is no quick fix, but here are some ideas to get you started.

For Toddlers and Preschoolers

• *Vary the representations of the word you are targeting.* If you are trying to teach the word *apple*, you must have photos, toys, drawings, and of course real apples, both red and green. Your child needs to know that it's not just a word that describes a specific picture in a book or on a flash card.

• *Try matching games.* For very young children, start with favorite "first word" books. Have a few of the items (stuffed cat, spoon, telephone, pencil, etc.) pictured in the book, on the bed with you. When you find one of the pictures in the book, say, "Hey, here it is, right HERE! This is a cat [point to the picture in the book] and this is a cat too [hold up the stuffed cat]!" Then let your child start making those same associations. You can have the matching items in a hat or a box, and let your child go find it, like a scavenger hunt. ("Here's an apple on this page. Can you go find one in the box?") What's even more fun is having your child choose things for *you* to find in the house. However, make sure your child uses the actual word, and doesn't just say, "Find this/that/one of these." It needs to be specific, such as "Go get a *toothbrush*."

• *Keep track.* With young children, the idea is to build upon success. Rather than having random words each week, you'll need to keep rein-forcing and reviewing them so that there are some old, some new. Keep lists. Making your own word book is helpful, as are taking pictures of newly labeled objects and putting them around the house (on the fridge, on the bathroom mirror). Even though your child likely cannot read yet, write the word clearly below the picture. You'd be amazed at how many children do make associations with pictures and words, even at ages 2 and 3. Keeping the new words and concepts fresh is help-ful and provides review. Even more, seeing the printed word paired with the picture reinforces the concept that written words mean something.

• *Move to verbs.* A good rule of thumb might be to start with 50 nouns, then begin introducing verbs. Some early favorites include: *eat, jump, sleep, cry, sit, go, fall, kiss, hug, brush, wash, walk, blow, open, close, push, take,* and *drink.* These are a little trickier because you can't hold them in your hand. However, they are fun to do! Little children just love to make us do things and feel as if they are in control. Make videos of each action you are targeting. (If at all possible, use your child or another family member or friend in the video.) You can watch them and reenact them together. For example, while watching the video you can say, "We're running! Look, now we're sleeping [snore, eyes closed]. What are we doing here?" You can also take action word flash cards and turn them facedown on the table. Each person picks one and has to tell the other person what to do. For example, "You *crawl!*" or "You *touch* something."

• *Provide first sound cues.* When your child can't think of the word, try to sound it out slowly, to see if it helps jog her memory. This is a great way of reinforcing the phonemic organization of the word at the same time. For example, your 2-year-old daughter brings a plastic spider to you and says, "Icky!" but you are trying to move her toward a more specific word, *spider.* You can say, "Oh, my, what is that thing? It's called a sssssspiiiii . . . ?"

• *Ask yes/no questions.* Let's pretend your daughter comes to you the next time with a caterpillar. She calls it a "bug," but again, you are trying to reinforce more specific words, and you're quite sure she has heard the word *caterpillar* many times. You could say, "Yes, it is a bug, isn't it? This one has a special name. Is it a rabbit? [She shakes her head.] Is it a monkey? [She shakes her head.] Is it a caterpillar? [She nods her head.] Ah, yes, what a smart girl you are! It IS a caterpillar." Notice how you used other animals that were much different from a caterpillar. It was quite obvious. But your daughter feels empowered and confident, and her lack of expressive use didn't put her in a corner. That's much better than saying, "What's the big-girl word for it? I told you already!"

• *Use puppets, dolls, and action figures.* I can't emphasize this enough. Children just love it when you make learning playful and fun. What's even more fun? A puppet that can't seem to remember the names of anything! It's good that your child is there to help. Let's pretend you are working on helping your child label actions. Have one puppet do one of the actions; for example, brush his teeth. He comes out of the pretend bathroom and the mother puppet is there. "Hi, Joe, what were you doing?" But Joe isn't good at using words either. He says, "I was . . . uh . . . doing something with my teeth." [He demonstrates.] "What?" she asks. I was . . . .uh . . . can you help me? What was I doing?" Children are the most empathetic beings, and I rarely find one who won't help a puppet in peril.

• *Remember to tie words with questions.* Action words tend to go with "What are you doing?" or "What did he do?" or "What is she doing?" Your child will need to know when to pull out the words she is learning. Nouns are to be used to respond to "What is it?," "What's that?," "What is it called?," and "What's this animal's *name*?" Prepositions go with questions that ask *where.* "Where is the spoon?" ("*In* the drawer.") "Where is the pillow?" ("*On* the bed.") and "Where is your shoe?" ("*Under* the bed.") Adjectives are used to respond to questions that ask "What did it *look like*?" ("It was *big* and *brown*, with *long* arms," etc.)

• *For computer lovers.* If your child is responsive to the computer, you can supplement these activities with some special software. My favorites are from Laureate Learning Systems (www.laureatelearning.com), including First Words and First Verbs. Another good program is Great Action Adventure, which is available from many vendors, including Amazon.com. However, be careful to use the software as a supplement, because your child still needs to learn how to play and learn language from people as well as from computers.

• *Pair gestures with new action words, prepositions, and descriptors.* We know that memory is enhanced when there is a multisensory association, so use your body! If you are teaching the word *face*, take your hand and make a circular shape a few inches in front of yours. For *jumping*, take the index and middle fingers of your right hand and pretend to jump them on the palm of your left hand. For *big*, make your arms go big, and for *small*, crouch down into a ball. For *in*, you can cup your left hand and put your index and third finger from the right into it. *In.* Say and do!

• *Offer choices.* When trying to elicit descriptive language, you can provide two choices, "Is that a soft cookie or a crunchy cookie?" Make sure you have one word your child already knows well (soft) and that is fairly opposite or obvious as the foil for the choice. This way, it will be quite apparent that the correct word is *crunchy.* This is much better than constantly peppering your child with open-ended questions to force the use of descriptive language. Keep it successful.

• *Teach categorical terms (animals, clothing, fruit, jewelry, drinks, vehicles, rooms).* The terms and the words associated with each are important to know and often are a struggle for children with vocabulary weaknesses. There are some good board games from LinguiSystems and Super Duper that can be fun to practice these words.

For School-age Children

If your child's receptive or expressive vocabulary is still functioning below an age 6 level or so, consider the suggestions in the preceding section. If your child is at or above this age, there are slightly different kinds of activities you can do:

- *Play the synonyms game.* In your conversational speech, see how many everyday words you can replace with a synonym. For example, for the next two weeks, you can say, "Okay, time for us to get in the *automobile!*" instead of using the usual word, *car.* Try to pick out 5 to 10 words to target each week, repeating them in as many contexts as possible. Some suggestions:

  - Do you want a *beverage*?
  - Please don't *quarrel* with your sister.
  - Let me see if I can *repair* this broken wheel.
  - Let's find something in this room that is *transparent.*
  - I am very *dismayed* that you forgot to wash your hands again!
  - Do you want the *indigo* cup or the *scarlet* one?
  - It's time to *depart*!
  - Which *blouse* would you like to put on?
  - Where are your *trousers*?
  - What are you *viewing* on TV?

- *Maximize your book-reading time.* Everyone knows reading books to your children helps them develop a love of reading and an ear for oral expression. But did you know how important reading to your children is for the expansion of their vocabulary? Because we tend to use the same limited pool of words in our speaking vocabulary (as do TV shows, which mirror common dialogue), *the primary way a child learns less-common words is through reading literature.*

So what can you do to help a child who is falling behind? Take a favorite book that your child has heard many times, and insert synonyms throughout it, instead of reading the actual words on the page. For example, you could insert "canine" in place of the word *dog.* Because the child is already familiar with the text, he can deduce the meaning with greater ease. Likewise, have your child read the book to you and see how many synonyms she can insert when reading to *you.* Because children like games, you can give a "point" for each synonym used. Remember, the idea is for it to be a synonym and not a rephrasing of the text—it must be a word-for-word substitution.

• *Use a digital camera.* With the advent of digital cameras, you have the opportunity to expand your child's vocabulary even more. For a fun summer activity, have your child take pictures of some of the daily routines in your life over the course of a day. Print them out and tape each one onto a page. Staple the pages together to make a homemade book. On each page, help your child describe what happened, using a new word on each page. Write it down, and read the book to your child over and over. See if he can remember some of the new words and tell the story back to you, without looking at the writing. For example, if you went to McDonald's, you can say:

> We *arrived* at McDonald's.
> We *entered* McDonald's.
> The *cashier* took our money.
> I *removed* the paper from the straw.
> I *sipped* the soda.

• *Make a personalized illustrated word book.* One mistake people make is to force a child to use a dictionary to learn new words. This usually backfires because the words that are used to explain the meaning are often foreign to the child. Student or children's dictionaries can be helpful if they are illustrated, but a better way to learn new words is to have your child make his own dictionary. When your child hears a new word in conversation or trips over one while reading a book, it can be a candidate for the "word book." Each word should have its own page. On this page, the word should be at the top. Let your child use markers or colored pencils. If the word has a funny spelling or pronunciation, help your child write out a way that will help him remember how to pronounce the word. For example, for the word *mystery*, you might write "MISter-ee" below it. The picture drawn should show the word being used in context so it is clear how to use it in a sentence. For example, the page for *mystery* might show a child noticing a treasure box under a tree and looking surprised. The sentences below the picture might be, "Rachel doesn't know who put the treasure box under the tree. It's a real *mystery*! She wants to find out more and solve the *mystery*." This would also help her tie another word (*solve*) with *mystery*, since they often go together. By drawing the picture and writing the context sentences, your child will be better able to recall the word and its meaning.

• *Board games.* Games such as Scattergories, Scattergories Junior, Taboo, and Password all help build semantic vocabulary use in school-age children.

Case Study: Angelique

Angelique was referred to the Student Study Team by her classroom teacher when she was in third grade. She was doing very well in math, art, music, physical education, spelling, language arts, and writing. Her problems were in reading comprehension, social studies, and science. Her teacher was also concerned because Angelique seemed to make irrelevant comments during class discussions. Sometimes she confused the class because she would speak in vague terms and use words incorrectly. When completing homework assignments, she took a long time to answer questions that required her to identify and explain new vocabulary words. Sometimes even understanding the question itself was difficult for Angelique. If Angelique studied long and hard, she was able to pass tests, but the marathon study sessions were taking their toll. Considering Angelique's A's and B's in other subjects, the C's and D's in reading, social studies, and science seemed curious.

In Angelique's case, she did not avoid social conversations. In fact, she was a bubbly and outgoing girl.

Angelique had initially been referred to remedial services in January of her second-grade year for extra help in reading comprehension. This small-group instruction had been helpful and had improved her vocabulary. Unfortunately, new words introduced in school outpaced these half-hour sessions held twice a week. Besides, many of the words in these supplemental classes were taught in addition to the ones piling up from her other classes. Without repetition and practice, the words became more and more of a blur. So by the time Angelique reached third grade, she was further behind her classmates.

Angelique's third-grade teacher made the referral to the Student Study Team in April. After discussing Angelique's case, the team decided to have the teacher and parent work on using some strategies. These were considered Tier 1 suggestions, based on the Response to Intervention (RtI) model they used. These interventions included modifying some of Angelique's classwork so that she was able to focus on fewer tasks with greater quality, without it impacting her grade. It also included allowing her teacher to modify the homework assignments to have fewer questions, so she was not staying up late trying to finish all the questions. However, Angelique's mother was still concerned and wanted to sort out what was going on. As in many situations, she pursued a private learning disabilities evaluation and paid for it herself. It wasn't that she didn't have confidence in the public school team; she just wanted an independent eye to take a look and was impatient to wait and see what happened.

The results of the evaluation showed there were no major disabilities or emotional issues present that could explain these difficulties, although Angelique's phonemic awareness was weak. Her ability for nonverbal tasks was somewhat higher than that for verbal tasks, although both scores placed her solidly in the average range.

However, both examiners did notice that Angelique would often ask to have the test questions explained because she "didn't know what she was supposed to do." She misunderstood several of the tasks, but she could complete them satisfactorily when shown a few practice examples. When she spoke, her language was vague. The psychologist recalled Angelique complimenting the "bottom dress" (skirt) the psychologist was wearing and referring to the pencil's location as being "inside [between] the pens." Due to these observations, a speech-language evaluation was requested as a follow up, and Angelique's mother asked the Student Study Team if that could be done at school.

Because Angelique still seemed a bit overwhelmed, the team decided to jump in and do some formal speech-language testing. At this point it was June, so it was scheduled for when school resumed in September, when Angelique began fourth grade. The results of the evaluation showed that Angelique had clear deficits in receptive and expressive vocabulary, as well as difficulty in related semantic skills and phonemic awareness. After a team meeting in October, the SLP recommended that Angelique attend small-group therapy twice a week to work on these skills, including phonemic awareness. By strengthening her phonemic awareness, Angelique would have a better way to "file" new words and remember them. In addition to the therapy, and no less important, were the modifications in the classroom that took place. These were carried out by Angelique's classroom teacher, with assistance and periodic consultation with the team and the SLP. By prioritizing and limiting vocabulary lists and assignments as well as restructuring tests to accommodate her weaknesses, Angelique's teacher was able to help her have a successful fourth-grade year.

Please note that it took several months to find the root of Angelique's problems. This is not an uncommon scenario; indeed, it is a typical, rather than an idealized, picture of what often happens to children like Angelique in a public school system. The delay between the initial referral and the time treatment begins is frustrating. The bureaucracy and legal requirements make much of this unavoidable. Sometimes supplementing a public school program with a private evaluation helps move the process faster. You can also help by letting your child's teacher know whether completing homework or studying requires extraordinary amounts of your child's time and energy or whether your child consistently resists doing the assignments unless you sit and help with each question. Children sometimes seem to cope well in the classroom but fall apart at home. Good communication between home and school can get the process moving more quickly and bring about solutions and strategies to allow your child to succeed and enjoy school.

The "Him Not Talkin' Right" Child: Morphological and Syntax Problems

I not goin' school today, Mommy. I sick. We goin' a doctor? Why you take me to doctor, Mommy? Him give me shot? Maybe yesterday I jump around too much. Tommy falled off and he have two cut now. I won' jump anymore.

—Pete, age 6

When Pete talks, his problem may be noticeable to you. However, for a parent who sees Pete every day, it's easy to get used to the way he talks and simply accept it as "something he'll grow out of." As we discussed in the first two chapters, Pete's speech is a bit behind that of his 6-year-old peers. In fact, his problem is more correctly described as an expressive language problem as opposed to an articulation deficit, because he is capable of pronouncing the words he is not using correctly. Also, he may not grow out of it, particularly if he doesn't get the right kind of help.

If Pete were a 2-year-old or a young 3-year-old, we wouldn't characterize him as having a speech problem. But he's 6 now and retains a babyish quality to the way he puts words and sentences together. If your child speaks this way and has already turned 4, he or she may need help to learn to speak correctly.

All children (and adults, for that matter) have difficulty with certain aspects of grammar. Did he play that song *good* or *well*? Would you like to come with *John and I*? Or come with *John and me*? These are typical problems everyone wrestles with as they develop language. Children may say *goin'* instead of *going*. Adolescents use certain words and phrases that are "hip" to their culture and may sound quite foreign to us dinosaurs. However, these are different issues from those of children who genuinely cannot put their thoughts together in a simple, grammatically correct sentence.

In this section I'll explain the kinds of grammar problems children may exhibit, how children are affected, and what parents can do to help.

Pete's kind of speech pattern actually is symptomatic of a language delay in two areas (morphology and syntax), but they typically go hand in hand, so I've included both in this section.

Morphological Deficits

A *morpheme* is the smallest linguistic unit. A morpheme can be a prefix, a root word, a suffix, or an ending such as *ed*, *es*, *n't*, or *s*. For example, in the word *unforgivable*, there are three morphemes: *un*, *forgive*, and *able*. Some languages do not use endings or inflections with their verbs or use plurals or possessives, so it is not uncommon for those learning English as a second language to struggle with the use of English morphology. In these cases, it would not be considered a disorder, but rather the normal learning process in absorbing an entirely new language system.

A child with a *morphological deficit* usually has the most difficulty using the correct endings with words, which is a type of an expressive language problem. The English language is filled with endings that change meaning. We change verbs by adding an ending to show present tense ("plays" or "play*ing*") or past tense ("play*ed*"). We use *s* to show something belongs to someone ("Daddy'*s* tie") and that there is more than one of something ("six car*s*"). When we use contractions ("I'*ll*"), the part following the apostrophe also serves as an ending. Of course, there are many exceptions to the rules in the English language, so you can expect a child who is already not quite clear with word rules to have difficulty with any words that don't follow the rules as well.

Most of us are fortunate enough to learn grammar rules simply by listening to others speak and imitating what we hear. It is not a conscious or direct process. For some children, though, it doesn't work this way.

Fluctuating hearing loss from frequent ear infections is a common cause of morphological errors, because endings are mostly high-pitched sounds that may not be heard when the ear is filled with fluid. Children will say words the way they hear them. Sometimes children with severe articulation problems leave off endings because it is physically hard for them to make the necessary sounds. Some children may be unaware of how their speech sounds to others, or they may have yet to learn the rules. Children whose overall development is delayed also may have difficulty learning morphological rules and speaking correctly.

Syntax Deficits

Syntax refers to the order of the words in a sentence. A *syntax deficit* is another type of expressive language problem. When babies and toddlers first learn to speak, they use phrases and shortened sentences with incorrect syntax. By the age of 5, children should be using grammatically correct sentences most of the time. Some children omit entire words (as well as endings) or put them in the wrong order. A child with a syntax problem may phrase a question the same way as a statement ("We goin' a doctor?") but add the proper inflection at the end of the sentence to let you know he would like an answer. At other times only the important words in a sentence are used, omitting articles, *is*, prepositions, and so forth. For example, a child with delayed syntax might say "Richie kick ball."

Characteristics of Children with Morphological and Syntax Problems

Children with morphological or syntax problems might do the following:

- May use primarily nouns to form sentences, with very few connecting words (e.g., "Dog . . . bone . . . dirt!")
- Use the wrong pronoun (e.g., say "Him over there" instead of "He is over there.")
- Omit words at the beginning of a question (e.g., say "You have candy?" instead of "Do you have candy?")
- Omit the word or contraction for *is* in sentences (e.g., say "It cold" instead of "It is cold" or "It's cold.")
- Confuse *has* and *have* (e.g., say "Mommy have a cold" instead of "Mommy has a cold.")
- Omit articles (*a, an,* and *the*) or use them incorrectly (e.g., say "I have balloon" instead of "I have a balloon.")
- Omit endings for past-tense verbs (e.g., say "I jump over it" instead of "I jumped over it.")
- Omit endings that show the possessive form of a noun (e.g., say "Mommy shirt is blue" instead of "Mommy's shirt is blue.")
- Omit endings that show plurals (e.g., say "three car" instead of "three cars")
- Overgeneralize regular verb rules to irregular verbs (e.g., say "I gived the doll a bath" instead of "I gave the doll a bath.")

Note: Many normal children persist in using the incorrect form of a few irregular verbs into the first grade or so. It's a problem only when it is pervasive, consistent, and in a child older than 5 or so.

How Do Morphological and Syntax Problems Affect a Child?

Toddlers and preschoolers are just learning how our language system works. Typically, nouns are the first element of language to be acquired, and for many children it becomes a challenge to move beyond that stage. They may be able to name just about any picture in a book ("Backhoe!") but still don't have the knack of putting them together in a sentence. Children who are "stuck" at this stage can become very frustrated. Imagine how hard it is to know so many words but not be able to express yourself to those around you! These children can be irritable at times and resort to expressing themselves in ways we may not enjoy. For example, Timmy wants the car that his friend is play-ing with, but can only say "car." His friend doesn't realize it's a request for it, and may think he's just making an observation, such as "Hey, you have a car!" Before long, Timmy may be grabbing it out of his friend's hand, which in turn leads to a struggle and a time-out. Without being able to formulate a more elaborate sentence, Timmy cannot ade-quately negotiate social situations.

As children become older preschoolers, we expect that more and more elements of morphology and syntax will be integrated into their spontaneous speech. When this does not happen, the other concern we will have is whether or not the child truly understands those language fundamentals. Let's suppose I have a 4-year-old boy named Jim who says, "The bunny jump!" If I ask him to point to the picture that shows the bunny "jumped" (perhaps from a group of pictures that show a bunny about to jump, actively jumping, and completing a jump), can he do it? If he says, "I have two car!" my first job is to find out if in fact he under-stands the function of plurals or not. Often, when there are significant morphological and syntax gaps in a child's expressive speech, there are related issues in comprehension, which are often too subtle for parents to notice on a casual basis. This is another reason why a good, thorough evaluation is so critical even when the difficulty appears to be quite straightforward: A child with these kinds of morphological and syntac-tical delays will be at risk for other reading and spelling difficulties in a short time, if the underlying deficits are not addressed.

Children who are new to a language or are learning two languages simultaneously often struggle to keep the grammatical structures of both languages straight. That's normal, and will usually resolve itself in time. Delays of this nature in a bilingual child would not be considered a "disorder" but rather a language difference. If your child is receiving speech therapy for other issues such as articulation, it doesn't mean we cannot support morphological and syntax development during speech therapy. However, in public schools it would generally not come under the umbrella of the special education program or required speech services unless there are similar difficulties present in both languages.

In school-age children, even typically developing children in the lower grades will struggle with certain elements of syntax and morphology. Common errors include "He seen it!" or "I have two loose teeths!" with irregular verbs and nouns still being misused. Children with greater difficulties will generally find that writing sentences and stories in school is a challenge. If Pete says, "I happy," that is what he will write. Connecting two related thoughts and putting them together to write a paragraph can be torturous for some of these children because the organization of the words (syntax) is still a puzzle. Children who have difficulty internalizing language rules for speaking may also have problems with other language rules needed for reading and writing. Most children of normal intelligence are able to overcome early problems with syntax and morphology in time, but we often see later difficulties with narrative and divergent language skills evolve in these children, as well as word retrieval weaknesses. In other words, the morphological and syntax problems may be more visible early on, but they may also be the tip of the iceberg in some cases.

What Can Parents Do to Help a Child with Morphological and Syntax Problems?

It is very important to get professional help for a child like Pete because a speech pathologist will be able to zero in on one skill at a time to work on. Each of the skills listed earlier may require weeks of concentrated therapy and practice before your child can be ready to try to incorporate it into his or her conversational speech. The speech pathologist can guide you with activities to do at home and share ideas about how to reward and praise your child for using the correct skill, as opposed to making the child feel inadequate when he or she forgets. Here are some more suggestions:

- If your toddler or preschooler is "stuck" at the one-word stage, try to reduce your speech to two words so the model is easier for him to reproduce. For example, if you are serving peas and your child says, "Peas!" you will want to stretch that by just one word. I'd go for "Eat peas!," "Yummy peas!," or "Green peas!"
- If you're trying to push from the one-word stage to the two-word stage, really focus on those verbs. When your child verbalizes a noun,

try to pair it with a gesture and the associated word. If he says, "Car!" you gesture and say, "Car *go!*" with the emphasis on the "go" part. Even if he just copies the gesture, he will start to understand that something goes after that word.

•   Use some drums! Bang on the drum for each word so your child can see how the words are connected. For example: "Cat-sleeping-on the bed!" Your child may only say, "Cat-sleep-bed," but if he's just at the one-to two-word stage, that's great. Once you want to zero in on that prepositional phrase, isolate that on the drums: "on-the-bed."

•   Use a variety of voices to make it fun. A sleepy voice, a LOUD voice, a baby voice, a cat voice. Do a copycat game and make the target phrase just one word longer than what your child typically says. So if your child normally says, "Phone gone!" you would perhaps emphasize the missing *is* and say, "Phone *is* gone" in your cat voice. Your child would then have to copy you. Switch roles and let our child take the lead.

•   Integrate gross motor movements. For example, if you want to get the word *is* into your child's sentence structure, tiptoe together and then jump as soon as you get to the word *is*. For example, you could say, "That fish . . . *is* swimming!" Hold your child's hand and jump up for *is*. Before long, he will be anticipating it and noticing it more in other contexts as well.

•   Children in preschool love to count. If you are trying to stretch your child's utterance and get those morphological and syntax elements in there, write down what he says with colorful markers, then count the words together. Use fingers (1-2-3-4): "Boy riding a truck" = 4 words. Now show your child how you can make it longer: "We can add a word or two before *boy*. We can say, 'A *big* boy riding a truck.' Let's count the words now. Wow, that's six! Look at all those fingers." When your child spontaneously produces longer sentences, count the words and show your child on your fingers how many words it was and give lots of praise for using those "big" sentences.

•   Your child's SLP should target one or two morphological or syntax concepts at a time. Make sure you emphasize the element (past tense verbs, plurals, missing articles, etc.) in your own speech throughout the week so your child can hear and notice it. So if the target is regular past tense verbs, after arriving home, you could say, "We stopp*ed* for pizza today, didn't we?" Your SLP may pair the *ed* ending with a physical gesture or a tap on the teeth to remind the child to get that sound for the *ed* in there. Whichever cues are being used should be incorporated into your own speech during this time so the child gets the linguistic input and pattern.

- A great DVD for this age group is *Teach Me to Talk* by Laura Mize, a speech-language pathologist. If you have a toddler or a pre-schooler who needs a jump-start in these skills, her DVD will show you some great strategies for working with your child at home (www.teach metotalk.com).

- Don't attempt to help children speak better by asking them to repeat sentences correctly after you when they speak incorrectly. When you focus so much attention on *how* your son or daughter is speaking and not on *what* is being said, you can unintentionally discourage your child from trying to talk to you at all. Also, in a child's mind, "Mommy doesn't like it when I say it this way" can easily be translated to "Mommy doesn't like me."

- Listen to what your child says, and then respond by rephrasing what was said, using the correct words and sentence structure. Emphasizing and repeating the missing words or endings helps, too. This "mirroring" also lets your child know you received the message. Here is an example of a helpful exchange between Pete and his father:

Pete: Daddy, we goin' a Gramma house today?
Father: *Are* we going to Grandma's house today? Yes, after lunch we'll get ready to go. We *are* going!
Pete: Melissa goin', too?
Father: Yes, Melissa *is* going, too. She *is*!
Pete: Her sittin' in the backseat, right?
Father: Yes, *she's* sitting in the backseat. She *is*.

- Use a patient, relaxed, and interested tone of voice when speaking with your child. Expressing impatience or dismay with the way she speaks can only make things worse.

- Find the time to work with your child at home if the speech pathologist sends home specific activities to do. Make it a priority. The more diligent you are about the exercises, the faster your child will progress.

Case Study: Jacob

Jacob was referred to me by his mother for a speech-language evaluation when he was 4½. She was concerned because Jacob was going to start kindergarten in nine months, and he was still "talking like a baby."

Working as a private practitioner on this case, I was able to schedule the testing the same week his mother called. When Jacob arrived for the evaluation, he was somewhat shy and reluctant to talk. He clung to his mother and hid behind her skirt. Using puppets and stuffed animals, I eventually elicited a quick smile and a few words. "He talks much more than this, really!" his exasperated mother told me. Not to worry. Any speech pathologist worth his or her salt knows it takes some time to draw out young children and win their confidence. The evaluation proceeded smoothly over the course of two or three sessions.

Jacob had very strong vocabulary skills and exhibited no difficulty following directions or comprehending what was said to him. He was, however, somewhat distractible for his age and clearly exhibited difficulty putting sentences together and using the correct forms of words. I wrote down what he said and counted the average number of words per "utterance," a technique called MLU (mean length of utterance), which showed the quantity as well as the quality of his language was a bit delayed. In addition, Jacob had some minor pronunciation problems that, along with his syntax and morphological errors, led me to suspect a possible hearing problem.

When I reviewed Jacob's medical and developmental history with his mother, she mentioned he had had several nasty and persistent ear infections in the past two years. "But he's fine now. He hasn't had a fever or complained of pain in a few months. Besides, I know he's hearing me because he answers me when I ask him questions. Unless, of course, he's in front of the TV; then I might as well be a potted plant. You know how kids are!"

If you've read the first few chapters, you can probably guess where I sent Jacob next. That's right, I sent him for a hearing evaluation by an audiologist. Guess what the hearing test showed? Jacob had a mild hearing loss, which affected his ability to hear higher frequencies, as well as residual fluid behind his eardrum, causing speech to sound somewhat muffled or distorted to him. At a testing three months later he still had fluid present in the middle ear and a mild hearing loss. Because it was a persistent and unresponsive condition, Jacob had tubes put in right after this second follow-up hearing assessment.

In the meantime, I began a speech-language therapy program with Jacob. He came twice a week for individual sessions, and his parents worked consistently with the activities I gave them to do at home. By the time Jacob began kindergarten, he was speaking much more clearly. We also worked on some listening skills, which were weak in a few areas. By the time Jacob finished his kindergarten, he was speaking at age level 90 to 100 percent of the time. He was phased out of speech-language therapy and has recently graduated from high school with honors. (Where does the time go?)

The "Whatchamacallit, Um, Thing Over There" Child: A Word Retrieval Problem

Sometimes when I try to think of what I want to say, uh . . . the words get um . . . jumbled up in my head. . . . When the teacher calls on me in class, I can't think of it fast enough, so uh . . . I just say "I don't know." I wish I wasn't so stupid.

—Jared, age 9

Have you ever momentarily forgotten a word? Well, it's a very common phenomenon that we all experience from time to time. Sometimes it may even be a fairly simple word that escapes you. It's a frustrating feeling, because you *know* you know this word. You may even "see" some of the letters in your mind, which helps your brain search through its files and pull the word you want. Sometimes you resort to selecting a word with a similar meaning to get past the awkward pause in the conversation. But you probably still rack your brain until minutes later it usually magically appears.

As children develop language, they store the newly learned words in their language "memory bank" so that they may use these words when they talk. For some children, tapping into this word store proves particularly difficult. Can they point to a cactus? Yes, but when they're asked, "What is this?" the answer may prove elusive. In a typically developing child, we always expect it to be easier to recognize a word than to say it. But for some children, the gap between these two skills is much greater. Children with other expressive language difficulties often exhibit word retrieval (also known as "word finding") problems.

Above, Jared describes how it feels to have a word retrieval problem. In this section we'll go over how to recognize and understand a child with Jared's problem and examine what can be done for children like him.

Word retrieval deficit refers to the brain's inability to pull words from its "file" quickly enough to use in the desired context. We all have moments throughout the day when our brain thinks of an idea to communicate to another person before our language center has properly pulled the words we will use. We start talking and expect that we'll think of them by the time we get to it. By saying "um" we give ourselves that extra second or two to get our thoughts organized. It's the lack of speed and lack of accuracy in naming that defines this disorder.

When I first visited Japan, I noticed that the word *ano* was used in Japanese conversations frequently. In my studies of Japanese, I had not come across that word in the context in which it was being used. It was interesting for me to find out that *ano* is the Japanese equivalent of *um*. In England, people tend to use *em* when stalling. So you see, we humans do need some time to retrieve our words!

In very young children who are learning to talk, we at times suspect a word retrieval difficulty when there is a big statistical gap between a child's receptive and expressive vocabulary scores. For example, the child may know what a *tissue* is, but when asked, can't name it. However, it's usually difficult to definitively diagnose this problem in young children because sentence formulation in the 3- to 5-year-old child is often filled with repetitions, pauses, and revisions that can be developmental rather than due to word retrieval deficits. It becomes more obvious when we begin working with an older child. After we teach a new word or set of words, we may notice that there is little recall of these words when presented in various contexts. In other words, the test scores on paper are part of the diagnostic process, but how a child uses and retains new words over time, and how these things impact a child during conversation or other narrative language tasks, can often be more telling, particularly in younger children, since at this writing, there are no specific tests for diagnosing word retrieval for this age group.

Children with severe autism and other developmental disabilities often have associated word retrieval difficulties, which can greatly reduce their expressive language. This is particularly apparent when there is a persistent use of a certain syllable ("eee!" or "dah!") to label just about everything, beyond the age of 3, and with little retention of new words explicitly taught and practiced.

By the age of 7 or 8, children should be more fluent in their speech and not grope for simple words they've used before. This is why, in the absence of other obvious speech or learning problems, word retrieval problems may be overlooked until the elementary or secondary school years. They are usually present in children with other expressive language disorders, auditory processing disorders, or cluttering.

Characteristics of Toddlers and Preschoolers with Word Retrieval Problems

- Exhibits a marked gap between the receptive vocabulary score (at or above normal limits) and the expressive vocabulary score (below average or lower)
- Shows a lack of ability to remember new words and use them correctly

- Overgeneralizes words, such as *milk* to mean any kind of drink (past the age of 24 months)
- Forgets the names of teachers, friends, and relatives
- Is often very animated with gestures and noises to compensate for lack of words
- Expresses obvious frustration ("I *know* it!" or perhaps just whining) when the word won't come and the child is unable to recall it
- Inserts lots of pauses throughout conversational language and "do-overs" with word choices ("He . . . uh . . . the um . . . bug—spider.")

Characteristics of School-Age Children with Word Retrieval Problems

As mentioned previously, it is not uncommon for word retrieval problems to go undetected until a child is in upper elementary grades or older. It is sometimes difficult to detect and may come to a parent's attention after an evaluation has been performed.

School-age children with word retrieval problems might:

- Possess average or above-average intellectual ability
- Exhibit other learning disabilities, often related to reading problems
- Use an inordinate amount of *ums, uhs,* or other stalls
- Exhibit grimacing, clenching of fists, blinking of eyes, or other signs of frustration when stalling
- Overuse vague words such as *stuff* and *thing* (e.g., "Put that thing on that other thing.")
- Use words that are similar to, but not as precise in meaning as, the intended word (e.g., "We went to uh . . . that sandy place on Saturday.")
- Talk around a subject or a word instead of identifying it directly (e.g., "Oh, it's one of those things that you wear in your ear. It's jewelry.")
- Make up words such as *a car loader truck* or *a twisty plant that goes up the house,* particularly after they have already been exposed to the correct word and used it on many occasions
- Have difficulty pronouncing multisyllabic words; often mispronouncing or omitting syllables (e.g., "veggables" for *vegetables,* "atainer" for *container*)
- Have difficulty completing fill-in-the-blank test formats quickly or accurately
- Complete multiple-choice or matching-column test formats with greater success than fill-in-the-blank formats or essays

- Need extra time to put thoughts together
- Raise their hand in class but often have no answer when called upon
- Find essay writing challenging

How Does a Word Retrieval Problem Affect a Child?

A child like Jared will tend to speak in a roundabout way. He may describe something with very little detail or use vague language showing poor semantic use. This is how Jared described his family to me:

> *I have a very nice mother who goes there to uh . . . um . . . her work—job, I mean. I forget the name of her company. She is in charge of taking those things that you see on TV and putting them into these little, little, uh . . . Oh! You know. Those things. She does that, but only on certain times. My dad drives all the way up the big highway, every day, in his car. Well, it's not a regular car, it's one of those big ones, you know what I mean. A . . . I forget!*

When I showed Jared a picture of a van, he easily identified it as a van. He then said, "That's what my father drives, you know, a van. I just couldn't think of it." Jared hears the word *van* on an almost daily basis, according to his mother. But in this conversation, Jared couldn't get it out.

This may or may not present a problem for Jared in social situations as a child. Most children are not as critical or as observant about this kind of a problem as adults are. However, if Jared is excited and he's trying to tell another child a story or explain something that happened, he may have to answer a lot of questions. At home, you may also have to play twenty questions sometimes to get to the bottom of what your child with a word-finding problem is trying to tell you.

Although this problem is frustrating at times, it is usually a more subtle language problem than others covered in this book in terms of the effect on your child's life on a day-to-day basis outside the classroom. The real challenge for a child with a word retrieval problem is in the classroom. The child's teacher may get very confusing messages from the child, which can lead the teacher to a mistaken conclusion. Consider this exchange in the classroom with Dimitri, a boy with a word-finding problem:

> *Teacher:* Dimitri, what is the name of the planet closest to the sun?
> *Dimitri:* It's . . . uh . . .
> *Teacher:* Dimitri, did you do last night's assignment?
> *Dimitri:* Yes!
> *Teacher:* Well, then, what is this planet's name?

Dimitri: Uh . . . it's that little planet that's so hot; it's not Pluto or Venus . . . it's uh . . .

Teacher: Can someone help Dimitri?

Anytime a teacher tells me a student is having difficulty passing tests, particularly when the child seems to know and understand the words in other contexts, I look for a possible word retrieval problem. Standardized tests are available for this purpose, but often the problem can be noticed by listening to the way the child responds to casual conversational questions. I usually use a combination of formal tests and observation to make this diagnosis.

One reason taking tests is so difficult for children with this type of problem is that the information tested generally is new. Since children with a word retrieval deficit need to use words over and over before they can be retrieved successfully from the brain's files, they have difficulty with new information. For this reason it is wise to limit the number of names, places, events, and vocabulary terms children like Dimitri must be expected to memorize at one time. When their brain becomes "overloaded," the words become a blur. This is particularly true if the words have not been used with any regularity. Dimitri's teacher should try to prioritize the words that are most important for him to learn and have him focus on those.

Because Dimitri's brain takes a little longer to find the information he is looking for, it helps if his teachers and parents show extra patience by waiting at least ten full seconds before asking him to respond to a question. The stress Dimitri feels to come up with an answer, *any* answer, will not help his brain function with any greater accuracy. In fact, timed tests and pressure for "fast answers" are extra obstacles for children like Dimitri.

Traditionally, many classroom tests use the time-honored fill-in-the-blank format. These open-ended questions are deadly for children like Dimitri. To try to remember a whole set of obscure words is torturous. If a child with this problem *does* do well, it may be at a very high cost: hours and hours of studying and assistance from you. Marathon study sessions take their toll on a family as well as the child. This is compounded if the child would like to participate in sports or music (in which such a child may excel and should certainly participate) and not spend *all* his free time studying to pass tests.

Often children like Dimitri are so overwhelmed by these types of tests that they stop trying or feel "stupid." If there is a list of words to choose from at the top of the test paper (referred to by teachers as a "word bank"), scores can literally go from a C or D to an A or B. This is one of the modifications discussed in chapter 4 that a child with an IEP could have incorporated into the school day. I have seen dramatic improvements in test scores with this little change alone. By changing the way the test is presented, the teacher can find out what the child *really* knows, and the child can be proud of a score that is a more accurate reflection of her knowledge. Imagine, such a simple, no-cost solution with such a tremendous return!

What Can Parents Do to Help a Child with a Word Retrieval Weakness?

Parents can help their child in the following ways:

1. Be patient with your child. Remember that it is difficult for your child to express himself clearly. Don't make him feel rushed.
2. When your child is "stuck" and can't think of a word, encourage her to describe the word or use another, similar word in its place.
3. If you think you know what that word is, tell the child the first sound or two to help him retrieve it. That will help him more than just giving him the answer.

    For example, if the child says: "I didn't get the page done because the teacher said we had to go out for . . . uh . . . um . . . " the parent can say: "Outside?"
    Child: "Yes, outside where we can play, just for a few minutes."
    Parent: "Oh, so she said you had to go out for . . . rrrrrreeee . . . ?"
    Child: "Recess!"
4. If the first sound or two doesn't help, offer the child choices (e.g., "Did you have to go outside for lunch or recess?").
5. Work closely with your child's teacher and team to modify written assignments and tests as needed. Remember, essays and "fill-in-the-blank" tests are particularly challenging for your child; multiple-choice or word-bank formats are much easier.
6. Help your child make associations when learning facts for tests at school. How does he remember Sacramento is the capital of California? Make a picture of a sack, a mint, and an *O* to make an association.
7. Sing those facts! Put them to music: "Sacra-MENTO, Sacra-MENTO . . . capital of California! California!"
8. Dance those facts. Stomp around or jump rope and say it over and over and over!

9. Listen to those facts. Have your child rehearse them on a tape recorder and listen to them while he drifts off to sleep ("Sacramento is the capital of California!") or while in the car.

10. Use a play microphone, a plastic tube, or a cardboard tube for your child to say them so they echo—anything to keep those facts being repeated over and over.

11. Play games with those facts—put the word on one side of an index card and the related fact on the other. (Sacramento—capital of California) Play *Jeopardy!*, memory, tic-tac-toe, or other games.

12. Help your child put spelling words into sentences because this is a particularly challenging task. You may find her sentences are often repetitive and show little creativity. Help her draw a context for the word first, then write a sentence to describe the picture on the actual spelling homework paper. Let the right brain's strengths help the left brain! For example, if the spelling word is *kept*, your child could draw a picture of a girl with a bird in a cage. The sentence could be, "Pam kept her parrot in a cage." Keep the drawing to pencil only, with a two-minute maximum time so the emphasis and time is not spent on drawing details.

13. Consider using some phonemic awareness/auditory discrimination software at home to boost these skills, such as Earobics, or even more intensive and comprehensive: Fast ForWord.

14. Check out Diane German's terrific website: www.wordfinding.com. It is filled with suggestions for school accommodations and other resources. (Diane is considered to be one of the leading experts in this area.)

How Would an SLP Treat a Word Retrieval Problem?

How does our brain's storage system work? Think of when you were stuck trying to remember the name of a recent acquaintance. Was it Janet or Joan? You remembered her last name began with a B. These are the clues you give yourself to work with as you try to "find" the woman's name. Ah! Judi Benton, that's it! Many times we use the sounds or letters in someone's name to help get us started. It may take a few minutes, but it often works. Likewise, we store words by linguistic associations. For example, I came from a big family. My mother would often call us by the wrong name. "Susan—no, Jen—Heather—no . . . Patti! Why did you leave your shirt here?" That is because there is yet another mental drawer filled with "children's names" and your brain goes to that. The more excited or upset you are, the harder it is to access it quickly and efficiently. The speech pathologist will want to help your child develop a stronger filing system as well as develop strategies for when the drawer is "stuck." Current research shows us that a typical child is able to say and use a word after hearing it in context approximately six times. For a child with a word retrieval disorder, they typically need to hear the word *twenty times* before it becomes a part of their expressive speech. For this reason, having a child say and use a word as well as hear it in stories and conversations all around them is one way to help it become part of their readily accessible vocabulary. Here are some of the ways the SLP might work on word retrieval:

- *Phonemic awareness.* In order to help your child's underlying filing system improve, it's important to get to the core of the language storage system itself. There are numerous programs on the market that can do this, but in most cases the SLP will use a combination of formal programs (such as Lindamood-Bell LIPS, Fast ForWord, Phonemic Synthesis Program) and informal, eclectic programs that we can pull from and use for this purpose.
- *RAN (Rapid Automatic Naming) charts.* These are simply pages of pictures—usually mixed with common words known as *high-frequency* words and less common words known as *low-frequency* words. The SLP may try to target words your child needs to know and work on rapid retrieval and making associations to help that process. The research is a bit mixed on this technique, but for some children it can at least help them target words they need to know.
- *Form linguistic associations.* You will notice that the SLP might introduce words in units—what we do with our mouth (smile, spit, cough, yawn, chew, etc.)—or in categories and their related members. This helps the child organize words into a linguistic filing system.
- *Teach new words with carrier phrases.* The SLP will help your child develop carrier phrases for new words, which can help him retrieve them in a pinch. For example, if teaching the word *entrance*, the SLP would teach it as "You go in the entrance" rather than defining it. The word itself should be used in the contextual meaning.
- *Compensatory skills.* When your child gets stuck or blanks out completely, it may be in a stressful or emotional situation. It helps to have rote, rehearsed phrases and a plan of action as to how to handle it. We try hard to reduce the "Oh, never mind . . ." responses.
- *Increase synonyms.* Because your child may not be able to retrieve the desired word, it's helpful to expand your child's synonym base for just such an occasion.

- *Reading fluency.* Recent research has found that poor oral reading fluency is associated with word retrieval problems. Programs that address reading fluency may need to be incorporated into your child's program.
- *Modifying tests.* The child with word-finding difficulties will benefit from modifications in how tests are presented, with multiple-choice, word banks, and true-false being a more appropriate way to test content knowledge in classes such as science and social studies. Tutoring in those subjects to help the new words "stick" better may be needed. Working with the classroom teacher and other professionals involved with the child's educational program is helpful.

Case Study: Jay

Jay was in the fourth grade and was getting by. He was consistently scoring in the C range on his social studies and science tests, but in other areas he was clearly an A or B student. His classroom teacher, Mrs. Jordan, happened to eat lunch with me, and as she corrected her latest set of science tests (between bites of turkey sandwich), she sighed as she reviewed Jay's paper. "He did so well when we discussed this in class the other day. I know he knows this. What happens to him when he takes these tests? Maybe he's just not a good test taker or maybe he needs tutoring."

Of course, any professional connected with the special education field has antennae that go up anytime a student has "unexplained" difficulty, particularly when it seems inconsistent with the child's ability. And so I began to examine Jay's test. All the multiple-choice questions were correct. In fact, the errors were primarily in the fill-in-the-blank sections, which were still, well . . . blank. So I began to ask some pointed questions, which led to a very interesting discussion.

Mrs. Jordan described how Jay punctuates his comments with an inordinate amount of hms and uhs, taking forever to get out a simple statement. Even when the sentence comes out, the words Jay uses are often vague. For example, when the class was asked how they spent their Thanksgiving holiday, Jay was eager to respond. "We uh . . . drove to my Mom's friend's little house up there. It's a . . . brown one by that big thing-uh-monnoment-uh-mon-U-ment . . . over in the town. You know, the one with the big ski things in it? We really liked it!" When Mrs. Jordan asked specific questions about the trip, Jay was able to supply answers. He did understand where he went and what he did; he was simply unable to express it clearly with clear, concise language. He often put himself down and sometimes muttered with frustration under his breath.

After hearing this and speaking with Jay's mother (who was getting quite frazzled trying to help him pass these tests and figure out what he was trying to say at times), I pursued a formal speech-language and learning-disability evaluation. The evaluation supported a diagnosis of a word retrieval deficit, with additional expressive language delays as well. Often children like Jay have other organizational and sequential problems that are consistent with a learning disability. Jay did show evidence of a mild learning disability

Learning disabilities are often defined as being a gap in a child's ability (which by legal definition is within the average range or higher) and his or her academic performance. To determine Jay's ability, a psychologist performed an IQ test, which supported our expectation that Jay was certainly not a "slow" child.

Language therapy was recommended for Jay, but what helped him most were modifications in the classroom and an increased understanding by his teachers and parents. I was able to discuss the diagnosis in simple terms with Jay, who was relieved to know he was not as "stupid" as he thought. The special education teacher provided assistance in the classroom and consulted with the classroom teacher to make sure the lessons, assignments, and tests were structured appropriately for Jay.

Jay continues to do well in school with modifications in the classroom and consultation between his teachers and parents.

The "I Don't Know How to Explain It" Child: Sequencing, Referential, and Divergent Language Problems

I know Tatiana is a bright girl. She gets straight A's in math and is a whiz in art, music, and PE! I think that's because she likes those classes better. She just sits and stares at the paper for half the period during language arts. If I prod her, she'll put a few words down every once in a while, but it's like pulling teeth. If she had a learning disability, she wouldn't be such a good reader, right? So she must just be lazy, I guess.

—F. G., teacher

Some children, even those with average or above-average intellectual ability, don't know where to start to explain something. For them to tell a story or describe what happened yesterday is a challenge. The inability to organize their thoughts logically affects what they say as well as what they write. Children with expressive language problems typically have difficulty with these types of tasks, even if their speech skills and grammar use are normal.

In this section we cover more about the kinds of language use problems children exhibit, how these problems affect children, and what parents can do about these problems. Typically, difficulties in these areas become apparent in first or second grade but may go undiagnosed until a bit later.

Sequencing Problems

Sequencing refers to putting things in the right order. Sequencing problems can take many forms. Some children have problems sequencing sounds, so that when they try to spell a word, they have difficulty figuring out which sounds to write down and in which order. When children have difficulty pronouncing long words, it is sometimes caused by a problem sequencing syllables. Some children have difficulty sequencing when trying to name the days of the week or the months of the year.

Tatiana's sequencing problem involves putting words (language) into some kind of order so that there is a cohesive, logical flow from thought to thought. Children who exhibit sequencing problems when they speak may be at risk for having other sequencing problems that can interfere with their ability to perform successfully at school. These are often part of a larger constellation of organizational weaknesses related to a *language-learning disability.*

Tatiana is a very good reader. Her problem is more subtle, so it is easy to miss. She is excelling in subjects such as art and math, because she doesn't need to do much writing or speaking in those classes.

Certainly most "normal" preschool children have difficulty with sequencing tasks. Even if they have seen a video twenty-five times in one week, it may be all but impossible to elicit any more than "The little boy was lost and they had a party and it was so funny!" As children reach first and second grade, the brain becomes more conscious of order. Left and right. Beginning and ending. First, second, and third. Stories have plots with a beginning, a middle, and an end. It is when these concepts and tasks present a special challenge that a problem may become more and more apparent. This is one reason why this kind of problem is typically diagnosed at a later age.

A child with a language sequencing problem can tell you bits and pieces about a story, a character, or a favorite part but often cannot start from the beginning and tell you what happened in an organized or logical way, even at the age of 10. One of the reasons why Tatiana may be hesitating to write a word on the paper during writing classes is that she doesn't know where the beginning of the story is. What should she say first?

Children with serious attention-span problems often have difficulty with sequencing tasks because they can't think about one thing long enough to get it organized. Their brains dart from subject to subject, never allowing enough time to put things in order.

Sometimes looking at pictures in the right order helps the child organize thoughts, but pictures are not always practical when you want your child to tell you about the incident on the playground at school today!

Sequencing problems present a special long-term challenge to children as well as to adults. As it can with many language problems, therapy can help your child improve these skills, but you should not expect a cure.

Referential Problems

"My sister and mom went shopping Tuesday, but she didn't buy anything." *Who* didn't buy anything? From this sentence, it's hard to tell.

Referential skills help the listener know who or what you are talking about. A child with poor referential skills will use too many pronouns *(he, she, it, they,* etc.) and indefinite pronouns (*this, that,* etc.) when she speaks. Referential skills are another component of expressive language that is important to a child's ability to communicate easily with other people. As with sequencing skills, referential skills are usually developed as a child reaches first and second grade. Weak referential skills are also sometimes one piece of a bigger language-learning disability profile.

Referential skills can be improved with language therapy but may need to be worked into other language activities and developed in time.

Divergent Language Problems

"Tell me everything you can about this picture." For many children like Tatiana, this kind of open-ended task presents yet another set of problems. If I showed Tatiana the same picture and asked her to "tell me what this lady is doing," I'm sure she could answer me easily. Answering a specific, direct question is a *convergent* task. Tasks that ask the child to speak about a general topic or thing, such as a picture, are called *divergent* language tasks. Tatiana may have difficulty "getting started" in these types of tasks. She may also have difficulty figuring out what's important about the picture. She may talk about peripheral details, such as a bird flying overhead and a blue car driving on the road, and may mention incidentally the raging fire that is the centerpoint of the picture, but knowing what's important and how to organize it is much more challenging for her.

Problems with divergent language skills show up when a child is asked to create a sentence with a particular word in it, a typical spelling homework assignment. What does the child say about it? The child may sit and think, stare out a window, write a word or two, and then get distracted with other thoughts.

When asked to write in a journal or about a topic such as snow, Tatiana would probably sit and turn over thoughts in her mind while the rest of the class is starting to work on editing their finished stories. However, if the teacher told her to write about a specific topic such as "what you like to do after school," Tatiana might have more success.

Characteristics of Children Who Have Problems Explaining

Children with sequencing, referential, or divergent language problems might:

- Have learning disabilities in other areas, such as reading or perceptual problems, or AD/HD
- Take an inordinate amount of time to get started with an answer to an open-ended question such as "Tell me about plants."
- Jump around when retelling stories, put events out of any logical order, or leave out essential information
- Start and stop in midsentence, changing words as the sentences unfold, such as "He . . . uh . . . I mean, she . . . uh, was going shopping, uh . . . well she had *gone* shopping, but it—I didn't know and uh . . ."
- Have particular difficulty talking about events or experiences that are out of sight. For example, he may be able to describe what you are wearing adequately because he can see it, but be unable to explain what he did earlier that day or on a vacation just a few days ago.
- Confuse *left/right* and *first/last*
- Think the listener is following the dialogue when in fact the listener is confused
- Have difficulty focusing on one task or paying attention
- Say "I don't know" or "Forget it!" rather than struggle to explain something

- Have difficulty answering essay questions
- Have difficulty writing stories with events in the correct order, although ideas may be creative
- Have difficulty putting months or days of the week in order
- Have difficulty initiating social conversations or thinking of things to say
- Possess much knowledge but have difficulty expressing it verbally and/or in writing
- Miss the "bigger picture" and focus on unimportant details
- Have word retrieval problems
- Be creative by nature, stronger in visual arts, music, drama, or dance
- Be very athletic

How Do Problems with Explaining Affect a Child?

Because children with expressive language problems often have difficulty "explaining," they may find chitchat very draining. They feel awkward if their search for the right words causes lulls in their conversations. But if they start talking too quickly, the rambling and starts and stops can leave listeners in the dust and the children feeling even more anxious.

In school, an expressive language problem is most likely to affect a child during classroom discussions and when writing essays. When asked to do a report, children like Tatiana will need help getting started and organized. Remember, the problems these children have when trying to explain verbally usually present a problem when the children are writing. They may need to be told very specifically what information should be included in a report.

These children may be able to answer direct questions quite well, particularly if the teacher is looking for a one-word answer, but they will likely struggle when it comes to answering essay questions and writing book reports.

There are several reasons for this phenomenon. Developing paragraphs and an outline requires an organized mind. To come up with ideas, you must be able to draw associations and recall information you already know and put it down on paper. The same organization and expressive language ability is required to give speeches or explain the results of a group science project. If these areas are delayed in your child, school may become increasingly tedious and overwhelming as time goes on. Your son or daughter knows the information, but explaining it or putting it down on paper is torturous.

At home, parents will probably need to ask several questions to find out the answers to questions such as "What happened at school today?"

A child like Tatiana may answer with a one-word response, such as "Nothing." Putting thoughts together, figuring out where to start, and thinking of what words to use can be exhausting, particularly after a long day at school! On other days, such a child may respond with a confusing answer such as "Okay; I just wish he didn't put the answers on the board until I was done. Yesterday it was only five minutes!" You may be able to piece together what happened, but the way it is expressed is confusing.

Socially, a child like Tatiana may be able to float along, without a huge impact on her ability to form and keep friendships. In my experience, most other children seem to be patient about drawing children like Tatiana out or asking questions to clarify something that confuses them. Tatiana may be perceived as a shy or quiet child. In fact, she may gravitate toward sports or the arts, such as painting or drawing, music, or dance. These are also considered skills that require right–hemisphere strengths, while language acquisition is considered primarily a left-hemisphere task. We often find that children with weak language are indeed stronger in associated "right brain" areas.

Your child may have difficulty in classes that require lots of report writing or oral reports. Using outlines and notecards will help, but chances are he will have more success in other kinds of classes, such as science labs, computers, math, arts, mechanics, woodworking, or other hands-on subjects. The areas in which your son or daughter finds success in school will also likely affect the career he or she chooses.

How Would an SLP Treat a Problem with Explaining?

Therapy to address problems with explaining rarely "cures" the child of the problem completely, although it can certainly improve it. Sometimes a child's naturally shy personality or a learning disability makes it difficult to significantly change what is essentially a weak style of communicating. Children with significant hyperactivity often will continue to struggle because their brain is going in many different directions at once, so therapy can be a challenge since the underlying issue is of an organic and perhaps maturational nature.

In therapy, the child will start by learning how to explain very short pieces of information or stories. Gradually the length and complexity of the task is increased. The focus may be on using descriptive words and phrases, retelling events or stories in order (sequencing), or simply knowing how to get started and mentally organize when asked an open-ended question. If the child's area of difficulty is referential skills, learning how to be specific and avoid vague language will be important, as well as keeping a good eye on the listener. The topic and content will need to be steered according to the response and interest of the person the child is talking to. What body language does he notice? Is this person able to follow what he's saying? Does her question or comment indicate she's confused? Typically, a child with weak expressive language skills will need to focus on nearly all these tasks at the same time to some degree.

Many speech-language pathologists also spend time helping the child to improve these skills in written language as well as oral language. Since reports and essays require organization and elaboration of language, they lend themselves well to language intervention, especially in the upper primary and middle school grades. There are entire books filled with therapy activities for language. The following are just a few things the SLP may do:

- *Teach the concept of "describing."* What does it mean if you ask the child to *describe* a picture? Part of the difficulty is the child's lack of awareness as to what kind of information goes with this request.
- *Work on expansion.* How do we take a simple sentence, such as "He has a cat," and stretch it? What kind of information can we add? If we cue the child into the "wh" question words (*who/what/where/when/why*), the child can play with adding detail to the sentence and making it longer. Counting the words in the sentences and making it into a game can make it more fun.
- *Reduce redundancy.* For example: "I see a boy. I see a building. I see a rainbow." The SLP may write it down so the child can see the visual pattern. Ah, they should be different! Pick out the nouns and plug in descriptors in front of them ("I see a *timid* boy") and switch out the verbs with spicier synonyms ("I *spy* a timid boy"), and voilà! A vanilla sentence has been transformed!
- *Clean up those vague pronouns!* Words such as *he, she, it, thing* are all relative. In narrative language tasks, we need to take great care that the antecedent is clear.
- *Get started on open-ended language tasks.* Because getting started is often challenging, there are tricks and strategies to help children have some surefire "go-to" phrases to use for this purpose, such as: "This is a story about a _____ who . . ."
- *Walk through sequencing stories and events that happened.* Helping a child walk through a sequence with numbered picture supports helps the child "see" order. Eventually, we will want to fade the picture supports and numbers, often by taking out one element at a time

until the child can re-create an entire sequence from memory. Building that inherent visual "picture" is critical to the process.

- *Teach and practice coordinating conjunctions* (*before/after, but, so, until, unless, because,* etc.). These are the building blocks of relating one event to the other and moving toward more developed narrative skills.
- *Use organizational software or graphic organizers.* Programs that help children organize information more visually are great building blocks for making the jump to better writing skills.
- *Work on perspective-taking and self-monitoring.* If you tell your friend, "Let's go with them to that place—I love their chili—what time is it?" the message becomes hard to follow. Using feedback, including writing it out and video- or audiotape, the SLP will help the child learn to listen to what he is saying, how it sounds to the other person, and how to modify it when the listener is confused.

What Can Parents Do to Help a Child Who Has Problems with Explaining?

If you suspect your child has a problem like Tatiana's, seek a professional's opinion. If your child has already been diagnosed with an expressive language problem of this type, here are some ways you can help:

- Be patient. Give your child extra time to respond verbally. Time pressure is apt to make her grab at verbal straws and become anxious.
- Avoid open-ended oral questions such as "Tell me about your ball game." Instead, ask specific questions such as "Did your teammates make any exciting plays today?"
- After watching movies, TV shows, or videos, help your child reconstruct the essential elements of the story. Draw pictures of important scenes together and help put them in order. Write captions under the pictures.
- Use family photographs to help your child talk about things that have happened. Try to take several pictures over the course of an event so your child can later put them in order and retell the event. See if she can tell someone else about the event without looking at the pictures. A talking photo album is a great way to preserve those memories!
- Help your child with independent open-ended projects, such as "Write a report about Paul Revere." Find out what information the teacher wants. Help your child develop an outline before she attempts to tackle the assignment, and show her how to take it one step at a time.

Otherwise your child will be overwhelmed with everything at once. For example, the Paul Revere assignment could be broken into four parts: (1) Write about Paul Revere's childhood; (2) explain what he did before the Revolutionary War; (3) describe what happened during the war; and (4) tell about what he did after the war and when he died.

• Look at your child's tests. If she is struggling with essay questions on tests, you may need to talk to the speech-language pathologist to discuss whether your child can be tested in another, more appropriate way.

As a parent, you may need to help your child with these kinds of homework assignments on a regular basis or hire a private tutor to avoid a nonproductive tug-of-war between you. Sometimes it helps just knowing your child isn't being lazy but has a specific kind of language disorder or deficit. You'll know you can't expect your child to excel at these types of activities any more than a clumsy child can be expected to excel at the balance beam. Understanding the situation can perhaps ease the guilt of feeling like you're "helping too much." A professional can guide you as to the best strategy for helping your child, who is apt to have unique needs.

Case Study: Jackson

Ten-year-old Jackson was well liked by his teachers and peers, but it was clear he was having some problems. When he was 8 years old and in the second grade, Jackson had been diagnosed with auditory and visual perceptual problems, which are a type of learning disability. Another specialist might have easily diagnosed him with dyslexia. These perceptual problems had become apparent when he had difficulty learning to read and spell. His handwriting was often "sloppy" and poorly spaced on a page. In fact, his desk was a mess, and his room at home was in equal disarray. Jackson was what we sometimes call a "loose" kid; he was a little unraveled, but oh, so lovable. Things got lost and assignments were frequently misplaced or accidentally forgotten. He received extra help through the resource room in school and a special reading program.

What wasn't apparent in the second grade, though, was that Jackson also had problems with expressive language. As he grew older, in addition to having the perceptual problem of putting sounds in order, it became clear that Jackson was having problems putting words and sentences in order as well. When Jackson was in second grade, his teachers and parents had recognized the trouble Jackson had with explaining things, but this was less of a concern at that time than his below-average reading and writing skills. His expressive language problems seemed minor in comparison to his other problems, so speech-language testing was not discussed at this time.

As Jackson's spelling and reading improved, he was expected to write longer stories with greater detail and a coherent plot. In class, discussions became more philosophical and abstract. Projects were assigned with fewer "restrictions" and greater room for creativity. Unfortunately, the "room for creativity" was too much room for a child like Jackson. Getting started was so difficult for him that he just didn't start at all.

Jackson's fifth-grade classroom teacher referred his case to the Student Study Team. She was looking for behavioral strategies to motivate him to complete these projects. His mother was also at her wits' end with him, with each project becoming a nightly battleground. Jackson was also less willing to take part in classroom discussions than he used to be. He was scoring in the B–C range on tests unless an essay question was asked. He usually bombed on those.

Since Jackson was already identified as a special education student, various strategies were discussed by the team. Perhaps he would do better on the tests if he studied more? Did he need more time to do the projects? Were they too difficult? I asked Jackson's parents for permission to perform a thorough speech and language evaluation to assess Jackson's higher-level language skills to see whether there was another reason for these problems.

On the language battery, Jackson excelled on the vocabulary subtests and language-processing tasks. However, when he was asked to describe a very busy picture or a construction scene, there was a pause for about a minute. He squirmed in his seat and nervously tapped a pencil.

"Well, uh . . . which thing do you want me to tell you about?"

"Tell me everything you can about the picture," I replied.

"Oh . . . uh . . . it's got that—I mean it looks like it's sorta a . . . a . . . guy laying bricks and the cat is looking into the house. Well—it's not really a house yet; the guys are building the house . . . I mean they are going to build a house. Oh, forget it. I don't know."

When I asked him to tell the story of his favorite movie, this is what he told me: ". . . Uh . . . well, I don't know. Yeah, I've seen it about a hundred times, but um . . . it's hard to explain . . . It's about a guy who does a lot of . . . has a lot of adventures. When he was almost killed, the big boulder almost fell on top of him and it really was radical . . . really radical. But first he was at his father's ranch for a while. The girl in the movie—Johanna—she took . . . uh . . . I mean she wanted to . . . hmm . . .

Well, they both really wanted to find a secret cave. But the guy that had—uh . . . that rock was so big, really . . . it was so radical."

Did you catch that? You are probably a bit confused and still know very little about the plot of the movie. If you asked Jackson something specific about that movie, he could tell you. It's not that he forgets, it's just that it all gets so scrambled up in his mind that it comes out wrong.

Jackson was diagnosed as having an expressive language disorder. With his other learning disabilities, he could also be called language-learning disabled. These disorders are typically interrelated. The missing piece to Jackson's earlier diagnosis had been his sequencing and organizational language problems. He also exhibited word retrieval problems.

Once his teachers and parents understood the obstacles Jackson faced, assignments and tests were tailored to help compensate for his language weakness. He was enrolled in weekly group "speech" therapy sessions (as I mentioned earlier, this therapy has more to do with language than with speech), which helped him develop strategies to improve his language skills and learn to organize his expressive language better.

Jackson will probably always have difficulty getting organized. Narrative writing and explaining and describing will probably never be his strong suits, either. But with increased understanding and the development of these language skills, Jackson can handle school with far less anxiety and negative impact on his self-esteem, and he will receive the help he needs to develop these much-needed skills.

Social Language and Playing: When Something's Just Not Right

Caleb is talking okay, after a little bit of a slow start. He's amazingly bright! At age three, he is already starting to learn to read. He's incredible on the computer and a whiz with puzzles. I just wish he had a little more interest in the other children. His eye contact is poor—I have to keep reminding him to look at me. His preschool teacher tells me he just wanders around or goes in a corner by himself. He doesn't seem interested in the other children. Sometimes he even talks to himself. His teachers are concerned, and so am I. Is he just shy or is it something more?

—Caleb's mother

Like Caleb, some children have plenty of words but don't seem to know how to—or want to—connect with other children the way we'd expect.

In part 1 of this book, I reviewed normal language development, but also social language and playing benchmarks. As you probably have figured out, in Caleb's case, there is cause for concern, but certainly not panic. We often will see very young children with social language and play difficulties who also have overall receptive and expressive language delays. When the difficulties are significant, we will want to rule out an autism spectrum disorder (See chapter 8, "Causes and Associated Conditions") because delayed language accompanied by social and play weaknesses is its primary identifying symptom. When the symptoms are obvious, a diagnosis is easier to determine. Up until recently, if there were only certain elements of autism present, a physician, psychologist, or team would consider *Pervasive Developmental Disorder* (PDD) as a possible diagnosis. However, as of this writing, the medical community is moving toward eliminating PDD as a separate diagnosis in favor of using autism spectrum disorder for this population. It has not been uncommon for us to have children come to our office with milder symptoms who were diagnosed as having autism by one doctor and PDD by another. Choosing between the labels has been a matter of professional preference, university training, or regional practice, but the diagnostic approach will likely become more consistent when the fifth edition of the *DSM* is released in 2013.

Other times, as in Caleb's case, the receptive and expressive language may be more developed, but the social language (pragmatic language use) and play skills are weak. With very bright children, we sometimes informally find that they are . . . well . . . "quirky." It's not a technical or professional term, but it is sometimes used to describe a child who is not precisely exhibiting enough symptoms of an autism spectrum disorder, but is perhaps not yet interacting as we might expect or like to see. We used to say these children "marched to the beat of a different drummer." Remember, we need lots of different drummers! In many work environments, such as engineering and technology, people often say these personality traits are common. I've found that highly artistic and creative children often have unique styles of play and interaction. The parents I've met of children like Caleb will often recall that they had similar play styles when they were children, or even confess to still being socially awkward. So Caleb's lack of interaction may be due to the fact that he's very bright and not interested in the humdrum preschool games the other children find so interesting, or he may just take after his dad. But does that mean we shouldn't perhaps help Caleb develop some stronger social skills? We'll talk more about that a little farther along.

On the other hand, it would also not be surprising to find out that Caleb is later diagnosed with Asperger's syndrome, which is a unique cousin of autism, having its own set of associated behaviors, which are discussed in chapter 8. (As with PDD, this diagnosis may also be phased out with the revised *DSM*.) However, there's so much more to the diagnostic process than a quick snapshot or a few symptoms. Because there is no blood test or X-ray or even a reliable standardized test (yet) for differentiating between them, the professional's clinical judgment about what is "normal" and what is not comes into play. In Caleb's case, we would want to know much more before assuming he has an autism spectrum disorder or Asperger's.

For example, I've had children come into my office for their first visit who made fleeting eye contact and said very little during informal conversation and attempts at play. If I were a physician and made a diagnosis based on that, I too might assume the child has a type of autism spectrum disorder. Yet after the second or third visit, a very different child may emerge. As children become comfortable, they sometimes blossom and begin to interact. They don't perform well on command, in unfamiliar places, and with new people. More important, sometimes the line between what is normal, disordered, or part of a family personality or learned behavior is very gray indeed. So what to do? Let's look at a few kinds of social language and play behaviors that might be of concern.

Social Language, Play Concerns, and Quirky Behaviors in the Toddler and Preschooler

• *Eye contact.* From the time your baby is a few months old, she should be getting your attention and responding to your smile on an ongoing basis. Babies and toddlers should care about what you are doing and how you feel, and about interacting with anyone else around. When you go to the grocery store, does your child flirt with the person in line behind you? If so, good! Does he laugh at your funny faces and egg you on to make them again? Great! Or does he seem more interested in objects and wandering, pulling things out, moving on to something else? If your child has great eye contact with you, but is less comfortable around others, that indeed may be due to simple shyness. Some cultures teach that it is not polite to look directly at others, so it's important to know if there is a cultural reason for a lack of eye contact. In cases where the shyness is extreme, one should rule out a social anxiety disorder or even selective mutism, but this is not a diagnosis that is commonly made until a child is a little older.

- *Seeking something they need.* A typical child should be bothering you to get something or seek permission. "Mommy, Mommy!" A tap on the hand, nudge, nudge. *You didn't respond? Now I'll say it louder.* "MOMMY!" A child who is too independent and gets everything himself is not taking the opportunity to socially interact and use language. Likewise, if your child gives up too easily and doesn't initiate getting your attention in the typical ways, something might be wrong.

- *Look, look, look!* As your child notices the world around him—the bug crawling up the wall, the scary picture in the book—he should be looking for your reaction to it, as well as actively seeking to show it to you. We call this "joint sharing" and "joint attention." You look at things together and react to them. From early on, children should be pointing things out to you and demanding that you watch every cool new thing they can do or see.

- *Copying what the other kids are doing.* By age 2 or so, your child should be watching what the other children are doing. If they're playing with Play-Doh, then chances are your child will want to as well. They're sitting over there and looking at books? *Me too!* Everyone's going on the slide. *My turn!* Even if your child's speech skills are delayed or if your child is shy, there should be a natural curiosity to follow along and mimic the play styles and activities of the other children for at least much of the time. By around age 3, the copying becomes more interactive with certain special friends.

- *Sounds, noises, and jargoning.* Babies are noisy, but as they replace those funny jargoning words with real words, the out-of-context sounds and babbling should diminish. Many times children like to make noises like their favorite animals, cars, trains, and planes. "Look at me, I'm a bear! Grrrr!" That's normal and a great way to start with some imaginative play. However, when there is chattering, laughing, or screaming outbursts without any apparent context, noises, and random jargoning or repeating of words and phrases, you should have it checked out. By age 3 or so, your child should be becoming increasingly aware of other children's observation and opinions of him, and should start modifying his behavior depending on who is nearby and who will see him.

- *Play.* Early on, toddlers and preschoolers do much exploration of their environment. They bang on drums, play with puzzles, pull toys, roll a ball back and forth, make cars drive around, put dolls to bed and feed them, do fingerplays such as "Where Is Thumbkin?," and sing songs, make Play-Doh cookies, and make their stuffed animals talk and interact. As they reach ages 3 and 4, they should be able to do these things in a negotiated way with other children. ("You be the dog, I'll be the cat.") Even if speech is limited, much communication can take place nonverbally in a typically developing child. A nod of the head, reaching out with the toy, a "follow-me" gesture to the playground, and a ready smile to acknowledge a peer's great attempt at art are all social communication. A lack of speech may cause a toddler or a preschooler to be more creative, but from watching children from other countries who are plopped into a completely foreign land, we know that children warm up and play together quickly. Play is a universal language! All too often, parents make the mistake of blaming the lack of social interaction entirely on a child's lack of articulation or weak language skills, but children of this age care very little about that, and will usually play with any willing partner. Regardless of a child's speech credentials, he should be playing with others by preschool age.

Children who spend too much time with electronic or computer games or TV may be at a disadvantage during interactive play. (Children under the age of 2 should not be watching television at all, according to the most recent recommendations from the American Academy of Pediatrics.) Passively watching TV or playing computer games does not promote social interaction and should be done sparingly in preschool children.

Social Language, Play Concerns, and Quirky Behaviors in the School-Age Child

• *Making friends.* Once in kindergarten, children start forming more meaningful friendships. They may change from day to day or week to week, but a desire to form friendships and connect with peers is normal and healthy. Children who withdraw and are uneasy, quite silent, or whispery outside their home environment, despite having had time to acclimate, should be checked for anxiety, including social anxiety or even selective mutism (see chapter 8). Of course, a child who prefers solitary play may not have a problem, and may be perfectly happy doing something she really loves, such as looking for bugs, which maybe isn't a pastime shared by her peers. There's nothing necessarily wrong with it, but there should be activities when the child wants to and does connect with other children in some way.

• *Negotiations in play.* Children's play is much about negotiation. They mutually decide what the rules will be, who will play, where to play, and so on. Children who are inflexible with rules ("rigid") can find it extremely difficult to make changes. "No; we *always* count to three, not five!" Significant inflexibility that leads to panic, crying, or upset should be checked out. Children who only want to play their own favorite games—their way—can find themselves very lonely. Play requires compromise and a reciprocity of spirit, and sometimes playing games or doing activities you'd rather not do. But you do it because your friend likes it. Likewise, children who can't cope with losing a game into their school-age years will struggle. As they say, "No one likes a sore loser," but for some children, losing is incredibly upsetting and difficult to logically understand.

• *What is the other child thinking? Do I care?* As with the preschooler, a child in school should naturally have some innate sense of who is watching and what they are thinking, and should modify his behavior accordingly. For example, if your daughter loudly proclaims, "Your dress is ugly!" to her classmate, it shows a lack of perspective-taking and empathy. It's not unusual for a preschooler to do this, but at some point, the realization that our words impact the feelings of those around us should develop. Does she anticipate a reaction? Does she notice or apologize? Or is she indifferent? Children who have little regard for or insight into what others are thinking or feeling will uniformly struggle with friendships. This is sometimes referred to as a *social cognitive deficit* and should be addressed with intervention to help develop these skills if it persists into the elementary years.

• *Using atypical facial expressions and body language.* If your child says "hi" but looks away and doesn't smile, how is that greeting interpreted by her peers? If he laughs or smiles for no apparent reason or walks rigidly, with arms that don't swing naturally, his peers might find it odd. Likewise, standing outside at recess with arms folded, looking down, and walking in circles will likely not induce the other children to seek him out for play. Some children have very little awareness of how they are perceived and don't realize the messages they are sending with their nonverbal communication.

• *Challenges with reading body language and facial expressions, and with situational logic.* Additionally, some children are poor interpreters of others' facial expressions and body language. They don't "read" them well, and so continue talking about a subject no one wants to hear about, interrupt when a private conversation is going on, or don't "get" that the classmate's sigh and averted eyes mean he doesn't want to hear the joke again. Picture interpretation and even understanding children's sitcoms can be very confusing. Why is she slapping her head? What does it mean when he grimaces and rubs his stomach after dinner and why is everyone laughing when he then asks for dessert? How does someone feel when chased by a snarling tiger? Children who can't read these emotions or who don't know what's logically in the mind of others are sometimes referred to as having "mind blindness," a term coined by Simon Baron-Cohen, a distinguished researcher in this field. Sometimes a child may insist that you are mad at him when you are not, and likewise may not know when you *are* upset because reading your body language and facial expression does not provide meaningful information to him. ("Can't you see we're in a hurry? Well . . . no.)

- *The tattler and staying with routines.* Children with social difficulties and rigid thinking are often quite the tattlers. They cannot cope with someone's deviating from the rules or the usual routine. It is distressing for them, and they want someone to stop it. They can become quite urgent. "Miss Smith, Miss Smith, Hannah is looking at the pictures in the book, and you told us to wait until after lunch!" The motivation is not the same as that of a traditional "brownnoser," who wants to gain the teacher's favor or a child deliberately trying to cause problems for a troublesome peer. The tattling is more due to a desire to keep the routines and rules consistent, which is an important distinction. The child is often surprised that his peers don't want to play with him after the tattling incidents and has little insight as to the effect of the tattling. Another related component is difficulty changing routines or deviating in any way from something that was planned. ("You *said* we were going to the store after lunch. We have to go *now!*")

- *The rhythm, cadence, and way your child talks.* Imagine these three sentences: "What's new with you?" "What's *neeew* with *yoooo?*" "What's—new—with—you?" Children have a natural way of speaking. Part of the "copying" behaviors we've spoken about also applies to how speech should sound. In preschool, it's not so much of an issue, but by elementary school, children whose speech is punctuated with awkward phrasing or is too monotonic for no apparent reason may elicit discomfort from peers. In terms of actual articulation or accent issues, my experience has been that children generally are fairly indifferent to it, unless they feel a child's speech pattern is associated with an opposite gender or sounds odd, like that of the Urkel TV character from years ago. Accepting all children and not excluding those with differences is a critical goal for schools, but it is a reality that a child who stands out as sounding "odd" may be a more likely target of a bully.

- *Oversharing and inappropriate questions.* Knowing the time, place, and audience with which to share a particular piece of information is important. Does your child announce to the fifth-grade class that he just farted, or that he had diarrhea at home yesterday? Sometimes sharing too much information can really turn off classmates. Likewise, asking personal questions or asking about flaws ("Why didn't you get an A? Why is your hair so fuzzy? Why is your backpack so dirty and old-looking?") can push them away as well.

• *Manners and relativity.* Manners are very situational and are like shifting sand. It's all relative. Suppose I want to talk to someone and tell her a secret. How close do I talk? Yes, I lean over and whisper, maybe even covering my mouth. But when—and where? What if I want to ask a classmate to share the glue? No, we need to keep a healthy body space for that. I'm wondering why that woman over there is so short. Can I ask her? These kinds of situations are not intuitive for some children. They need the rules explained very, very clearly because they don't just "pick it up" by observing and need a hands-on crash course that can walk them through as many situations as possible.

• *Picking up the subtle signals: humor, sarcasm, idioms, and slang.* As children move into the third and fourth grade, communication becomes much more socially driven and less literal. Some children who perform extremely well in academic situations, where learning is straightforward, often find the most challenges during recess, lunch, and before/after school because the structure is looser and interacting with peers is less predictable. "Yeah, *right!*" means exactly the opposite. The difference is in the intonation, and matching it to the situation and the speaker's body language. A lightning-quick interpretation we make all the time, but one that is too complicated for some children. Children with social-pragmatic difficulties often think very literally. "You're going to Disneyland? *Get outta here!*" For some children, that sounds like a request for them to physically get up and leave. As children get into middle school and high school, they develop slang that is specific to their age and school. It's almost like a dialect. If your child speaks like a polished college professor and uses extra-perfect grammar, it will sound stilted around peers. The ability to "code-switch" (change the way we speak given the audience, place, and time) is important, and it's a difficult concept for some children.

What Can a Parent Do to Help a Child with Social Language and Play Challenges?

The first issue for you as a parent is to sort out whether your child's difficulties fall into the "passing phase" category (maybe your child is new to the neighborhood or school, just got over a serious illness, or recently experienced a family tragedy) or the "quirky-kid" category (which might include the "apple didn't fall far from the tree" situation or simply a personality that is hardwired as such), or are part of a larger condition, such as an autism spectrum disorder, including PDD and Asperger's; social anxiety; or something else. Are there other auditory processing or receptive/expressive language weaknesses that are exacerbating the situation? Sometimes the term *semantic-pragmatic disorder* is used to describe cases where there are social/play issues combined with certain expressive language traits, but it's been used less frequently in the United States in the last few years. Is your child displaying only a few of the issues I discussed above in isolated situations, or are you wondering if I came into your home and followed your child around for the day? Chances are, you may need an objective eye to help sort it out, although as I mentioned, even qualified professionals can still disagree on what exactly to call it.

Once you've got a little better picture of the underlying nature of the social and play behaviors that are impacting your child, you'll want to sort out how to handle the situation. Public schools' resources are stretched extremely thin, so your local district may or may not be coop- erative in providing intervention unless there are other diagnosed issues that are impacting school performance. Ideally, a group setting is the way to go in nurturing these skills. Some schools have a variety of programs set up with clever nicknames such as the "lunch bunch" (to teach recess and cafeteria behaviors), which can be run by a special educa- tion teacher, a speech pathologist, a counselor, or a psychologist. Many private practices also run social skills and/or play groups. There are some good programs out there that also work on helping the child "think social." My favorite programs incorporate the teachings of Michelle Garcia Winner, who has written and presented extensively on this topic. (See appendix B.)

Aside from direct intervention, the key will be how your child learns and integrates the skills that are introduced and taught in the therapy set- ting, so communication between you as a parent and the professional running the program is critical. How should you coach your child at home to integrate the new skill? What should you do if she forgets? How can the teacher facilitate your child's use of the newly learned skills? As with playing a piano or learning any new skill, practice makes perfect.

Aside from these suggestions, there is more you can do:

• *Facilitate playdates.* Your mission is to find even just one child who has similar interests or hobbies as your child. Don't be disappointed if your child chooses a slightly younger child. A year or two younger is fine, and may be a better companion for your child. Children with more significant social delays may select a child even younger or another child with similar disabilities. That's fine. Companionship comes in all sizes, and compatibility is key. Is your child passionate about rocks? Building with Legos? Playing the Wii? Whatever it is, you may need to make the effort to set it up, including calling the parent, picking up and delivering the child, and initiating the second visit. Don't be a pest, though. If the parent says the child is "busy," move on to another child after the second rebuff. Some children just don't click, and that's okay. It's sort of like dating. At your house, you may need to set up several activities for the children to choose from. Discuss in advance how your child will make suggestions and respond to his friend's replies. Have a tasty snack, and keep the visit on the short side (one to two hours) until the children are more bonded. Linger a little and eavesdrop if you can to get a sense of how it is going, but don't step in and coach in front of your child's friend. If necessary, call your child outside and inconspicuously provide a nudge if needed. Provide obvious choices rather than lecture. ("Do you think Timmy's enjoying watching you play that Wii game for the tenth time? Or do you think taking turns might be a better idea?") Praise him for making better choices. Let him think he came up with them all by himself. Positive attention to the things he is doing right is much more helpful than picking apart what he didn't.

• *Model good social skills.* This may sound funny, but over the years I have had parents who bring their children for social language development, then proceed to exhibit some rather inappropriate social skills themselves. Children watch what you say and do. They can't implement something they haven't learned. In addition, talk your child through the decisions you make during the day. Teach them to observe and analyze how people interact. "Stuart, did you notice how I said 'What a nice haircut!' to your aunt? That's called a compliment. Compliments make people happy. One or two a day is just perfect. Let's try to think of a compliment we can give your sister."

• *Target one behavior or skill at a time.* It is really important that a clear and definitive goal be verbalized and targeted. Have your child write it down and draw a picture of the desired behavior and put it on the fridge. For example, this week's goal might be to ask a question once and wait for the parent's response before repeating the question again and again. The steps might be written this way:

1. I make sure my parent is ready. I wait until she is off the phone and not having a conversation with someone else.
2. I stand about three feet away and say her name. ("Mom . . . ?")

3. I wait for her to look at me. I count to five slowly, but very quietly so no one can hear it. Mom will say, "What is it, Jeff?" (Or maybe "What, Jeff?")
4. I will ask my question or say what I am thinking once.
5. I won't say it again.
6. Each time I do this, I will get a point.

It's important to enlist your child in the writing and drawing elements of this so there is more personal investment and greater recall. Don't forget to have some kind of nice treat at the end of the week if your child accumulates enough points.

• *Start with external motivators.* What do I mean by that? "External" means outside. We often think that a child will be naturally internally motivated to acquire new social or play skills, or to expand his way of thinking or perspective-taking, but that's not always the case. Many times, children are quite content as they are. You may need to use a reward or a treat to motivate your child to do the work and make changes in behavior and way of thinking. With time and maturity, it may be less necessary.

• *Monitor for mental health and neurobiological issues.* Sometimes quirky behaviors can become such that they interfere with the quality of life and warrant further attention from professionals. For example, the child who can't stop touching each brick as she walks or must count each step she climbs might be exhibiting signs of obsessive-compulsive disorder. The fifth-grade child who is literally peeing in his pants because he's afraid of going into a public restroom because there may be a bug in there may have anxiety. The artistic seventh-grade girl who sits in the corner and is suddenly talking very little may be exhibiting depression. The sleepless high-schooler who recently began talking loudly and incessantly while invading everyone's body space with little regard to their reactions or the teachers standing nearby may have signs of a bipolar disorder. The boy who makes "inappropriate" barking or sniffing noises, repeats certain words and phrases over and over, and winks at everyone may have Tourette's syndrome, a neurological disorder. Children with quirky personalities sometimes have other issues that emerge and need professional handling along the way—sometimes urgently. See chapter 8 for more information on how these conditions can impact the communication process.

• *Accept and love your child "as is."* Well, *of course I do*, you're thinking. *But it would make me so happy if he acted like the other kids his age.* Okay, sure; that's understandable. But the reality is that sometimes that may happen and sometimes it might not, despite all your best efforts and expensive therapies from world-class clinicians. If your child begins to feel as if he's always being "fixed," it can start to backfire. He may feel you are embarrassed or disappointed that he has these difficulties. Your relationship needs to have a healthy balance between supporting growth in the areas that are challenging for your child and not making it the primary emphasis of his daily life with you. It's a tough line to walk, but you can do it!

How Would a Professional Treat a Child with Social Language and Play Challenges?

The professional (usually a speech pathologist, but not always) would need to employ a number of strategies to help your child learn how to think and act socially in an age-appropriate way. Sometimes these can work and help, but some children with these difficulties are just not programmed to think or respond socially the way the rest of us do. If they are happy, as my daughter says, "It's time to chillax." Quirky makes the world go round, and perhaps your solitary daughter will find the cure for cancer, as she spends her weekends ambitiously working out complex formulas. The long-term goal may be to help her know how and when to employ the strategies to use in social situations, even if she chooses to socialize on a much smaller scale, and to have the skills to enjoy a healthy partnership with a mate if she wishes, as well as congenial relationships with coworkers and family members. For children with more severe disabilities, the goal may be less ambitious and may focus more on the functional nature of interacting within their own environment. Here are some strategies that might be used and goals that might be addressed in therapy:

• *Facilitated games and play.* Children with social language and play delays may need to be taught very specifically how to play. For toddlers and preschoolers, starting with puzzles, shape sorters, and pretend play might be in order, with modeling and explicit teaching. Using action figures and stuffed animals to develop a simple story is a great exercise. "Let's pretend the pig and the cow are going on a trip. Where can they go?" Making the characters talk in the first person and move themselves is important because we want the child to take on the perspective of each character. ("I better go pack now! Oh no, I almost forgot my toothbrush. Here it is! Are you almost ready?") With school-age children, simple board games that use dice and turn-taking are a good start, as are simple card games. Helping a small group of children sort through games on their own and negotiate which ones to play, who will go first, and where they'll set it up are the kinds of things we work on in social language-play sessions. With older children, navigating how and when to use text messages, what to say on Facebook pages, and how to play age-typical video games in an interactive way with peers might be addressed.

- *Alerting to facial expressions and body language.* A crowd of people is looking at something "over there" and pointing. What is it? How do they feel about the monkey being loose from his cage if they are laughing? Wrinkling their noses? Your child will need to learn to alert to body language and interpret what he sees. *How do I feel? My hands are up to my mouth, I'm trembling, and my mouth is agape.* Learning to interpret facial expressions and body language is an integral part of any pragmatic program. "Emotion charades" are a great way to practice.

- *Conversational skills.* Let's pretend I just told you I went on a vacation last week. What might you say in response? For many children, there is no response or a completely unrelated one ("What's for lunch?"). Helping children stay on topic and reciprocate with an appropriate follow-up is crucial, particularly in the elementary school and older years. Tying that in to body language, eye contact, and facial expressions is the ultimate goal. *Where do I stand and look when talking? What if someone walks up and tries to join our conversation? How and when do I end the conversation?*

- *Thinking, feeling, and opinions.* As children move into elementary school years and older, this is important not only during interpersonal interactions, but also for reading comprehension. Why is the boy hiding the broken vase? What will his mother think when she sees the flowers in a puddle on the floor? Why did the girl say "thank you" for a gift she didn't actually like? Understanding motivations, inferencing, reading others' emotions, and perspective-taking are critical for higher-level communication and reading comprehension. When perspective-taking is limited, it's also sometimes hard for a child to understand the difference between their opinion ("Chocolate is the *best* ice-cream flavor. That team is the *worst* team ever.") and fact, which can come across as pushy, opinionated, and even argumentative since the child sees things in very black-and-white terms. "How could anyone say that strawberry ice cream is good? They're wrong. Chocolate is good.") Teaching children about opinion and perspective-taking—and the consequences of not appropriately respecting others' opinions—is essential in learning to get along with peers.

- *Social conventions and manners.* No, farting in class is not something that your classmates will appreciate. Yes, they may be laughing, but that doesn't mean to do it again. Your friend didn't return the call? No, don't call again every five minutes. These are usually sprinkled in as the situations arise or are brought to the attention of the instructor. The SLP may make books or use dolls or puppets to emphasize the key topics.

- *Video modeling and role-play.* There are some excellent DVDs and software available that provide good models for children. Research on the benefits of video modeling is fairly solid in that many children are more comfortable watching others on a TV screen than in person, and thus getting the information "in" this way can be helpful. Some of my favorites can be found on these Web sites: www.modelmekids.com, www.socialskillbuilder.com, and www.teachtolearn.com. (Their play skills hierarchy for toddlers/preschoolers is unique and helpful.) Watching children's TV shows and dissecting what's happening and why is a way SLPs show situations in action and work on interpreting reactions.

- *Facilitating carryover.* While we work on teaching a variety of skills I described above, the therapist's biggest and most important role is to help the child integrate these skills into other settings. The goal is not to learn how to participate in reciprocal conversations in our therapy setting, but to transfer those skills across settings. This often becomes the greatest challenge. Parents and teachers should be supporting the specialists who are working on these issues to encourage carryover, but the problems tend to arise when the child needs continual prompting, cueing, and rewarding to use the skills he's learned. Why are some children more successful than others? My experience has been that some children genuinely don't care what their peers think. If they want to pick their nose in seventh-grade science, they will do it—and maybe just wipe their fingers on the cover of their book. It doesn't matter to them if their peers are grossed out, so there is little incentive to modify their behavior. Making a child care about the opinions of others in his environment (but not too much) is a very tall order. These are the situations that are the hardest for all concerned. The child knows what to do, but just opts not to do it because the natural motivation is just not there.

Case Study: Jasmeen

Jasmeen, a 4½-year-old, was brought to our practice due to concerns about the way she was interacting with her peers at preschool. Her mother reported that at home Jasmeen was animated and played well with her siblings and one girl who lived three houses away. Her speech and language skills were largely quite functional, but after doing some in-depth testing, we discovered that her receptive and expressive language skills had some gaps. Jasmeen didn't always understand what people were asking her to do (following directions), and she struggled with expressing herself during tasks that were more complex, such as explaining what happened. On paper, the standardized tests found that her overall scores were within the low-average range, but these specific areas impacted her.

As is my custom, I secured permission from Jasmeen's mom to contact the preschool teacher. She gently explained that Jasmeen spent much of her three-hour school day wandering around, interacting very little with the other children. During "Circle Time," she was not following what the others were doing, and sometimes was singing songs to herself while the teacher was reading a story to the class. Outside, she liked to swing on the swings nearly every day and sometimes would look at her peers and smile. There were only brief periods where she'd interact with her classmates, and it was usually to tell them to move (not very politely) or to take something they were playing with, without asking. The teacher was concerned and asked for any suggestions that could be of help. In an ideal world, it would have been best if I could have physically gone to the preschool and observed Jasmeen, but, alas, time did not allow for that, so I needed to rely on the description from her mother and the teacher for input.

During the testing, I engaged Jasmeen in a number of play opportunities, including feeding a bird puppet we call Pepe with a host of imaginary foods, playing a simple board game (Barnyard Bingo from Fisher-Price), and making several stuffed animals plan a birthday party for a stuffed cat using our toy birthday cake set. During the play with Pepe, Jasmeen fed the puppet and smiled, but said very little spontaneously as one would expect. During Barnyard Bingo, she easily matched the colors and the animals, but lost interest quickly and tried to dump everything out. She responded well to the pretend birthday cake scenario, picking up and moving her stuffed animals, but she didn't talk for them. She spoke about them ("He gotta present") or made suggestions ("Miss Patti, let's have the cake") but she wasn't pretending to be my stuffed animals or investing in the imaginative element. I spoke to her stuffed goat ("Hi, Goat! Do you think we should blow up some balloons for the cat's birthday party?") but she would look at me and say, "I have balloons at my house!" At her age, she should have been able to switch perspectives and relate to my characters as *though I wasn't there. Using voices other than her own to sound like her cat or goat—as I did with the monkey and the dog—should have been typical play.*

Jasmeen was the type of child who is often in a bit of a gray zone. We discussed whether or not she should she be referred to a developmental physician, a psychologist, or a team for further study, but decided against it just yet. Her parents were apparently not as concerned as the teacher and seemed to have arrived for the assessment a bit reluctantly. We decided to start by having Jasmeen receive services at our office for a few months to see if we could make some headway. From a diagnostic point of view, her receptive, expressive, and social language/play skills were not disordered enough that they'd likely qualify for a diagnosis of autism, but she could possibly have met the criteria for a diagnosis of PDD. (Again, the diagnosis of PDD may be phased out after 2013.) Whether her issues were severe enough to qualify for special education intervention in the public school system was iffy. I discussed this with her parents, but they were quick to dismiss any talk of working with the public schools because they were very uneasy having Jasmeen "labeled" or having her enter school with preconceived opinions about her. Since Jasmeen's parents felt strongly about it, I did not push the issue and decided to give it a little time.

Jasmeen's program with our practice consisted of one individual session a week to work on the receptive and expressive language skills she lacked, and one group session a week to integrate the skills she learned. The concept of playing and talking at the same time was one we practiced and her mom reinforced at home. Soon Jasmeen was making exclamations ("Look, he ate three candies!") and verbalizing more. We used roleplaying, homemade social story scripts (using Carol Gray's model), and video modeling DVDs (see appendix B), and even worked on how to move and talk with toys. In group, Jasmeen learned how to interact with her peers in an age-appropriate way, including playing games, negotiating, politely refusing, complimenting, and participating in group activities as they do in preschool, such as "Story Time" and "Circle Time." Each week a new skill was introduced and practiced, with coaching for carryover at home and at school. Jasmeen responded beautifully, and her teacher reported that by the end of the school year, Jasmeen was largely indistinguishable from her peers, except for a few remaining quirky traits that still needed work, such as singing to herself at inappropriate times. She still has moments when she is distractible, so we continue to monitor her for a possible attention deficit disorder. Jasmeen now attends a private school, where she does well with the smaller teacher to student ratios. Interestingly, several years later, her mother brought in her younger sibling for similar issues.

Jasmeen's case worked out well and had a largely happy ending, primarily because hers was not a serious difficulty. The program we offered was a "lite" kind of intervention, and for some children with mild problems, it may be enough. Other times, though, a child needs more than speech-language therapy. Children with moderate to severe social language difficulties may benefit from an educational environment or a class setting where these skills can be nurtured all day long and facilitated with their peers through ongoing professional support. This can be done in a regular classroom setting or with a special class placement, depending on the child's academic skills and other accompanying behaviors. For children with mental health issues (anxiety, obsessive-compulsive disorder), a program called cognitive-behavioral therapy (CBT) done by a psychologist trained in it can be enormously beneficial. Another option for children on the autism spectrum is RDI (Relationship Development Intervention), a program developed by Steven Gutstein and his associates that teaches children and parents joint-attention and interaction skills. Some children have problems that should be considered for medication so that the underlying glitches in their brain wiring will allow them to have more control and ability to apply the interventions they are learning. Others find dietary changes and vitamin supplements from homeopathic practitioners helpful, although research on these approaches is still lacking. There is no one-size-fits-all approach, and it is largely driven by a family's long-term goal for their child, the child's ability to progress, and the available resources.

7

Understanding Listening (Auditory) Problems

As we discussed earlier, language is both receptive and expressive. Since receptive language refers to how well we comprehend language, a listening problem can have an impact on a receptive language weakness. After all, if information is not getting heard as it was intended, it will be difficult to comprehend. In many cases the term *receptive language deficit* is used interchangeably with *language processing deficit* or even *auditory processing deficit*. It can also be considered a Specific Language Impairment (SLI). Much research stills needs to be done in this area and professionals often disagree on the terms to use. Sometimes it is difficult to tell whether a child is having difficulty comprehending what people say because the ears are not processing sounds correctly or because the linguistic part of the brain is not processing what the ears are sending. Some tests are available to help answer this question, but in many cases, there are multiple related issues occurring at the same time.

In this chapter I describe the difficulties faced by children with common listening problems. I discuss auditory processing disorders, in which the auditory pathways are not working properly; auditory memory problems, where children forget much of what they hear; and language processing problems, in which children have difficulty comprehending what is said to them. As always, I explain how these conditions affect the children at school and home, and I detail what parents can do to help them cope.

The "What? Did You Say Something?" Child: An Auditory Processing Problem

Eddie is a very bright boy, but sometimes I just don't understand what is wrong with him. I know he hears me because we've had his hearing checked by several people. But sometimes I call his name and he never looks up. When I call on him, I usually have to repeat the question because he's been daydreaming or tuning me out. He also doesn't pay attention to the other children during class discussions and is distracted by every little noise in the hall or outside. When I work with him one-on-one, he does much better, but I don't have the time to do this with twenty-five children in my classroom. What can I do?

—Miss Donnelly, second-grade teacher

Children like Eddie are a real puzzle. Parents and teachers know they are bright, yet something is not quite right. Although it's true that a very creative and gifted child can respond to being bored in school by daydreaming, many children have a weakness that prevents them from listening in a normal way. It is out of their control.

When a child is of preschool age, you expect listening to be a challenge, particularly when the child is required to sit for long periods of time. A problem like Eddie's may go unnoticed until second grade or even later, because so often it seems like something the child will grow out of or that it is just a matter of controlling the child's behavior. In this section we'll look at ways to recognize and understand that children with Eddie's problem may have an auditory processing disorder, also known as APD, or a central auditory processing disorder (CAPD). It is also written as (C)APD. Having an auditory processing disorder means that Eddie's ears are able to hear sounds, but his brain perceives sounds and speech in a different way than a typical person does due to the inefficient or inaccurate delivery of the information by the auditory nerve pathway. We often start seeing warning signs of it in younger children, but the tests given to confirm it are primarily for ages 7 and older. One test, called the Auditory Skills Assessment (ASA), published in 2010, can be administered as early as 3.6 years of age, but it is considered a screening tool only.

There are many symptoms associated with auditory processing disorders, so one child may not have the exact same presentation as another. Professionals in the field still sometimes disagree about what tests to use, how to interpret them, and how to treat auditory processing deficits. Sometimes psychologists, teachers, and learning disabilities consultants use the term "auditory processing," but in a more generalized way to mean difficulty understanding verbal language, whereas speech pathologists and audiologists are referencing a very specific condition that audiologists would diagnose with a battery of tests. If a professional is using this term, unless an audiologist has confirmed it, it is more likely being used as a synonym for the processing of oral language.

If you are worried that your child may have an APD, you should rule out other reasons your child may be struggling to process spoken language, including the following:

1. *Inattention and/or hyperactivity.* While it is very possible for a child to have difficulties with attention span with or without hyperactivity (AD/HD) as well as a central auditory processing disorder, it is often hard to tell which is which. The primary difference between the two conditions is that the child with AD/HD has pervasive difficulty sustaining attention for most tasks that require prolonged attention (other than watching TV or playing video games), which would include doing written homework, reading silently, or organizing a school project. These are not auditory-based activities. The source of the inattention is within the child, and is not specific to listening, but listening activities may certainly be just as challenging. Children with APD may have an excellent attention span for anything visual and do just fine completing worksheets or other assignments, assuming they are confident with the content, but their difficulty is more evident during listening-based activities, which is usually whole-class instruction, discussions, or conversation.

2. *Lack of receptive language knowledge.* Remember that if your child's receptive language skills are a bit behind, it stands to reason that he won't be as attentive or able to process spoken language quickly. This could be due to a lack of exposure (if the child is new to a language), a lack of stimulation, or an inability to retain new language concepts. It is of course not unusual to have both situations happening at the same time, but the underlying linguistic issue would need to be addressed; it may be the primary culprit.

3. *Classroom or teacher setup.* For some children, the teacher's voice may be unduly quiet and whispery or hard to understand. The classroom may have poor acoustics, noisy kids, or too many groups being taught at the same time. This is not necessarily an auditory processing disorder (although it might very well exacerbate it) but is due to the fact that the verbal information is not being inputted appropriately.

4   *Neurobiological and mental health interference.* Imagine how hard it would be to focus and listen if you were preoccupied with persistent worry thoughts. *What if my teacher calls on me? Will the other children think I'm stupid?* Some children have to cope with compulsions to perform rituals (such as counting their steps when walking or starting all over when they make a mistake on their paper) that make it difficult to attend to oral instruction. For some children with anxiety or obsessive-compulsive disorders, it may be hard to focus on anything else. If a child has sensory issues, her clothing may be scratchy or too tight, the classroom too hot or cold. *What did the teacher say?* Consider the child with Tourette's who is trying to inhibit tics, such as blurting out a noise or a word. This struggle can be so consuming that it makes it hard to listen to what the teacher is saying. Any one of these children may also have an auditory processing disorder, and in fact, that is not uncommon. However, it is important for the specialists to tease out what component of the observed behaviors is due to these other issues and what part is truly caused by auditory deficits.

5. *Obstructive sleep apnea.* You've probably heard this term before. It refers to a disorder that is caused by a mechanical malformation in the airway that creates a difficulty when the muscles are relaxed when sleeping. It results in snoring and a momentary stopping of breathing, and often a reduction in nighttime oxygen intake. Children with enlarged tonsils and adenoids are at risk for this, as are children with small mouths. When boys go through hormonal changes and their voices deepen, it can be exacerbated. The resulting lack of restorative sleep can cause a condition called a "cognitive fog." One of the features of a cognitive fog is a slowness of language processing, inattention, and reduced memory. If your child has these symptoms (particularly if the processing issues seem to be getting worse) along with daytime sleepiness, treating the sleep apnea will often result in noticeable improvement in these areas.

6. *Chronic health problems and medications.* When your body is not cooperating and you are uncomfortable, it is very hard to stay focused on what anyone is saying, let alone to process or remember it. Children with chronic health problems may exhibit symptoms of an auditory processing problem, but the etiology (and thus the intervention) is very different. Likewise, some medications can cause a child to be sleepy and less alert, making it hard for him to listen attentively.

7. *Intellectual disabilities and/or autism spectrum disorders.* Children with intellectual disabilities and/or autism spectrum disorders usually

have associated difficulties in listening and reduced auditory skills, but in general they are considered a part of the overall language or cognitive disability, rather than a separate disorder.

What Kinds of Difficulties Are Associated with an Auditory Processing Disorder?

There are many facets to auditory processing disorders. Your child may have one or two areas of weakness, while another child may have just about every one of them. The job for the speech pathologist and the audiologist is to dissect the difficulties your child is having, through observation, formal testing, and talking with adults who interact with the child on a daily basis, across settings. Ideally, the diagnosis should be reached as part of a team process, but at the very least, it should attempt to rule out the myriad of "look-alike" conditions that could cause similar symptoms to be observed. A key component of the audiologist's assessment will be to examine the function of the right ear versus that of the left ear. There is typically a "right ear advantage" (it performs the tasks with greater accuracy) for auditory processing, but the gap between the left and right ear performance needs to be assessed to determine if it's within normal limits. A left ear advantage or too large of a right ear advantage should not normally occur. When an APD is suspected, the SLP or other specialist will refer to an audiologist for further testing and confirmation. Some of auditory tests might include:

- *Auditory figure-ground.* This refers to how well a child can pick out a person's voice from background noise. In a typical scenario, a child with auditory processing issues hears everything with equal importance and cannot localize to the source or suppress the background noise the way he should.
- *Dichotic listening tasks.* In these types of tasks, words or sentences are presented into the child's right and left ears via headphones at the same time. The child is directed to repeat the word heard on a given side (left or right) first, but needs to repeat both words correctly.
- *Auditory (time-) compressed sentences.* One test we give takes a sentence and literally compresses it so that there are no gaps between the words, and the time between the phonemes is reduced. It makes a sentence such as "You are wearing a purple dress" sound like "Youarewearingapurpledress." For children who can't process language quickly, the normal speed at which we process language is too fast.
- *Pitch, duration, and pattern awareness.* These tests ask the child

to identify whether or not the presented tone is high or low, long or short, or if there are two sounds heard or one.

• *Phonemic awareness.* Children with poor auditory skills often have at their core weak phonemic systems. That is, it is challenging for them to perform a variety of sound manipulation tasks because their underlying grasp of the phonemic elements of speech is weak. We start working in earnest with these skills when children are around 4½ to 5 years old. They are the basis not only for auditory processing, but for reading and spelling as well. Some of the phonemic awareness skills we check would include identifying the first/last/middle sounds in a word, identifying rhyming patterns, synthesizing separate sounds to make a word (*b-e-l-t* put together auditorily says *belt*), counting syllables in a word, and synthesizing given syllables to figure out what word it is (*buh-tter-fly* put together says *butterfly*).

• *Auditory closure.* If you heard the sentence "I think we will be 'eaving at 'ee o'clock" it would likely be fairly easy for you to fill in the blanks and easily process the sentence. (I think we will be leaving at three o'clock.) For children with weak auditory skills, it is not as easy to do. They cannot fill in the blanks and thus are more impacted in noisy situations. *Auditory closure* is the ability to fill in those missing pieces.

• *Auditory memory.* Speech pathologists, psychologists, and learning consultants generally test for this, as do some educational audiologists. It is one of those "gray areas" that straddles both auditory processing and other language-based learning disabilities, including Specific Language Impairment (SLI). For more about this, read further in this chapter about the "I Forgot What You Said" child.

How Is APD Confirmed?

Auditory processing disorders are diagnosed by an audiologist, although a speech-language pathologist or other professional typically makes the referral for the testing. The evaluation takes place in a soundproof room specially equipped to accommodate this kind of testing. Headphones are placed on the child's ears, and she is asked to perform various listening tasks, such as repeating words and sentences heard in the headphones. The child is presented with words and sentences in different ways, with noise in the background. At this time you may find only a handful of places in your state that do this kind of testing due to both the expense of the setup and the relative newness of our knowledge about this disorder. Your child's speech-language pathologist or ear-nose-throat physician can help you find someone who does this testing. You may have to go to a university or a city to have this done. An APD is most appropriately diagnosed as part of a team process. Other conditions may also be present, such as a learning disability, AD/HD, language deficits, or sensory integration deficits, and thus a comprehensive evaluation is best.

Characteristics of Children with an Auditory Processing Disorder

Children who have an auditory processing disorder may exhibit a variety of behaviors. Remember, however, that a diagnosis is made based on the results of audiological tests, not soley on the basis of observation of these behaviors. Children with auditory processing disorders might do the following:

- Listen much better in a one-on-one setting than in a group or in an open space
- Have difficulty staying focused on what someone is saying when there is noise or other distractions in the background
- Have difficulty listening for long periods of time
- Confuse or forget what people say; misinterpret what was said
- Exhibit word retrieval difficulties in conversation
- Say "Huh?" or "What?" frequently
- Not turn around or react when someone calls their name
- Be easily distracted when listening
- "Zone out" during whole-class instruction
- Have difficulty sounding out words when learning to read
- Have difficulty spelling words
- Exhibit speech problems
- Exhibit problems learning new words
- Exhibit difficulty with reading comprehension

How Does an Auditory Processing Problem Affect a Child?

An auditory processing disorder can manifest itself in a variety of ways. Below are some of the most common difficulties associated with this disorder:

- *Getting your child's attention.* At home, you might find it difficult to get your child's attention if she is in the next room, especially if the TV or the washing machine is on. Once you do get her attention, it may be difficult to keep for more than a minute or two. If a radio is playing in the background or if siblings are running around playing, you may find it impossible to have a meaningful conversation.

- *Misunderstandings.* "But you *said* I could!" It's not at all unusual for this to happen even with a child without an APD, but misinterpreting, mishearing, and misunderstandings come with the territory. (For tips on how to minimize this, read further in this chapter.)

- *Noisy environments.* Due to acoustical conditions, having a conversation in the car or on the phone may also be very difficult, particularly if a radio is playing in the background. If your child plays on a sports team or attends noisy club meetings, she may seem "lost" or "tuned out" at times. These situations present a special challenge for a child with an auditory processing disorder. People's voices are competing with each other, and in a large room or an outdoor area, the acoustics make it difficult for the child to hear clearly.

- *School issues.* School is probably the place where an auditory processing disorder affects a child the most because of the intensity of the listening required, the amount of time in which listening is required, and the number of distractions present. And because of the relationship between auditory processing disorders and speech, reading (sounding out words), and writing, a child may need extra help in those academic areas as well. However, an auditory processing disorder need not be a permanent or debilitating problem and can be managed so your child can function successfully at school with the right help.

Children with this problem may also have difficulty comprehending what they read as well as what they hear. However, when reading, the child can go back and reread the passage until it has "sunk in." With listening, there is no way to recapture the words unless they are written down. These problems may be significant enough to warrant a special-education label of "learning disabled" in school.

Children with an auditory processing disorder may have problems keeping up their grades, particularly if a teacher teaches primarily by lecturing. This is especially true for classes such as social studies and science. Thus it is important to properly diagnose this problem so accommodations can be made for the child in the classroom. The audiologist, speech-language pathologist, and learning disabilities teacher should work together to adjust classroom lessons so your child can learn successfully.

Children with an auditory processing problem may seem to ignore the teacher, daydreaming as Eddie does. They may watch the other children to make sure they are following the directions correctly. This copying behavior may be easily misinterpreted by the teacher.

However, with therapy and understanding, these children can function successfully in the classroom and at home.

Therapy for Auditory Processing Disorders

Testing and diagnosing this problem have become more common in recent years, but treatment programs are still being developed to address the problem. Most audiologists prefer to wait until a child is 7 or older before making a firm diagnosis, to give the child's system time to mature.

To help a child with this disorder experience success at school, it is critical to make the classroom as quiet as possible. Having carpeting on the floor and making other acoustical improvements can be a huge help. For the most part, a teacher should treat the child as though he *does* have a hearing problem, because most of the recommendations are appropriate for a child with a hearing impairment, and that is how the child is functioning. For example, the child should sit close to the teacher, who should speak slowly and simply while facing the child. Writing directions and key pieces of information on the eraser board helps. Repeating and rephrasing important information may be necessary.

Therapy is usually provided by a speech-language pathologist or audiologist. The therapy plan should be developed based on your child's individual needs. While there are many common areas of weakness, a skilled clinician needs to pick and choose the activities that will best meet your child's needs. It's not a one-size-fits-all disorder and thus treatment should be designed with great care. A prepackaged or published program should be selected only if appropriate, and even then, only the applicable elements within the program should be used. At this time, there is no single program that is available that addresses all areas of auditory processing for any particular child.

It is important that the clinician work closely with your child's classroom teacher, as the teacher will need to modify how she presents information and how she asks the child questions. To maximize hearing, the child will need to be encouraged in the classroom to use good listening behavior. Therapy should be systematic and sequenced, building on one skill, beginning at an easier level, and gradually getting more difficult. Strategies that ask the child to consciously think about the learning process are often called *metacognitive skills*. These would include subvocalizing and visualizing information (see below) as well as compensatory strategies to make listening situations less taxing. Having a child listen to stories and answer questions or follow a series of directions is not helpful unless specific strategies are being practiced.

The following include some therapy goals and strategies that are often used with children who have auditory processing disorders:

- *Establishing a listening "set."* One of the first things to do is help a child work on transitioning his focus from other activities (writing, playing with something) and attend to auditory information. Most children—but not all—do better when their body is still and their eyes are on the person talking. Learning to be aware of distractions and using internal strategies to inhibit them can be helpful. In addition, there are different levels of auditory focus that are needed, depending upon the task at hand. If you are waiting to hear the weather forecast, you "keep an ear out" for when the commercial is over, but your vigilance is different than if you are being given important instructions as to where and when to meet someone on Thursday. A child needs to learn how to jump into the most effective listening mode when important information is about to be given.
- *Sustaining auditory focus and attention.* Listening tasks with gradually reduced visual support are important, especially after the age of 7. These activities might include listening to a story without pictures or attending to a teacher providing instruction. Stretching a child's ability to listen for developmentally appropriate intervals of time is critical.
- *Improving auditory discrimination/sound awareness.* This means your child will work on listening to sounds and learning how they are different. Children with APD tend to have difficulty hearing differences among similar words such as *want, went, when.* By improving auditory discrimination, your child will differentiate similar-sounding words better. The SLP may also work on listening to different tones and determining if they are high or low, as well as on the order of the sounds. A computer-based program such as Fast ForWord is an excellent tool for providing intensive intervention for these skills. Other methods, such as the Lindamood-Bell LIPS program, can also be effective if sufficient practice is provided. Some reading programs for children with decoding weaknesses or dyslexia, such as the Orton-Gillingam, Slingerland, and Wilson programs, work on these skills, as well as on phonetic awareness.
- *Improving phonemic awareness.* This refers to the way in which your child can organize/process sounds and syllables when they are put together and taken apart. Children with APD often can't tell you that *c-a-t* is *cat.* When they hear *mar-ble* it is hard to put it together as "marble." These are called auditory blending skills. Other phonemic awareness skills include identifying the first and last sound in a word (not the letter), hearing rhyming patterns, and telling how many syllables are in a word (auditory segmenting). Research shows that phonemic awareness skills are critical not only to children with APD, but also to children with difficulty learning to read and spell. By working on these skills, your

child should improve in these areas as well. (See "Phonemic Awareness Training Software" in appendix A.) The Phonemic Synthesis Program (Jack Katz) is a terrific way to work on sound blending.

• *Pitch pattern and duration awareness.* This is especially helpful for children with flat-intonation vocal patterns or who have trouble comprehending subtle changes in melodic contours, such as for sarcasm, emotion, or added emphasis.

• *Listening when background noise is present.* Once the child has mastered the above skills, it is helpful to practice them in background noise. Of course, you would start with soft talking for short periods of time (two to three minutes) and slowly build up to books on tape or a talk-radio station. Listening to music is not as helpful, as it utilizes a different part of the brain. It is important to alternate the position and the distance of the sound source (usually a boom box) from behind the child, left to right, and from behind the person speaking.

• *Improving auditory closure.* Another skill to incorporate is deducing meaning when part of the message is missing or not heard. The child needs to learn to use context clues to figure out what may have been said.

Compensatory Strategies

• *Attending to the speaker's mouth for additional clues (lipreading).* Because children with APD often have compromised hearing in noisy situations, it may be helpful to teach lipreading, also known as speechreading. This allows the child to use visual skills to look at the speaker's mouth to help figure out what was said.

• *Learning how to initiate asking for clarification if the child cannot hear or understand what was said.* Children with APD often have gotten used to letting information "pass over their heads." They hear it, but they don't process it well. The clinician will want to help the child learn to be a more active listener. The child will need to pinpoint where the problem lies. *Do I want the teacher to repeat that? Say it louder? Explain it?* Sometimes these are called compensatory skills because the child is learning to compensate for the auditory problems.

• *Helping the child learn to control the environment so the message is more easily understood.* This means the child will need to be a more active participant in troubleshooting the interfering factors around him. We sometimes call this "self-advocacy." The child cannot rely on the people around him to do this. For example, if it is noisy outside, he should initiate closing the door or the window. If the person is talking across the room and is hard to hear, he should move closer to the person speaking, ask the person to speak louder, or ask the person to come closer.

Therapeutic Listening Programs

There is a type of treatment, called *therapeutic listening,* that is used by some practitioners to treat auditory processing disorders. Therapeutic listening involves having the child listen (usually through headphones) to carefully selected and modified music on CDs for a prescribed amount of time per day. It is felt that if the child is exposed to certain frequencies and combinations of sounds, his ability to listen to speech will improve. This technique is usually administered by a speech-language pathologist, an audiologist, a psychologist, or an occupational therapist. The most common therapeutic listening programs are Tomatis and The Listening Program.

In 2004, the American Speech-Language-Hearing Association (ASHA) issued a position statement on the use of one kind of therapeutic listening program, Auditory Integration Training (AIT), indicating that a review of available research did not support its use as being effective and that it should be considered an "experimental" and non-mainstream intervention.

Today, it is not uncommon to find that specialists such as occupational therapists and educational therapists as well as SLPs use therapeutic listening programs, typically in a private setting. Public school programs generally do not offer these kinds of programs due to the expense and because they feel it is still an "alternative" kind of treatment. Some practices routinely recommend starting with a therapeutic listening program when auditory weaknesses and inattention are primary symptoms, including for use with children on the autism spectrum.

Some children who have related sensory integration difficulties exhibit a hypersensitivity to certain sounds, such as blenders, lawn mowers, or hair dryers. The children sometimes hold their hands over their ears because it's too irritating to them. We call this *hyperacusis,* and some children with auditory processing disorders have it. When this difficulty impedes the child's ability to tolerate the noise at recess, at a movie theater, in a noisy multipurpose room, or at a party or restaurant, it may be worth a try to see if your child responds to one of these programs. Practitioners report that children are less irritable and have a better attention span after undergoing these programs. I've had several parents report very dramatic changes in their child's listening and language development as a result of undergoing a therapeutic listening program. But in a number of cases, other parents have also reported to me that there seemed to be little noticeable benefit. So the results of these programs vary from child to child.

Assistive Listening Devices

A device called an *FM system* (also called an *auditory trainer*) can be very useful for a child with an auditory processing problem. To use an FM system, the teacher attaches a mini microphone, which receives the teacher's voice, to a clip worn on the collar. This is wired to a small transmitter that can be clipped to a belt or the top of a pair of pants. The student wears headphones, a loop, or other device, which is wired to a receiver that is clipped to a belt, a harness, or the top of a pair of pants also. This technology allows the child to hear the teacher's voice with far less distraction, although other children's voices can still be heard. Most important, it helps the child input auditory information with greater clarity, which improves auditory discrimination. It helps the child stay better focused on what the teacher is saying, and the child doesn't tire as quickly from listening. Newer versions are increasingly wireless.

Sound-field systems require the teacher to wear a microphone clip on the lapel, but instead of being transmitted through a headset, the teacher's voice is broadcast through a portable speaker. The advantages of this type of setup are that the system can travel from class to class, and that the teacher's voice can be heard more clearly by the rest of the class as well. There are other models that deliver the sound in a speaker that is easily hung in place of a ceiling tile. While this does not allow the system to move from room to room, the location offers multidirectional diffusion of the sound, benefiting the entire class. Using a sound-field system reduces wear and tear on the teacher's voice. The teacher can also monitor it for static interference. Best of all, the child with APD is freed from having to wear the headset, which is sometimes awkward for children trying to "fit in," especially in the older grades. There has been research that shows using a sound-field system is helpful for children with ADD as well as for children with other auditory-based learning disabilities. The disadvantage of this system is that since the speaker is several feet away from the child, the teacher's voice has some space to diffuse and is not as close to the child's ear. As with the FM system, the child with APD will still have difficulty hearing peers during discussions unless the microphone is passed around, which is usually a bit impractical. Flat-panel displays that look more like a picture on the wall than a speaker are another new technology.

IDEA regulations require that assistive listening technology be included in the IEP, if appropriate. If the audiologist feels your child needs this type of support, make sure it is written into the IEP. Most companies that provide these systems allow a thirty-day free trial to see if it is helpful. Most systems cost $500 to $1,000, similar to the cost for the FM systems. (See material on assistive listening devices in appendix A.)

I have worked with a few children who have retested in the "normal" range on these tests and who no longer displayed any observable listening weaknesses after receiving intensive therapy for a year or two. (These particular children, however, had minimal accompanying speech, language, or learning weaknesses.) But for many if not most children, an auditory processing problem is only one piece of a bigger learning disability; therefore they may always struggle in some way with listening tasks. However, good therapy can not only help the child improve these skills, but also teach lifelong compensatory strategies.

What Can Parents Do to Help a Child with an Auditory Processing Problem?

If your child has been diagnosed with an auditory processing disorder, the audiologist who diagnosed the problem has probably given you plenty of practical tips. If he or she hasn't, ask. This is particularly necessary because each child is different and, depending on the results of the evaluation, may have specific needs. The following are general suggestions that are somewhat universal for children with auditory processing problems:

- Don't try to have a conversation if your child is in another room. Walk directly to where your child is before speaking.
- Make sure your child is looking at you and ready to listen before beginning a conversation.
- Reduce the noise level in your home when having a family discussion or conversation. Go into a quiet room, turn off the TV, or close a door if needed.
- Use books on CD (no pictures) in the car and at bedtime to practice auditory focusing and attention. Try to gradually increase the amount of time your child can listen.
- If your home is noisy due to tile or hardwood floors, consider carpeting your living areas. This will improve the acoustics and make it easier for your child to hear.

- If you find yourself in a noisy situation, speak just a little more loudly. This will help your child focus on your voice and ignore the background noise, which is difficult to tune out.
- Speak slowly and pause between thoughts. This gives your child time to process what you say.
- Repeat and rephrase important messages. If your child can read, write them down in a conspicuous place.
- Consider direct therapy from a trained professional to remediate the associated auditory and language deficits.

Case Study: Ramon

Mrs. Edelman, Ramon's third-grade teacher, stopped me in the teachers' room one day. She was wondering what to do with Ramon. She was sure he had a hearing problem, especially since he still had tubes in his ears as a result of past ear infections. But the school nurse double-checked his hearing and assured Mrs. Edelman it was normal. Now what could she do? Ramon didn't seem to hear her much of the time. When she called on him, he didn't know what was going on or answered a related question but not the one she asked. He frequently said "What?"

The teacher told me Ramon's reading was in the low-average range— just low enough that he was struggling, but not enough for him to qualify for special education services. He seemed to be a bright boy but frequently copied other children's work. She guessed that he must not be paying attention. Mrs. Edelman knew that something was not quite right, but since Ramon was not failing, she was hesitant to push for testing. "What should I do?" she asked me.

I observed Ramon informally in class on several occasions. When he paid attention, he seemed to keep up with the rest of the class, but his attention was usually fleeting. Mrs. Edelman continually had to prompt him to look at her. He was seated near an open window, where he could hear a lawn mower humming throughout the lesson, and he looked out the window frequently.

When I spoke with Ramon's mother, she expressed exasperation with him at home. "He doesn't listen," she said. "I ask him to do something and it's like it goes in one ear and out the other! For instance, if I ask him to go upstairs and brush his teeth, get on his pajamas, and pick out a book to read, I can go upstairs in twenty minutes and find him sitting there, fully clothed, reading a book."

Ramon's mother and teacher filled out a referral form for our school's Student Study Team and requested testing to find out the source of

Ramon's problems. The learning disabilities teacher did an evaluation and found Ramon had some strong skills in many academic areas, especially math and spelling. However, it was noted that Ramon was memorizing most of the words he knew how to read and spell, because he was unable to figure out how to read or spell made-up words, such as "fip" or "tibe." He had no idea how to go about sounding them out or spelling them. Since Ramon was not failing in reading or spelling, his problem had easily escaped notice.

He also needed to have the test questions repeated often, because he misunderstood what the evaluator said. He needed frequent breaks from the testing because he became easily "overloaded" from all the questions and concentration.

On the speech-language evaluation, Ramon scored very high on the vocabulary tests and even did well on most of the language and listening tests. (It is not uncommon for children with auditory processing disorders to do well on listening tasks in a quiet environment or for short periods of time.) The tests that did give him trouble were the tasks that asked him to listen to sounds such as t-oa-s-t or syllables such as el-e-va-tor and figure out what the word was. These tasks, along with those that tested his ability to remember a series of words or long sentences, were below average. However, overall Ramon's testing was not low enough to qualify for a special education classification.

With his parents' permission, our team referred Ramon to an audiologist for an auditory processing evaluation. The testing showed a clearcut, significant auditory processing disorder. Ramon was unable to perceive speech clearly with even a minimal amount of background noise or when part of the message was missing. Thus he now qualified for a special education program, which allowed us to tailor an individual program for him, combining therapy with changes in the way the classroom teacher presented lessons and tests.

The audiologist asked us to try an FM listening system to help keep Ramon focused on the teacher's voice. We also moved his seat so he was close to the teacher and away from the window. The teacher was asked to write directions on the eraser board and speak more slowly. Other suggestions for teaching strategies were included on Ramon's IEP. (See chapter 4 for a full explanation of the IEP.)

At home, Ramon's mother and father realized they would need to be patient with him. They no longer tried to give him long directions or have conversations in the kitchen while the dishwasher was running. When they needed to get his attention, they waited until he was looking at them before talking. In the car, they turned off the radio and spoke slowly and clearly so that Ramon could focus on their voices. On the soccer field and basketball court, they helped his coaches understand how difficult it was for Ramon to follow a coach's voice from 20 feet away. His coaches agreed to pull Ramon closer to help him comprehend what they were saying. These and other suggestions have helped Ramon's family cope very well with his weaknesses in auditory processing.

Ramon is now in eighth grade. He no longer needs any direct therapy services for his auditory processing disorder. In fact, tests show his problem is now clinically "mild." He is still classified as a special education student, however, because teachers still need to meet with the SLP from time to time to review his progress and ways in which they can modify their instructional methods to accommodate his needs. If the school had an audiologist on staff, he or she would be the primary specialist involved with Ramon's program. However, since Ramon's school, like most public schools, does not have one, Ramon is tested each year by an audiologist with whom the district contracts for this service. Ramon resisted wearing the FM system after a year or two, so it was phased out. Ramon is pulling A's in math, science, art, PE, and social studies with no help, although he needs to take careful notes and study with diligence. He works very hard for his grades. Language arts are still difficult for Ramon. His spelling and reading skills are weak but in the C+ range.

Unfortunately, due to a shortage of audiologists with experience in assessing APD, it is often difficult to find someone trained to diagnose and treat APD. Other times, we find some audiologists using criteria for diagnosis or recommending expensive treatments that fall far short of the recommended guidelines set forth by the two organizations that support audiology practices in the United States: The American Academy of Audiologists (AAA) and the American Speech-Language-Hearing Association (ASHA). Some SLPs and audiologists feel that APD is over-diagnosed and merely a manifestation of an SLI or of attention deficit disorder. In addition, budget cuts have made continuing education and buying updated testing materials a challenge, so sometimes the school SLPs do not have the time or the tests they need to properly screen for it. More and more, it seems that the symptoms themselves are treated without going the extra mile for the diagnosis. Sometimes it can't be avoided, but at the very least, employing many of the strategies and compensatory techniques can be helpful, if it is shown to be helping the child.

The "I Forgot What You Said" Child:
An Auditory Memory Problem

Yesterday Mrs. Sauer was telling us what to do, and I couldn't remember what she said, so I asked Jamaal 'cause he's smart. When she caught me askin' him, she got really mad because she said I should pay attention better, but the words just fly out of my head like a bird.

—Tamina, age 5

Do you know a child like Tamina? A child who looks right at you and seems to be listening but can't remember what you said? Maybe you can relate to Tamina's mother. She's at the end of her rope this morning. Is Tamina ignoring her, or has she truly forgotten to go upstairs, brush her hair, and bring down her spelling book? What exactly *is* she doing up there?! Tamina's mother gets so exasperated . . . especially after repeating those directions for the second and third times in ten minutes. Is Tamina deliberately trying to test her patience?

In this section I discuss a kind of listening problem Tamina is exhibiting, how it affects children, and what parents can do about it.

Interestingly, Tamina is a crackerjack when it comes to remembering where pieces of a puzzle go or how to get to her aunt's house. If she can remember those things, then why can't she remember what people say?

The brain doesn't have one specific place for memory. In fact, there are many kinds of memories stored in different places and ways by the brain. You can remember smells, tastes, emotions, songs, events, and what your mother looked like as she tucked you in. These are just a few of the kinds of information stored by our brain. Once the information is stored, it becomes part of our memory.

When children like Tamina have difficulty remembering what people say, it is not because they can't hear the words or understand the message. It is because their brain cannot hold onto the words long enough for them to make sense of the message. The word *auditory* refers to the way we hear and interpret sounds and words. Tamina has an *auditory memory deficit*. It is a common type of listening problem that can seriously impact a child's ability to succeed in school. Sometimes psychologists and learning specialists call this a deficit in "working memory" because it is auditory information that needs to go to the "short-term" holding tank in our brain. It can also cause enormous frustration for parents and teachers.

Auditory memory develops in a child from a young age. It is a gradual process that requires intact hearing acuity, attention span, and remembering during the course of a typical day. Simple activities such as listening to stories read aloud, talking with a parent, and following along with songs and rhymes help a child develop auditory skills. Even with the best hearing and stimulation, however, a child may for many reasons still have an auditory memory problem.

If Tamina has difficulty keeping her attention on what is being said and is easily distracted, it will be even more difficult for her to remember verbal information. Therefore, attention span problems will also impact or cause an auditory memory problem. Medication may help children with attention deficit disorder, a type of attention span problem, to stay focused longer, thus improving auditory memory skills.

Auditory memory problems are often not detected until a child is in school or is given a thorough speech-language evaluation for other problems, such as speech delays or language weaknesses. Unlike speech problems, listening disorders are often not the kind of deficits that jump out at you if you are not looking for them. It is easy to assume the child is willfully disobeying the parent or teacher or just not paying attention.

To give you an idea of what it would feel like to have an auditory memory problem, read these directions quickly out loud: *Draw a large purple and red flower above the green door, but first underline each word with a p or an f in it; cross out the second large triangle to the right of the small blue circle.* Now close your eyes and see how much of that you can remember. Did you remember it accurately? Chances are you remembered something about some shapes and a flower, maybe the letter *p*. But if you are like most people, the information was not stored. Reading the information also allowed you to see the words. When a child hears it only, the words linger in the air. There is not even a printed word to remember.

While you were reading those directions, you certainly understood each one individually, right? But when they were put together and spoken quickly, your brain could not hold onto them. When a child has an auditory memory problem, the same thing happens, except only a small amount of verbal information is needed to produce the same confusing effect.

Children with learning disabilities, short attention spans, speech and language problems, and other kinds of listening problems often have auditory memory deficits. Many people consider it to be an associated condition of an auditory processing disorder or specific language impairment (SLI). This problem can be diagnosed with any number of tests given by a psychologist, a learning disabilities specialist, an audiologist, or a speech-language pathologist. A typical way to test for an auditory memory problem is to say a series of words and numbers and ask the child to repeat it. As the series presented gets longer and longer, the child not only may have difficulty remembering the exact items but also typically may forget the *entire* thing once it gets too long. Another way to test auditory memory is to ask the child to respond to directions, which also get longer and more complex as the test progresses. A child whose only problem is a weak auditory memory will get the directions correct nearly all the time if you repeat them several times without any further explanation. However, if you say them once or very quickly, the child may get only part of the direction correct or just say, "I forget what to do."

Auditory memory difficulties can be short-term, such as when you ask someone to repeat something back immediately, or they can be longer-term, such as when you ask someone to recall that same information ten minutes later or even twenty minutes later. Very few tests are sensitive enough to identify these kinds of difficulties. My favorite is the Auditory Processing Abilities Test (APAT). It is amazing to see the discrepancy in some children's auditory retention as just a very brief period of time elapses, and this cannot be determined with a traditional auditory memory test since some children have great short-term memories but poor longer-term memories.

A child who doesn't understand the directions or who gets confused even though she can accurately repeat them has language *processing* problems. These are discussed later in this chapter.

Characteristics of Children with an Auditory Memory Problem

Children with an auditory memory problem might do the following:

- Have difficulty remembering oral directions, details of a story heard, or characters' names
- Watch what other children do before attempting to follow a verbal direction
- Remember only some parts of the direction, usually the last thing that was said
- Have a history of frequent ear infections as an infant or a toddler
- Have difficulty listening to lectures or discussions for long periods of time; may tune out after a while
- Have difficulty repeating back a multistep direction verbatim
- Have difficulty taking notes during class lectures; say the teacher "goes too fast"

- Have difficulty taking tests given orally
- Forget new words or concepts heard during a class lecture or need repetition and drills for them to "stick"
- Stumble over multisyllabic words; mix up syllables or mangle words when saying or writing them
- Learn more easily when watching what others are doing, or when using a hands-on approach
- Need to reread written information several times for it to "sink in"
- Have difficulty paying attention
- Forget new names easily
- Have difficulty memorizing their phone number, address, words to songs, poems, prayers, math facts

How Does an Auditory Memory Problem Affect a Child?

A child with an auditory memory problem is going to be at some disadvantage at home, but unfortunately the weakness will be more pronounced at school. Therefore, in the absence of other speech, language, or learning problems, an auditory memory deficit may not become noticeable until a child is 6, 7, or 8 years old. A delay in diagnosis is especially likely if the problem is mild.

Tamina's mother may remind her that she wants to leave for Grandma's house after lunch, only to find that Tamina's left to go play before her mother has even finished washing the lunch dishes. It's not that Tamina is trying to be difficult, it's just that she forgot what her mother told her. If her mother asked her, "Where are we supposed to go after lunch?" it may have jogged her memory, or perhaps not. Tamina may remember hearing about going to Grandma's, but the "after lunch" part may have escaped her.

Learning the words to songs and nursery rhymes is difficult for preschool children with auditory memory problems. This may cause frustration or embarrassment at times, but in my experience, children of this age seem generally unaware of this kind of problem. As children enter kindergarten, learning letter names and sounds may be difficult because these are primarily auditory memory tasks. If they can make associations (A is the letter in sister Ashley's name), they may remember it better.

It is a challenge for a child with an auditory memory problem to listen to a story and remember it the way other children do. As Tamina listens, she may comprehend what is being said, particularly if the sentences are simple and short. Unfortunately, as the sentences grow longer and more complex, the words become a mental blur. When the story is over, she may have trouble remembering any new words that were introduced, the characters' names, or other details related to the story.

In early grades, where learning is more hands-on, children often work together in groups, so if a child forgets the directions, it is easy for that child to watch what the others are doing. For these reasons, a child with an auditory memory problem may compensate for the weakness for some time, although reading and other language skills may be a challenge.

As stories, characters, and plots become more complex and filled with more details, there is more to remember, and the child will find it increasingly difficult to follow along. New words and concepts are discussed and taught at a quicker pace. Directions for worksheets and projects explained by the teacher grow more complex. A child with an auditory memory problem may begin to really fall apart in the second grade, particularly in the last half of the year. If the child is a strong reader, he can read back written directions several times or study the stories at home to help the information sink in. Although this strength helps the child compensate for a few years, it is exhausting for the child and for the parent, who has to spend so much extra time to help keep him going in school. The child may come home cranky and worn out and especially resistant to doing even more work at home.

Therapy for Children with an Auditory Memory Problem

The classroom teacher may need to work with the specialists to present new information, directions, and stories in a different way (or give fewer details) so your child is not too overwhelmed. These modifications should be included in your child's IEP (see chapter 4).

There are many ways a therapist or a teacher can help children improve their ability to listen and remember what they hear. Often the focus is on teaching the child to use visualization, subvocalization, and self-gesturing to aid in memory. The specialist may teach the child how to take notes in a way to remember key points from a classroom discussion. Additional emphasis may be placed on teaching good listening behaviors such as maintaining eye contact with the teacher, keeping the body still, and requesting clarification when confused.

At this time there is a lack of research proving the value of traditional listening "drills" that require a child to remember a series of words, numbers, sentences, or directions of increasing length. My experience shows that without teaching the child how to do it better, this kind of practicing has little benefit.

What Can Parents Do to Help a Child with an Auditory Memory Problem?

If your child has been diagnosed with an auditory memory problem, you will need to be careful about the way you speak to your child. Try to do the following:

- Get your child's full attention and eye contact before continuing to speak. ("Tamina, look at me. I want to tell you something.")
- Make sure you are in a quiet place when having a conversation. Turn off the TV, radio, dishwasher, and so forth.
- Remind your child to keep from touching or handling objects while listening (no tapping pencils, doodling, etc.).
- Keep your words short. Avoid long directions or complex sentences when speaking.
- Speak slowly, and pause between thoughts.
- Emphasize and repeat key points and directions.
- Give one direction at a time; wait until the task is completed to give the next one.
- If your child can read, write down the directions so she can refer to them as needed. Numbering them in order helps; for example, (1) Make your bed, (2) put away your toys, and (3) brush your teeth. If not, use pictures and sketches instead.

Children with auditory memory deficits need after-school time to relax, play, and participate in activities that are not so frustrating and challenging. It may help a child's self-esteem to get involved in sports, learn a musical instrument, take up dance, or try any other "nonschool" activity. But therein lies the dilemma: How do you help the child keep up with the class unless you spend considerable after-school time going over what was missed the first time in class?

Most schools set approximate time frames for children to spend at home each night on homework, depending on the grade level. Try to stick to the recommended time frame. If your child needs a great deal more time to keep up with the class, speak to your child's teacher about it.

Case Study: Sarah

Sarah first came to my attention in November of her first-grade year. She was having some difficulty learning to read and spell, so her classroom teacher referred her to our Student Study Team for help. She also had difficulty following directions as well as grasping her pencil the right way when writing, so her printing was a bit sloppy. Since Sarah was one of the youngest children in her class and had no preschool experience, the team decided to take a conservative approach. She was given remedial reading help three times a week. The classroom teacher was given some strategies to try in the classroom to help Sarah learn her letters and sounds. For example, Sarah was given clay to squeeze to help her strengthen her fingers so she could hold her pencil better, and she used a larger pencil with a special rubber grip. The teacher tried to give class directions in a simpler way, demonstrating what to do when possible. Sarah's progress was monitored every few weeks for several months.

Sarah's mother was concerned at this point. Her husband had had a learning disability as a child and remembered having problems from the very beginning, as Sarah was now experiencing. Her parents were anxious to prevent Sarah from getting too frustrated or feeling bad about herself. They worked with Sarah at home daily to help her learn her letters and spelling words.

By January, Sarah was doing better with her reading and spelling skills. She wasn't setting the world on fire, but she was making slow, steady progress. She still seemed lost at times when given directions, but she sat near a very patient little boy who would help her, so she was able to keep up in class. The classroom teacher also tried to check on her frequently to make sure Sarah understood what she was supposed to do.

At the end of the year we discussed having Sarah repeat the first grade, but we felt that Sarah would suffer more harm to her self-esteem by being held back than by possibly struggling in second grade. Besides, she had already made friends with several children and was on the tall side, so we decided to place her in second grade.

In second grade, Sarah was quiet in class and rarely volunteered to answer questions. Her reading and spelling skills were marginal. She usually seemed to be paying attention, but her teacher would call on her at times, and Sarah would not always be able to answer the question. In fact, the teacher found that Sarah was not able to recall the question at all. When it was rephrased or repeated, she would often be able to answer correctly. Although Sarah was not a stellar student, she plugged along in second grade until April.

Sarah began giving her mother and father a hard time about going to school. She was clearly not enjoying school. In class she seemed more and more tuned out. She had to have things reexplained often and, to keep up, looked more often at what the other students were doing. By this point in the year her classmates were able to read and spell on a much more advanced level than Sarah.

Sarah's second-grade teacher referred her to the Student Study Team again. This time a complete educational evaluation was performed to find out the source of Sarah's difficulties. The psychologist found Sarah's IQ to be overall solidly in the average range for her age, but he did find that she needed to have the directions repeated, sometimes several times, before she would answer the questions. She also couldn't repeat a series of numbers (8–3–5–9) when asked, which could be symptomatic of an auditory memory problem. Sarah also showed some problems with drawing tasks and tasks that asked her to match shapes. Yet on other types of tasks, Sarah's scores were well above her age level. This kind of contrast (high scores in some areas, very low scores in others), in addition to Sarah's performance in the classroom and normal IQ, indicated the presence of a learning disability.

The learning disabilities teacher found that Sarah had a great deal of knowledge about many things. However, she clearly demonstrated difficulties with oral directions and sounding out words using her knowledge of phonics. When she saw a word she didn't know, she just guessed any word that began with the first letter.

The speech-language evaluation was also interesting. Sarah had an enormous vocabulary, naming even the more obscure pictures with ease. Her speech was clear and appropriate. Her stories were full of details but somewhat weak in organization. However, her biggest problem was auditory memory. When asked to repeat this sentence: "John gave his brother a large brown basket," she responded: "John's basket is brown." When asked to repeat this: "Each girl wore a pretty blue hat and white gloves," she said: "The girls had hats and . . . I forget." On all the sentences longer than this, she simply answered, "I forget." When asked to follow oral directions, she performed poorly. Similar results were exhibited on any task that asked her to listen to long pieces of information and answer questions about it.

Based on Sarah's test scores, classroom performance, and behavior at home, she was diagnosed as having a learning disability, with auditory memory as a primary weakness. Sarah was able to receive help right in her classroom from the special education teacher and speech-language pathologist. Since there were several "problem listeners" in the classroom, lessons for improving listening were introduced each week to the whole class. The teacher modified the way she gave directions and presented new information. By adding these services and making some changes in the classroom, we were able to help Sarah enjoy school again. She is now a happy, although still sometimes challenged, fourth-grader.

Like all people with learning disabilities, Sarah will never be cured. However, she can learn successfully by using methods that are designed for her special needs.

In cases such as Sarah's, lately I often find that resources are stretched so thin in most school districts that children like her are overlooked since they manage to stay afloat, academically speaking. This may be due to incredibly hardworking children and parents who pay a huge price by forgoing afterschool activities and family functions on the weekend, just so the child can pass. Often, the child is not disabled enough to benefit from special education services, but has enough challenges that school is overwhelming. Districts who use a Response to Intervention (RtI) model can often provide some strategies and assistance, including modifying assignments. Alternatively, private schools that offer small classes and more opportunities for "hands-on" learning may be a good match for a child such as Sarah, as long as the curriculum is not overly rigorous. Look for more information on school selection in chapter 9, "Answers to Your Questions."

The "I Don't Understand What I'm Supposed to Do" Child: A Language Processing Problem (AKA Receptive Language/Auditory Comprehension)

I'm concerned about Manny. He's always been shy, but as he's getting older I'm beginning to think it's more than that. He's fine as long as he's playing with his friends or doing something physical, but he avoids conversations at all costs. He seems confused at times. I don't think he's a slow child, but he doesn't always seem to know what's going on. He's been defensive lately, which I'm not at all happy about. In school, he struggles to follow class discussions, and he often has no idea how to do his homework when he gets home. Thank goodness our neighbor is in the same class, because I'd never know what he's supposed to do. He reads well, but he doesn't seem to always understand what he read.

—Mother of Manny, age 8½

Children like Manny are more common than you think. Because he hasn't had serious behavior problems (*yet*) or struggled with reading or writing, Manny's problem has not stood out to his teachers or parents. Yet something is clearly not quite right, and his mother knows it. Is he "slow"? Is he simply a child who doesn't like conversations? Or is something else going on here?

In this section I discuss how to recognize and understand children with language processing problems and describe what can be done for them. Manny is exhibiting what is often referred to as a *language processing disorder*. It causes him to have difficulty comprehending what people say. The words float around in his mind and need time to be "processed" by his brain before he can really understand them. When someone talks too fast or says too much at once, the thoughts get even more scrambled, and he can't make sense of any of them. This problem has several names, which tend to be used more or less interchangeably: *receptive language weakness/deficit/disorder delay, language comprehension,* or *auditory comprehension deficit.* In younger children, or those with more pervasive language deficits, receptive language *delay* is typically the preferred term. However, I feel the term *language processing problem* also describes Manny's problem, because the words people use, the "language," is what is causing his confusion. The words are going in clearly and accurately via the auditory channel, but his brain can't interpret them efficiently.

As with several of the other problems we've discussed, a language processing problem often goes hand in hand with other kinds of speech, language, and listening problems, or learning disabilities. If Manny had exhibited one of these other problems, he might have been diagnosed earlier, because the speech-language pathologist would have tested his language processing skills as part of an initial comprehensive evaluation. But since Manny belongs to the group of children whose primary problem is language processing, he avoided a diagnosis for some time. The effects of the problem are now slowly creeping into his life.

In toddlers, preschoolers, and children with more significant disabilities, difficulties with language processing and receptive language directly impact their ability to remember and learn new words and concepts. These weaknesses with processing language can be caused by a variety of conditions including developmental disabilities, autism spectrum disorders, recurrent ear infections, inattention and hyperactivity, and even a mild hearing loss. Sometimes we have no idea why a child's receptive language is stalling. Anytime your child's expressive language is delayed, it is especially critical to rule out an underlying language comprehension weakness.

We often find that children who persist in speaking in one- or two-word utterances (usually nouns) longer than expected have delayed receptive language skills. When hearing questions, they often zero in on the noun and can't make heads or tails of the rest of it. For example, the question "Where did you find that ball, Joey?" requires a response. For a child with a language processing problem, the words that jump out might be *ball* and *Joey*. If we want to get Joey talking more and putting sentences together, we need to help him make sense of all those other little words in between the nouns! Sometimes, we later find that these children have auditory processing disorders, but usually they do not. It typically is truly a language-based disorder and not due to any kind of auditory pathway deficits. This can be confusing to parents because many teachers and professionals use the terms *auditory processing* and *language processing* interchangeably, but for a speech pathologist or audiologist, these are two separate disorders, though they are related and sometimes overlap (as described earlier).

Children with mild language processing problems are easy to miss at younger ages because conversation is less complex and there are fewer listening demands. As children grow older, they are asked to process and use more and more language. Children's play begins to take the form of jokes and ribbing. They watch TV shows that require understanding of what the characters say and why they are saying it. Characters talk about how they feel; they argue, try to persuade, and come up with all kinds of crazy ideas and stories. In school, more and more lessons are centered on listening to the teacher explain math principles, science concepts, and so on, and on listening to other students talk about any variety of things.

A child with a language processing disorder will miss a lot of information in all these situations. The following are some common problem areas for children with language processing disorders or delayed auditory comprehension of language:

Toddlers, Preschoolers, and Children with More Significant Disabilities

- *"Circle Time."* While everyone else's children are following along, a child with a language processing problem may look confused. Fingerplays and hand movements that follow along to the music may be hard to "get" because the words are flowing quickly and are hard to follow. The more overwhelmed your child gets, the more tuned out he may be.
- *Following directions.* Teachers often rattle off directions that may be too long or complex for your child to process. ("After you finish up with your project, I need all of you to meet with me in the art area. If you haven't finished it, please lay it carefully on the top of the blue cubbies.")

School-Age Children

- *Confusion with learning concepts through lecture-style teaching.* As children move from third grade to the fourth grade and beyond, classroom instruction is primarily oral and requires listening. For children who struggle to process language quickly and efficiently, concepts can be misunderstood or unclear, resulting in struggles with homework, in class discussions, and when taking tests.
- *Confusion with assignments, projects, and reports.* Nothing is more frustrating for your child than to work hard on an assignment, only to find out he completely misunderstood what to do and did it wrong, or that he didn't realize it was due on Friday. Special projects are usually discussed and explained in class, and a child with poor language processing often misunderstands the instructions.
- *Humor.* It is very abstract and requires a higher level of processing. Children with language processing problems may not "get the joke."
- *Idioms.* These are expressions we use that, taken literally, mean something entirely different from the intended message. What does someone mean when they say they are "under the weather"? Does it mean it's going to rain? "Put yourself in my shoes" and "Get outta here!" are other examples.
- *Long, complicated directions.* These tend to get "tangled" in the child's mind. It isn't so much that he doesn't understand what it means to "write something on the top line," or "circle every word with a long vowel," or remember what to do, as with auditory memory problems. It's just that the child needs time to process one piece of information before the next one is given, or else he gets totally confused. This is also true when Manny's mother tells him to look in the "left side of the top drawer of Jessica's dresser for the pair of scissors." Too many positions (first, second, top, left, right, etc.) in one sentence are too much to process at once for him.
- *Stories with lots of characters and events.* Listening to these may get confusing. The problem also surfaces when you try to explain the family's vacation agenda or plans for the afternoon if it requires several stops, times, and people's names.
- *Inferencing and reading comprehension.* As stories become more intricate, the subtext of the message in the story may become confusing. The child needs to keep track of details and process them, drawing conclusions and working with language on a much higher level. Children with poor oral language processing frequently have similar difficulties with reading comprehension since we essentially "talk to ourselves" when we read. However, when reading, we can slow

it down to match our processing rate or reread it if needed, which is not the case when we process spoken language.

- *Poor expressive language.* It stands to reason that a child's expressive language skills will typically not be stronger than the receptive skills. That is, if you don't understand it, you are hard pressed to use it, but that is not always the case. When children have weak expressive language skills, it is typically much more obvious. However, receptive language understanding may not be so obvious in casual conversation, so it is usually better detected with formal testing.

How Are Receptive Language Problems Diagnosed?

Receptive language problems are diagnosed by observing a child in different listening situations as well as by administering several standardized, formal tests. Does the child seem confused? Does the child frequently need to have the teacher reexplain the directions or instructions for an assignment? Can the child listen to a story and understand what is happening?

In these cases the speech-language pathologist has to act as a detective. Does the child have difficulty processing or comprehending the information because he doesn't know what certain words mean? For example, the child will easily become confused if a character fed a *kid* on the farm, if the word *kid* is not understood. Therefore, testing a child's vocabulary is an important part of understanding the root of his confusion.

Another skill the evaluator will want to check is the child's auditory memory, discussed earlier in this chapter. If the child can't remember what is being said, comprehending it will be difficult if not impossible. Many times a child has a language processing problem *and* an auditory memory problem. The primary difference between the two problems is that the child with an auditory memory problem can comprehend and process what was said but quickly forgets it, perhaps even before responding. The incoming message jumps out of the child's mind. It can also be considered a problem with "working memory." The child with a language processing problem may know what was said, but misinterpret, rather than forget, it. Again, in many cases there is a combination of difficulties present.

Obviously, a hearing problem will also have to be ruled out. If certain other symptoms are present, the speech-language pathologist or other specialist may want to have an audiologist test for central auditory processing problems, discussed at the beginning of this chapter.

If a child has difficulty keeping her attention on one thing, an attention deficit disorder (AD/HD) may cause her to function as though she has a language processing problem. In this type of case, treatment for AD/HD will improve the child's ability to focus on a message long enough to comprehend it. It is often more challenging to diagnose children with inattentive-type attention deficit disorders, because there is typically no associated hyperactivity. Petit mal seizures should always be ruled out, which is just one more reason to have a qualified medical physician make this diagnosis.

In cases of children with intellectual disabilities, language processing ability will always be affected, as are all language and listening skills. Weak language processing skills are part of a bigger, more global problem for a child with cognitive delays, and it would not be appropriate to diagnose this child as having a language processing disorder per se, although the clinician would likely indicate delayed or weak receptive language skills.

Characteristics of Children with a Language Processing Problem

As with all speech, language, and listening problems, a child may manifest only one or many outward behaviors of a language processing problem. Children with a language processing disorder might do the following:

- Misunderstand or confuse what is being said
- Need directions explained several times and sometimes need demonstrations
- Need an unusual amount of time to think before answering a question
- Watch what everyone else is doing to figure out what to do
- Make comments that don't fit the discussion
- Have difficulty following the plot of a TV show or a movie; ask questions that reflect a lack of understanding of the critical points of the story
- Have other speech, language, listening, or learning disabilities
- Have a history of frequent middle ear infections
- Have unexplained behavior problems or dislike school
- Tune out or not pay attention during listening tasks

How Does a Language Processing Problem (or Receptive Language Weakness) Affect a Child?

In toddlers and preschool children, weak receptive language skills are often observed as the child "tuning out" when people are having conversations around him. The child may be playing contentedly, but not really *listening* to anyone. When expressive language skills are severly delayed, receptive language is the first thing an SLP will be checking. Because younger children are more active in their playing (going on slides and swings and running around), there is less emphasis on conversational language skills, and receptive language demands are fairly low in social situations. As children reach preschool, the linguistic demands increase and the associated behaviors may become more obvious.

In elementary school, a child with a language processing problem may eventually feel a bit left out and may begin to react to that by avoiding or tuning out conversations. Children like Manny can feel very isolated when everyone in the group is laughing and they don't quite know why. "Maybe they're laughing at me?" You can see how easy it would be for Manny to become defensive or hostile when he doesn't quite understand what people are saying. The problem can manifest itself in a number of ways:

- *Conversation*. When everyone else is participating in an intense dinner table discussion, Manny might sit passively or begin playing with his food or his fork. With friends, he might unconsciously avoid conversational situations by initiating physical activities such as bike riding, playing tag, or roller skating. As he grows into a teenager, team sports or creative pursuits such as drawing, dancing, or music may become his focus.
- *Self-esteem*. Children who have self-esteem problems are already at risk for misinterpreting what people say to them or about them. Compound that with a language processing disorder and you may see a child who is very evasive or defensive during conversations, particularly when a confrontation or a heated discussion is taking place. Feeling confused when your friends understand something tends to lower a child's self-esteem, which is why many children with this problem feel that they're stupid.
- *Off-topic comments*. Sometimes children with a language processing problem make comments that are related to, but perhaps a little bit off, the topic you are talking about. That's because they are not quite sure what the point of the discussion is at times.
- *Verbal humor.* As discussed earlier, understanding humor is sometimes difficult for students with a language processing problem. That is not to say they are not funny. They can make *you* laugh in any number of ways, with slapstick (doing gross things or making faces) or by mak-

ing simple jokes. It's when someone else uses *language* to make a verbal joke such as with a pun or a play on words, rather than, say, sticking straws up his nose, that they get thrown. You may see them laughing when everyone else does, but they really don't know what is so funny.

- *Reading comprehension.* Because reading involves processing language, a child with this problem may have to read very slowly or read something several times before it makes sense. This can be a time-consuming chore, and children tend to get very anxious when they see everyone else on page 12, and they're still on page 8. So they may speed up, but they really do not understand what they're reading.

- *Understanding test questions.* Taking tests can be frustrating for a child with a language processing problem. If the questions are read by the teacher orally, the child will be at a disadvantage because she may not have enough time to process the question before needing to write the answer. If the questions are written, they should be phrased clearly and simply, or the child may easily misinterpret what is being asked.

Children with mild language processing problems will need to work extra hard in school to keep up with the class, but it can be done. Choosing a career that takes advantage of a child's other strengths will be important.

Therapy for a Child with a Language Processing Disorder or Receptive Language Delay

Intervention for a child with a language processing disorder depends on a number of factors. Are there other related problems, such as weak auditory memory or learning disabilities? How severe is the problem? How old is the child? In some cases, therapy may be appropriate to work on certain listening skills and improve a child's ability to process certain language forms, such as idioms or humor. Typically, children with mild problems are taught ways to compensate for the problem. These children are usually phased out of a formal program in a year or two. As with many forms of listening disorders, there is no cure for a language processing disorder, but children can certainly improve and develop their ability to comprehend language through therapy and good teaching.

For toddlers, preschoolers, and children with more significant disabilities, therapy will likely focus on the following:

- *Learning word meanings.* In the very young child or the child whose receptive language is progressing slowly, the emphasis will be on learning the meaning of individual words, and then processing them when they are embedded in slightly longer contexts. In the beginning, this may be just a single word, then two or three, and eventually a short sentence! Typically we start with nouns, then move quickly to action words (verbs), spatial concepts (*on/in/under/behind/on top/bottom,* etc.), and early descriptors (*big, little,* colors, etc.)

- *Drawing attention to the "little words" in a sentence.* All those little functor words (*to, at, with, is, by,* etc.) are often ignored by children who are comprehending primarily nouns. The SLP will want to introduce one concept at a time and teach it. Auditorily, the word will need to be emphasized throughout the session and the week. ("Daddy is *at* work. You made this picture *at* school.") Visually, the SLP may find it very helpful to pair the word with a gesture or sign of some kind. It doesn't need to be a real sign that anyone else knows. After all, the point is not for the child to sign to other people but to draw attention to the word and visually associate it with the word. By having a sign associated with the verbal production, the child can also retrieve it for better expressive use.

- *Answering "wh" questions.* From the youngest ages, the "wh" questions pose a challenge for children who struggle with language processing. For toddlers, preschoolers, and children with language delays, these questions would start with who, what, and where. In conversation, you may find that your child struggles with questions such as, "Where did you put the car?" or "What did you find in the basket?" Even if expressive language is an issue, we'll want your child to be able to find and show you the item regardless. It will be helpful to start with just one "wh" type of question at a time.

- *Yes/no questions.* "Would you like some juice in your cup?" A child who has trouble with language processing may key in to the words *juice* and *cup* and not realize what you are asking. Instead, he may repeat part of the question or not respond at all. Sometimes pairing the verbal response with the associated nod or shake of the head requires a bit of gentle "hands-on" help and practice.

- *Pronouns.* "Give the ball to *her.* Now give that to *me.*" Pronouns are relative, and they change from situation to situation. Children with language comprehension problems frequently struggle with them. The SLP will want to introduce each one—or pair (such as *he* and *she*)—at a time.

- *Comprehending prepositions and spatial concepts.* "Go put the ball *next to* the chair." A child with receptive language processing weaknesses may know he's supposed to do something with the ball, but what that is may not be clear. We often find pairing prepositions with gestures or signs helps not only to mark them in sentence structures, but also to associate the word with its meaning.

- *Comprehending negation.* "We *aren't* going to the park." It may seem clear to you, but a child with a receptive language delay may hear "going to the park" and miss entirely the first part of that sentence.

- *Attending to storybooks.* Your child may enjoy sitting and listening to you read while looking at the pictures, but how does he respond when you ask questions? "Which bear is looking for the honey? What is the baby bear doing in her bed?" A child with an auditory comprehension problem may very well get fussy and irritable when you try to ask questions. They aren't a predictable part of his story, and he may not know how to answer them. Keep questions simple at first to avoid undue frustration. Using storybooks to not only learn language that's on the page but also to attend to what's not on the page is good practice.

- *Following directions.* Attending to a direction, holding onto it in our working memory, sustaining focus, and carrying it out requires a delicate weaving of skills, not the least of which is comprehending it. "First go hang up your jacket, then find a yellow crayon and sit down." Two of the key words in that direction are *first* and *then*. They signal to us what the order is supposed to be. Therapy will work on helping your child key in to these important parts of the direction, as well as master the listening and attending behaviors to carry it out.

- *Learning how to visualize.* If I told you I had lunch yesterday in Paris, at a little outdoor bistro, I bet you have already imagined it. Can you see the tables and chairs? Hear the music? Children often "hear" the words spoken, but don't create an image in their minds. When they hear "She went to school," they need to know that "she" requires them to imagine a girl, and that "went" means it happened already. The child has to learn to break down each sentence and picture it correctly. Later the child can work up to picturing complete sentences and stories. One program for visualizing stories is Lindamood-Bell, which provides specific training in this and publishes materials. Another program that addresses visualization strategies was developed by this author as part of a larger metacognitive-based approach (a Metacognitive Program for Treating Auditory Processing Disorders by proedinc.com).

For school-age children, therapy will likely cover these areas:

- *Understanding test questions.* What does it mean if the test says, "Explain how the main character intimidated his younger brother.

Describe his favorite method for doing so and the impact it had on his brother." Your child may fully understand the book but do poorly on the tests. If the test had asked, "What kinds of mean things did the boy do to his brother?" your child could probably ace it. But the way test questions are worded can make the difference between an A and an F. The SLP or specialist who works with your child will need to help him interpret these kinds of questions so he can show off how well he really does understand the book.

• *Understanding complex directions*. Oral instructions, but also written instructions, can be hard for children with processing problems to process. When projects and multistep directions are involved, the child might come home and have absolutely no idea what to do. Perhaps he thinks the book report is due a week from Monday but it's actually due next week *on* Monday. Children like Manny often need a buddy who is a good student, to call him up and check these things out. The speech pathologist or instructor will need to help Manny learn to use strategies to dissect the direction, write down key pieces of information, and visualize what the final product will look like.

• *Understanding inference*. The story said the girl "peeked behind the couch and quickly ran back inside, her mouth wide open, breathing hard." It didn't exactly state outright that she saw something scary or shocking, but there are clues the reader should pay attention to that lead us to that conclusion. Some children can understand language at a very literal level, but struggle to go to the next step and put all those pieces of the puzzle together. This often becomes more apparent around fourth or fifth grade. In the context of reading comprehension, a good reading tutor or teacher can assist your child in learning how to understand inferential reasoning, as can an SLP or a special education teacher. However, it's helpful for you to know that this kind of difficulty is indeed part of a bigger language processing difficulty and not specifically just a "reading" problem.

• *Understanding idiomatic expressions*. "Give me a hand." "He's a pain in the neck." "Don't beat around the bush—give it to me straight." These are examples of idioms. They are often confusing to nonnative speakers of the English language, but they are also just as likely to be challenging for children with poor receptive language skills. In many cases, each of the most common phrases will need to be directly taught so it can be understood since these children don't typically deduce meaning well from context.

• *Understanding puns and verbal humor.* Sometime in second and third grade, it starts. First the knock-knock jokes, then the riddles and the puns. For children with language processing problems, these go right over their head. Helping a child dissect a simple joke and understand why it's funny is often part of the therapeutic process.

• *Understanding multiple meanings.* School-age children with poor language processing often struggle with words with multiple meanings. What does it mean if you "ran up his electricity bill"? What is someone trying to tell you when they say the weeds will "spring up" after the rain?

• *Classroom and teaching modifications.* In a public school, the emphasis of the intervention may be on adjusting the teacher's expectations and teaching style within the classroom rather than on "fixing" the child. Since a language processing problem impacts the child's ability to take in information, the school may need to provide extra help or support in the classroom. Science, social studies, reading (comprehension), and other subjects may need to be retaught in small pieces on a simpler level. However, most schools do try to achieve this within the regular classroom with help from special education teachers, paraprofessionals, and/or the speech-language pathologist.

What Can Parents Do to Help a Child with a Language Processing Problem?

As with all speech, language, and listening problems, patience is an important virtue for any parent who has a child with a language processing problem. You can help your child by keeping these thoughts in mind:

• Speak slowly. Children with processing problems can comprehend better when speakers slow down from their typical pace.
• Make sure your child is looking at you and "ready" to listen before you talk.
• Use body language and gestures to help make your point.
• Repeat and paraphrase important messages, and ask questions to make sure your child has processed them. ("Be home by six o'clock. Make sure you're here by six o'clock. . . . When do you have to be home?")
• Pause between thoughts to allow time for your child to process the idea. ("After dinner, I'd like you to babysit Emma. . . . You can watch TV together or play a game. . . . Just make sure you're both in bed by ten thirty.")
• Keep your sentences short. In other words, if you are upset with your child, say, "I'm very upset right now. . . . What you did makes me

unhappy," rather than "You know, every time I tell you to do something it seems you just do whatever you want. I'm very annoyed because what you did was totally uncalled for. . . ."

- Encourage your child to ask questions when she doesn't understand. Children with a language processing problem already feel "dumb" at times, so they often hesitate to ask questions. Let your son or daughter know that asking questions shows a person is listening and cares enough to really understand what someone is saying.

- Explain idioms, or other figurative language, if you use them or hear them being used with your child. Don't assume she knows what you mean when you say "Keep a lid on it."

Case Study: Andre

Andre appeared to be a typical fourth-grade student in most respects. He was a B–C student in most subjects and had not presented a major concern to his past teachers, although several had expressed a feeling that something "just wasn't clicking" with him. When the SLP asked them to file a formal referral, they usually backed down, saying he wasn't failing and that they had to deal with students with far more serious problems first.

However, by April, Andre's classroom teacher and his father were very concerned with his poor attitude. Andre was combative when asked to do assignments at home and goofed off in class instead of paying attention. He was having more and more trouble passing tests, but this was attributed to his poor attitude and lack of studying.

Although he continued to struggle, he got through the rest of the year. In fifth grade, as he grew comfortable with the teacher, Andre expressed feelings of "I'm dumb" more and more. A number of interventions were attempted through the Student Study Team, but little change was observed. The SLP requested permission for some testing to make sure Andre didn't have any other underlying language or listening problems, and the special education teacher also did some testing for learning disabilities.

The testing revealed that Andre had a high-average IQ with strengths in many areas, including visual-spatial skills. However, his performance on listening tests revealed a significant problem with language processing. He understood what words meant when they were presented in isolation, but in the context of a paragraph or complex directions, he became very confused and frustrated. The learning disabilities testing showed problems with reading comprehension.

The teacher changed the way she structured questions asked of Andre and how information was presented to him, and his stress level was reduced. Intervention by the special education teacher and speech-language pathologist helped him develop compensation strategies and function more effectively in the classroom. As he began to feel more successful, Andre's attitude began to change. He developed a new understanding of why he felt so stupid at times and began to take more pride in his superior math and art abilities. He stopped putting himself down and took chances in answering and asking questions. Since his homework was tailored to his individual needs, he was less resistant to doing it. His parents supplemented his public school program with private therapy, and in high school, with private subject-area tutoring.

Andre, like the other children we've discussed, will likely continue to exhibit weak language processing skills, which often persist into adulthood when college students try to read and comprehend complex information in textbooks or soak up lectures. However, its effects were most likely significantly minimized by the intervention he received and by his gaining a new understanding of himself. Andre is now the owner of a very successful plumbing business.

8

Causes and Associated Conditions

Each child presents a unique set of abilities and challenges, many of which don't fit the textbook, or classic, profile. Although I have described many of the most common speech, language, and listening problems in previous chapters, there are many more that may be affecting your child. In this chapter, you will read about some of these causes of speech, language, and listening problems as well as special conditions that bring their own set of unique issues.

This chapter discusses serious topics such as abuse and neglect, lead poisoning, and oxygen loss to the brain. It also covers other problems that can often contribute to speech, language, and listening problems, such as frequent ear infections, mouth breathing, and thumb-sucking.

In addition, the chapter contains information on associated conditions such as Down syndrome, cleft palate, attention deficit disorder, autism, and cerebral palsy. Many children with these handicaps have physical, mental, or medical conditions that require a great deal of attention or running back and forth to the doctor. Therefore, it's natural for parents to push aside things such as how well their child speaks or listens, especially when they are celebrating getting through the child's latest surgery. However, it is important to remember that helping children improve language and listening development will also have a profound effect on their future.

Common Causes of Speech, Language, and Listening Problems

Usually the first question a parent asks me after an evaluation is "Does my child have a speech problem?" followed by "Did I do something wrong?" I think, deep down, that is the fear of most parents whose child—the child they love with all their heart, the child they would die to protect—is not developing normally. Could they have unwittingly done this? The answer is usually no.

We in the speech-language pathology field focus our attention on determining a child's present speech and language skill level through an in-depth evaluation. This gives us valuable information that tells us how we can capitalize on the child's areas of strength as well as facilitate growth in the weaker areas. It also helps us to know which techniques will probably be more successful than others. The purpose of the evaluation is not to find fault with parents, make them feel guilty, or analyze marital problems or lifestyles.

Your speech-language pathologist may suggest *changes* in how you interact with your child to facilitate growth with certain skills, but you should never take this as a criticism of your parenting style. The goal is to make the most of the time you have with your child. Some children need a more aggressive approach than others. It doesn't mean that what you've been doing is wrong; it merely means that your child has special needs and may require more attention, or a different kind of attention, from you than a typical child who is learning to speak. Other times there may be contributing physical factors (such as orthodontic problems, hearing problems, and allergies) that need to be addressed before clear speech can be achieved.

In this chapter I discuss what we know about these causes of some speech, language, and listening problems. I hope this section provides some reassurance, as well as advice, about how to avoid a similar problem in a younger sibling. Regrettably, there is still much research to be done on this topic. We don't have all the answers.

(In alphabetical order)

Abuse and Neglect

Perhaps the most frustrating cases we see as clinicians are children who came into this world with great potential or who *could have*, but do not, progress as expected because of their parent's or caregiver's actions.

Communication problems in children can sometimes be caused or worsened by the following:

- Drug or alcohol abuse by the mother during pregnancy.
- Poor prenatal nutrition.
- Abuse by neglect—these are situations where babies and toddlers are basically left alone or in front of a TV set for the better part of their day; they may also be malnourished and often are removed from the home and placed in foster care by state agencies.
- Physical abuse—unfortunately, there are documented cases of children who have suffered brain damage from physical abuse by a parent, stepparent, or other caregiver.

As you can probably guess, the parents of these children are generally not apt to seek help for them, for a variety of reasons. However, you may have adopted a child or care for a foster child whose problem is a result of these kinds of abusive behaviors. Or you may know someone whose child is at risk because of a substance abuse problem during pregnancy. These children need help right away because, although the odds are against them, with aggressive, early treatment, tremendous improvement *can* take place.

In speaking about "abuse by neglect," I am not referring to the amount of TV a typical child watches but about the television being used as a babysitter. Television programs can't ask questions or hold conversations with a child. Some educational programs on public television stations offer excellent benefits to the children who watch them, but someone needs to show interest in a child for meaningful language development to occur.

Congenital Conditions

Some conditions are present at birth and predispose a child to speech and language delays. Some of these are Down syndrome, cerebral palsy, cleft palate, congenital deafness, and Hunter's syndrome (these are discussed later in this chapter). Sometimes a child loses oxygen during the birth process when the umbilical cord is wrapped around the neck or if the child temporarily loses heart function. Children born as a result of traumatic births following an incident such as the mother's falling down a flight of stairs or being involved in a car accident should be watched carefully for later problems.

Premature babies are not necessarily as at risk as they were years ago. With early intensive medical intervention and technology, premature babies without permanent birth defects can recover completely, catching up with their peers in a few years. Recent studies do not indicate any higher prevalence for language or learning problems for these children than for full-term children. However, if there was oxygen loss at birth, inadequate medical care, or other extenuating health issues, the risk does increase.

Fluctuating Hearing Loss from Frequent Ear Infections

Children who have had frequent ear infections in the first three years of life are at risk for speech and language delays. Defining "frequent" is difficult, but I would consider three or more infections in the first three years often enough for the child to be closely monitored. Many children referred for speech and language delays have a history of ear infections. Additionally, difficulty with remembering information (auditory memory) and understanding spoken information (auditory processing) may persist long after the hearing ability returns to normal.

Inherited or Imitated Family Speech and Language Deficits

It is not uncommon for a speech-language pathologist to treat brothers and sisters for similar speech problems. Whether this is due to nature or nurture has never been proven conclusively. It seems remarkable, though, that a child who is exposed to many, many different correct speech models (through friends, television, and neighbors) throughout the day would copy the one sibling whose speech pattern is distorted or agrammatical. Yet we do see these patterns in families happen sometimes.

The family patterns I have encountered tend to be mild articulation problems (lisps, distortions of *r* or *l*) and language delays or learning disabilities. Sometimes a parent also displays the same problem during our initial meeting and may or may not be aware of the connection. I have treated parents and children together for articulation problems when the parent initiates interest in correcting his or her own problem. It is not impossible to remediate a child's articulation problem if the parent continues to speak incorrectly, but it is more challenging!

Lead Poisoning

Lead poisoning is still a very serious problem in the United States. Your child does not have to eat chips of lead-based paint to become lead-poisoned. Research shows that children are being poisoned by inhaling the dust in the air from lead-based paint or by drinking water contaminated from lead pipes. A simple blood test can determine whether your child is suffering effects of lead poisoning. Ask your doctor to perform this test if you are concerned. Your local health department may provide free screenings for this problem.

Lead-based paint was sold before 1974, when the federal government passed a law banning it. This paint can be disturbed merely by opening and closing a window with an old coat of paint on it. When renovations are done on an old home, lead-based paint is often disturbed. Visiting an older home undergoing renovations for a long weekend can be enough to cause a problem, if only temporarily. However, even short exposures *can* have long-term repercussions for a child.

A child only needs to inhale a small amount of contaminated air to be poisoned. If the lead problem is not corrected, the poisoning can soon result in permanent learning and behavioral disorders. Children under age 6 are considered to be at the greatest risk for lead poisoning. The adults in the same home may have no symptoms at all, because their bodies can fight off the lead poisoning more easily. A child with lead poisoning will typically become agitated and cranky and may in time develop attention deficit problems and learning disabilities (including language problems) if the lead source is not identified and removed. Early detection and removal of the source will prevent permanent problems.

Lead pipes also can contaminate your water source. Before buying a house, have the water in your home checked for lead, even if it is not mandated by your state real estate laws. If your child is found to have lead poisoning, you will need to locate the source. Don't forget to have your water examined for a high lead content.

The Centers for Disease Control and Prevention in Atlanta, at (404) 639-3311, can refer you to proper resources and current pamphlets on this subject.

Intellectual/Cognitive Disabilities

This is a difficult diagnosis to make at a young age, because intellectual testing is often unreliable, except on a gross scale, before age 7. This is one reason why school systems tend to call all children who are behind their peers in two or more areas before this age *developmentally delayed* unless a physician or a psychologist makes a more specific diagnosis. These children have difficulty in most, or all, developmental areas. They typically have delayed milestones for nonspeech skills such as walking, playing appropriately, manipulating puzzles, and self-care such as dressing and feeding themselves. Sometimes they do these things at the proper age, but the quality of their skills is poor. Intellectually disabled children never completely catch up, no matter how much intervention they receive, but their prognosis is much improved with early and appropriate therapy. Speech, language, and listening will be a lifelong challenge for these children. Today's public educational system, however, is staffed and trained to accommodate and develop *every* child's skills to the highest possible level. You can and should take advantage of every opportunity to help your child achieve the most he or she can if your child has an intellectual disability.

Mouth Breathing

A child with ongoing allergies often finds it difficult to breathe through the nose, forcing him into the habit of breathing through the mouth. Enlarged adenoids or tonsils can contribute to the problem. Breathing through the mouth causes the tongue muscles to become off balance, in a forward position. Children who consistently breathe through their mouth sometimes develop a "lispy" quality when pronouncing words with sounds such as *s* and *z*, because their tongue lies forward between their teeth. Therapy to correct the lisp typically is more effective if the child's nasal passages are cleared and breathing through the nose is relearned. If the child's tongue muscles have had a long time to become unbalanced, a forward swallowing pattern also may need remediation before the lisp can be successfully corrected.

Neurobiological and Mental Health Disorders

Children with neurobiological and mental health conditions often exhibit symptoms of communication disorders. Sometimes they do have speech, language, or listening difficulties as well, but other times their condition is mistaken for a communication disorder. We also often find that children on the autism spectrum or those with "quirky" personalities have one or more of these accompanying issues. In many cases, there is a genetic predisposition to them. Here is a quick snapshot of some conditions that may impact your child:

• *Anxiety.* Anxiety can come in all shapes and sizes. Sometimes it's as subtle as a child who is too frightened to answer a teacher's question lest she get it wrong; or it can be a severe social anxiety that makes interacting with other children at school difficult. For children who suffer with anxiety, worry thoughts can be very preoccupying. It's hard to process what someone else is saying if your mind can't stop thinking, such as *What if I am late for the bus? What will I do?* It is easy to assume that these children don't understand the teacher's question because they may be "tuned out" and consumed with their own thoughts. For some children who are working on social language and pragmatic issues, the lack of carryover may not be due to a lack of knowledge in terms of what to do, but the lack of ability to carry it out. For example, the child may fully know how to initiate conversation and join a group (intellectually) but be frozen in fear when the opportunity arises to transfer that skill in a real-life situation. In these cases, a clinical psychologist and/or a psychiatrist can make all the difference. Research shows that interventions such as cognitive-behavioral therapy (CBT) are extremely effective for children whose lives are impacted by anxiety; it is sometimes paired with medication.

• *Obsessive-compulsive disorder (OCD).* Children with OCD often have rituals they feel compelled to complete. It may be tapping a pencil exactly ten times, erasing any misformed word they've written, counting their steps, or touching every child three times before leaving the class. If you get in the way of their completing these rituals, you may find their emotional regulation suffers and a "meltdown" may occur. Many times the rituals are done secretly, especially if the child is intellectually and socially fairly normal. They realize that these kinds of behaviors are *not* normal. It is easy to assume they can just stop doing something, but for them, it is not a choice they feel they can make. For example, there have been times that I've gotten referrals for children who are assumed to have some kind of auditory processing disorder because the child won't "listen" to the direction, such as "Put your name at the top of the paper." But a child with OCD, whose perfectly aligned pencils fell out of his case, *cannot* move on until the pencils are exactly where they are supposed to be. The teacher interprets his actions as not following directions or, even worse, being defiant. In playing games with their peers, they may resist any attempt to change rules, as inflexibility and an aversion to change often accompany OCD behaviors. Like anxiety, it is responsive to cognitive-behavioral therapy and medication.

• *Tourette's syndrome (TS).* Children with Tourette's sometimes can be quirky, and may also have any number of accompanying mental health conditions, although TS itself is very much a neurological disorder and can range from very slight cases to severe. People with TS have tics, which are repetitive sounds, movements, or actions they have little control over. These tics change over time, and come and go. Children with Tourette's may develop vocal nodules if they clear their throat or bark repeatedly for long periods of time, which are common tics. In these cases, identifying and treating the TS is critical to managing any related voice problems. Children with TS often have bouts of stuttering, which may be exacerbated by stress (even happy stress, such as a trip, a holiday, or a birthday). Currently there is little or no available research on the efficacy of traditional stuttering treatment for children whose disfluency is rooted in TS; however, in situations where it is ongoing and causing frustration, it may be worth trying. Children with TS may also struggle to inhibit their tics in the classroom. When that happens, it is difficult for them to focus on the instruction because all their energy is being used to restrain their tics. This is one reason why many in the field urge teachers and classmates to avoid demanding that children with TS do so. Conversely, some children with TS take one or several medications that limit the tics but which make them sleepy and lethargic. When the medications wear off after school, the tics can increase so much that sustained attention for homework is in short supply. In most cases, there is a comorbid AD/HD component, which can make behavioral control a challenge. Last, because some tics are considered socially unacceptable (spitting, picking their nose, making fart noises with their mouth, copralalia—cursing or saying socially unacceptable things) it is easy to think they are intentional. With TS, they are not done for a "purpose" but are tics. Because the feeling of releasing a tic is often pleasant, particularly if it's been restrained, the child may smile or seem content afterward, but again, this does not necessarily mean he is happy that he just spat and upset his parent or teacher. Confusing? Yes, for the child and for the adults. If you have a child with TS, check out the Tourette Syndrome Association's Web site, www.TSA-USA.org, for a wealth of information. There is a terrific DVD called *A Teacher Looks at Tourette Syndrome* featuring Susan Conners, an engaging teacher with Tourette's syndrome herself.

Oxygen Loss from Trauma

If your child's oxygen supply is restricted, even for a short time, permanent brain damage can occur. This is another type of traumatic brain injury (TBI). Traumatic brain injury is exhibited by a regression or lack of improvement in your child's speech and language skills. In infants, TBI is more difficult to detect by behavior alone. You may find your child's crying patterns to be different, eye gaze less focused, and general alertness changed. A neurologist is a medical specialist who can tell you whether your child has suffered brain damage as a result of this type of trauma. If your child has experienced one of the following events, the attending physician will undoubtedly also know to check for this. Some events that cause a loss of oxygen to the brain include the following:

- Near drowning
- Near suffocation
- Reaction to a medical procedure
- Choking
- Temporary loss of heart function or pulse

For more information about speech, language, and listening issues related to traumatic brain injury, please refer to the section "Autism, Cerebral Palsy, Hearing Impairment, and Other Special Conditions" later in this chapter.

Seizures

Children with a history of seizures, whether from a high fever, an unknown origin, or a seizure disorder such as epilepsy, are at greater risk for developing language deficits. Sometimes a baby or a toddler may even show a regression in language development for a period of time following the seizure. Often speech, language, and listening functioning may improve or resume its previous level with time. However, repeated seizures sometimes can result in permanent brain damage, which could have an impact on a child's speech, language, and listening skills. Children who seem to suddenly develop "ADD-like" behaviors in elementary school or later should be checked for petit-mal seizures, which can mimic these symptoms.

Selective Mutism

While the name of this condition suggests there is a choice (selective) and that the child is unable to speak at all (mutism), neither of these accurately describes what is really happening for a child with selective mutism. This condition is a form of anxiety. Typically, the child is normally communicative at home, but extremely unresponsive in public places, such as school. The child may not verbally respond, point, or indicate any response when asked a question. Any pressure that is put on the child to talk will often result in a further "shutdown." A fear of failure or of doing or saying something wrong often is associated with this condition, and children who suffer from it are extremely sensitive to reprimands of any kind. Other times the child may whisper or speak in short, telegraphic phrases or only to a favorite friend or adult. Children with selective mutism often have accompanying receptive or expressive language weaknesses. Because the nature of this communication difficulty is psychological in nature, the SLP will need to work closely with the treating psychologist or psychiatrist if there are accompanying speech or language difficulties. However, an SLP would not be the primary specialist who would treat selective mutism.

Teeth, the Jaw, and Your Child's Bite

When a child has untreated orthodontic problems, it sometimes will make pronouncing words difficult. For example, a significant overbite, crossbite, or underbite may cause certain sounds to be difficult to pronounce clearly. If, in addition, the child has a high, narrow palate and/or a tongue thrust, these factors can work together to make certain movements necessary for speech difficult. In most cases, a speech pathologist can help the child find another way to make the same sounds until the problem can be corrected. If this approach is unsuccessful, it may make sense to wait until the child's orthodontic problems have been addressed. During the orthodontic process, the child may have a large appliance for palate widening installed in the mouth, which would further hinder clear speech and make waiting a few weeks for the child to acclimate to the new appliance an appropriate course of action.

As a general rule, crooked teeth do not interfere with speech production.

When a child has missing front teeth, some sounds, such as *f* and *s*, are slightly distorted until the new teeth grow in, but typically there is no discernible change.

In some cases a child may have an adequate bite but still may demonstrate difficulty with appropriate jaw movements during eating and speaking. If a child slides the jaw from left to right or favors eating on one side, there may be a problem with the jaw muscles. Because the tongue is rooted in the lower jaw, where it goes is directly determined by where the jaw goes. If a child's jaw is not coming together in the correct way, the tongue will not go to the appropriate position when speaking. Muscle-based speech deficits are common in disorders such as dysarthria and hypotonia.

Thumb-Sucking and Bottle-Feeding Past Age 1

Many children suck their thumb or use bottles sporadically past age 1 with no apparent long-term effect on their speech. However, if a child does so on a daily, consistent basis, the habit can often cause the tongue and lip muscles to become off balance, resulting in a tongue thrust. These habits can also push the front teeth forward and cause future orthodontic problems. Tongue thrusting can result in a distortion of the s and z sounds. *Sh, ch,* and *j* can also be affected. When the child tries to pronounce these sounds, the tongue pushes between the upper and lower teeth as when making a *th* sound, instead of the correct sounds. Unless your child is on a special feeding program under the supervision of an occupational therapist or a speech therapist, try to wean your child onto a regular cup by age 1.

Thumb-sucking is a very difficult habit to break. What works for one child may not work for another. Some strategies work for a day or two, then lose their novelty and are no longer effective. It will take trial and error, time, and consistency for you to know which one will help the most.

To help your child break the thumb-sucking habit, try these strategies:

- Work on daytime sucking first. Since watching TV often prompts a child to pop her thumb into her mouth, set boundaries. If necessary, have your child wear a glove during TV time. When the thumb goes into the mouth, the TV goes off. Start with short intervals of time (five to ten minutes), then build up to a whole half-hour show. Some people find chewing bubble gum helps.
- Some people report success by taking an Ace bandage and lightly wrapping the arm, from a few inches below the elbow to a few inches above. When the child goes to such his thumb, the resistance from the wrap makes the thumb-sucking position either impossible or uncomfortable. This is especially effective for nighttime, when the the child is not even aware of what he is doing during sleep. However, take extra care not to wrap it too tight so circulation is not affected.
- Consider a reward chart. Every time your child can watch a whole half-hour show without thumb-sucking, you put a star or a sticker on the chart. When your child gets five or ten stickers, she earns some kind of special reward.
- In the beginning, try giving your child something to do with her hands (coloring, blocks) while watching TV to distract her from thumb-sucking.
- Once TV watching is conquered, add a new activity. Since traveling in the car often induces thumb-sucking, use that as your next goal. Start with short trips to the store (five to ten minutes), and give rewards on your chart. If necessary, use the glove in the car, too.
- Your next goal may be working on eliminating thumb-sucking after dinner, because thumb-suckers tend to do so when they are tired. Break

down the evening into smaller parts, such as from seven to seven-thirty. Reward the child for keeping the thumb out. Each week add an additional half hour: 7 to 8 P.M., then 7 to 8:30 P.M.

- Once your child's thumb-sucking is under control during the day, begin tackling the nighttime. You may find the glove helpful. Some people use a splint that you can buy at the drugstore for broken fingers, while others use the Ace bandage approach (see second bullet on previous page).

If you need more ideas, a pediatric dentist, orthodontist, or speech pathologist may help. The book *My Thumb and I: A Proven Approach to Stop a Thumb or Finger Sucking Habit for Ages 6–10* by Carol Mayer and Barbara Brown is a good resource as well. (It is available from Amazon.com.)

Unknown Causes

For many children, speech, language, and listening delays emerge for little apparent reason over time, becoming more noticeable at 18 months to 4 years of age, depending on the severity of the delay. Less severe communication deficits, such as articulation problems, stuttering, voice disorders, and processing difficulties, may be less noticeable or absent at this young age. It is not uncommon for them to go undetected until the elementary school years.

As speech-language pathologists, we do our best to pin down the cause of the problem. However, we accept that *in many if not most cases, we never know why a child's speech, language, and listening develop differently or more slowly than the average child's.*

Autism, Cerebral Palsy, Hearing Impairment, and Other Special Conditions

For some children, speech, language, and listening are particularly challenging tasks. When a child is born with, or acquires, physical or mental handicaps, it is the beginning of a new and sometimes daunting journey for the parent. *What will happen to my child? Will she ever be able to communicate the way other children do? What should I do to help my child make the most of these developmental years?* These are natural questions to ponder. Unfortunately, most of these questions are not easily answered at birth or in general terms. The old axiom "Each child is unique" really does hold true.

For example, ten people with Down syndrome can speak and function on ten different ability levels by the time they reach their twentieth birthday. Some people with Down syndrome grow up, work, and even marry. Others need more help with day-to-day activities, speak with great difficulty, and are less independent. Although there are common bonds that tie certain groups of children, what one child needs may be different from what another child needs. Education and speech-language therapy is not a one-size-fits-all proposition.

Only time will tell what the future holds for a child with one of these conditions. For now, parents can help their child make the most of all the special help and experiences life has to offer. Attitudes have changed in the past few years toward children with handicaps and special challenges. They have access to all kinds of therapies and technology that can make a big difference in their quality of life. Thus they can enjoy their childhood and do most of the things that any "normal" child can do.

In this section I briefly outline the nature of some special conditions and the associated speech, language, and listening issues of each, along with a short discussion of what kind of intervention you might expect. Although there are hundreds of neurological, muscular, and intellectual conditions and syndromes, I have selected the most common in the interest of space.

If your child has a special condition not described here, the American Speech-Language-Hearing Association can put you in touch with a specialist in your area who might be able to answer your questions. Phone numbers and addresses are included in appendix A. Many other organizations, public and private, that are devoted to helping children with handicaps are listed as well.

Attention Deficit Problems (AD/HD)

Some children who come to see me are very bright, yet have difficulty staying on task. Their minds are quickly and furiously checking out the pictures on the walls, the games on my shelves, and the objects on my desk. They want to touch and experience them all, and all at once. Everything distracts them, even themselves, though never intentionally. In years past the term *attention deficit disorder (ADD)* was used to describe this condition. The preferred term is now *AD/HD*, which includes children with or without the hyperactivity component. When a child has an attention deficit problem, listening and attending to a conversation or a classroom lecture is difficult. In a quiet room at home the problem may be less noticeable. But because a classroom is decorated with colorful posters, has the sounds of pencils being sharpened, and so on, these children have far more difficulty getting work done in school.

Most children with AD/HD function as though they have auditory memory and language processing problems. This is because the information they hear is not "getting in." They may tune out someone's voice and focus on another sound or something they can see, such as a bird or a squirrel in a tree out a nearby window. They can't remember or process a message that is not received in the first place. With medication (usually Ritalin, Concerta, or Strattera), physical maturation, and the use of coping strategies, children with AD/HD can improve their listening skills. However, listening and staying focused on someone speaking will probably always be a challenge for these children, even into adulthood.

Another issue for children with AD/HD is taking turns in a conversation or a classroom discussion. They are typically the children who call out answers and forget to raise their hand. Sometime they may repeat an answer someone else said or answer a previous question. This is not due to rudeness or insubordination. Rather, a child with AD/HD is typically impulsive by nature and acts quickly, without being able to process what other people say or wait for their turn. If they wait too long, their brain will have moved on to another thought by the time the teacher calls on them. When they do raise their hand, they will often say "I forgot" when the teacher asks them for their response.

In conversations, children with AD/HD also may have some difficulty at times keeping focused on the topic being discussed. They often digress from the question you ask and go off on many other related tangents. They may ramble and tell events out of sequence. They may interrupt the other person speaking, particularly at inappropriate times. Although they may be poor communicators at times for the reasons discussed, they may not necessarily have a language disorder, in the traditional sense of the term, in addition to their attention span problem. Sometimes they do. The two are so closely intertwined, it often may be difficult to tell. But because a child with AD/HD often functions as a child with a listening and/or language problem does, many of the suggestions for parents presented in chapters 6 and 7 hold true.

Autism Spectrum Disorders

Autism spectrum disorders (ASD) are a group of biologically based disorders of an unknown origin that affect the way a child communicates and interacts with the world. In 1994, the American Psychiatric Association developed specific criteria as outlined in its *Diagnostic and Statistical Manual IV* (referred to as the "*DSM* book") for diagnosing pervasive developmental disorders, which include the following subcategories: autistic disorder, Asperger's syndrome, pervasive developmental disorder-NOS (not otherwise specified), Rett disorder, and childhood disintegrative disorder. However, as of this writing, the 2013 *DSM*'s editors are seriously contemplating eliminating the Asperger's and PDD subcategories and instead considering those children to have a degree of an autism spectrum disorder. Most experts in the field of autism prefer the term autism spectrum disorder (ASD) to describe these related disorders.

No two children with ASD are exactly alike. However, they exhibit many common traits. Textbooks routinely state that delays are in the areas of social behavior, speech development, and sensory integration, but what does that mean? Here are some things you should look for.

Social Behavior and Autism Spectrum Disorders

Let's start with social behavior. When children share an activity or a conversation, it is called a *joint-attention* activity—that is, each person monitors the other's reaction and responds accordingly. Children with ASD have difficulty relating to how someone else is feeling. They may:

- Not notice when someone comes in or leaves the room; they often need to be prompted to say "Hi" or "Bye" each time and they may repeat your request verbatim. (You say, "Johnnie, say bye to Daddy." Johnnie says, "Johnnie, say bye to Daddy.")
- Often take an adult's hand to show they want something or to get help with something. Use the hand as an instrument, but not necessarily relating to the adult it is attached to. Not smile or express gratitude when helped.
- Avoid looking directly at people, except when prompted.
- Seem not to acknowledge, notice, or point out things in their environment to another person. (Not show you something of interest, such as a funny scene in a TV show or a picture they drew.)
- Have difficulty playing "pretend" games with puppets, dolls, and action figures. Not attempt to make them talk to or look at each other.
- Have difficulty taking turns. If you stop taking turns, will not prompt you to take your turn. Sit and wait indefinitely or continue the activity without you.
- Laugh, cry, or scream at inappropriate times and for no apparent reason.

- Have difficulty understanding or using facial expressions/gestures normally. If you look angry, scared, or shocked, they do not react.
- Have difficulty initiating or maintaining a conversation or an interaction except to get something they want or to talk about their favorite topic. Ask very few questions, such as "What's that?" or "Where are we going?"
- Be unusually focused on one theme, such as trains, maps, or memorized facts.
- Often be more interested in the parts of toys (spinning the wheels on a car) than actually playing with them in a make-believe way.
- Be resistant to physical touching, or conversely, readily hug almost anyone, including strangers.
- Often be very rigid with routines and inflexible with change. Get very upset when you sit in the wrong chair at mealtimes or vary where you put things.
- Like to line things up.

For more information on social language use, see chapter 6.

Speech-Language Characteristics of Children with Autism Spectrum Disorders

While lots of children have delayed speech and language skills, children with autism spectrum disorders have very specific language behaviors that set them apart from other "slow talkers." What concerns an SLP is the type of errors a child makes, not just the number of words he says or doesn't say. He may:

- Repeat things out of context, such as TV commercial dialogue or words to a song.
- Use jargon or nonsense syllables as words, beyond age $2\frac{1}{2}$ (may use real words in addition).
- Repeat a question that's asked, or the last part of it, instead of answering it (called echolalia).
- Not follow the normal pattern of language and concept development. For example, they may be able to name letters or numbers before being able to answer simple questions.
- Be delayed in terms of the amount of language used. They may not talk at all, or may just use single words, usually nouns.
- Speak with an unusual or unnatural intonation pattern. They may sound robotic, "singsongy," or whispery.
- Like to repeat one word or phrase over and over (called perseveration).

- Have difficulty comprehending what people say.
- Be very "independent"; going to get what they want rather than getting your attention and bugging you for it, either with gestures or with words.
- Not use gestures in a typical way. They may not nod for "yes" or shake their head for "no" as toddlers. Generally they do not accompany speech with gestures, such as to show something was really, really big.
- Have difficulty consistently performing tasks such as pointing to pictures unless you guide their hand or prompt them.
- Have difficulty generalizing words and phrases into new situations. If you play a game with the question "Where's the bird?" you may be able to teach the child to say "in the tree." However, if you use a different representation of a bird (toy) and put it somewhere else (in a house), the child cannot make the jump and therefore may just echo the question.
- Have difficulty with yes/no questions. (You say, "Would you like some cake?" The child may respond with silence, or echo the question or the word *cake*.)
- Not usually say "I don't know" or ask "What does that mean?" even if asked a question they couldn't possibly know the answer to, such as "Where is your tibia?" Instead, usually will not respond, or will echo the question or the last word.
- Not respond when someone calls their name. Often have to be taught to say "What?" as well as to look at the person when someone is addressing them.

Sensory Behaviors of Children with Autism Spectrum Disorders

Sensory information helps us perceive our world through sight, sound, smell, and touch. Children with these disorders often *under*react (hyposensitive) or *over*react (hypersensitive) to sensory input. One child may be hypersensitive to sound (he wails when you grind the coffee) yet hyposensitive to pain. Either way, it is clear the child is not perceiving things in the environment in a typical way. Children with an autism spectrum disorder may:

- At times appear "deaf" and unresponsive to sounds or talking, and at other times appear overly sensitive and bothered by commotion.
- React to sounds such as blenders, lawn mowers, and so on as though they are uncomfortable, by putting their hands over their ears, crying, or screaming.
- Have only a few foods they will eat, which are often bland-tasting and have softer textures. We call them "picky eaters."

- Be extrasensitive to strong smells or like to smell everything, even things such as cans, plastic cups, or clothing.
- May be very picky about clothing they wear, preferring only long or only short sleeves, even when the temperature dictates otherwise. May have favorite clothing they wear over and over. Often they are very uncomfortable with the labels in shirts.
- Flap their hands or arms—when excited or upset—in a repetitive way.
- Have some weaknesses with fine motor skills such as buttoning, zipping, or writing letters on lines.
- Have difficulty with gross motor skills such as riding a bike, balancing, or climbing on playground structures.
- Amuse themselves by spinning things.

Strengths of Children with Autism Spectrum Disorders

Children with autism may:

- Be unusually interested in letters or numbers, even children as young as 18 to 24 months old.
- Be very good with puzzles and building toys.
- Have a good memory for finding things, or remembering places they have visited, things that happened, or routines.
- Have an extremely good attention span for watching TV, playing a computer game, or other self-directed, independent activity.
- Be very good at drawing/art (usually after age 5 or 6).
- Be musically inclined.

The symptoms for these disorders present themselves during the first three years of life, although more typically by age 2 to 2½. Children with more pronounced symptoms, or a greater number of symptoms, are typically diagnosed with *autism* or infantile autism. Informally, it is sometimes referred to as "textbook" or "classic" autism.

Children with *PDD-NOS* (pervasive developmental disorders, not otherwise specified) have *some* autistic characteristics, yet not as many or as severe as a child with classic autism. PDD-NOS basically says the child is displaying *some* unusual language, sensory, and social behaviors that cannot be otherwise defined as a learning disability or a language disorder.

In addition to the symptoms discussed below, children with *Asperger's syndrome* usually have a favorite topic/interest (such as maps or addresses) that dominates their play and conversation, even when inappropriate. (An 8-year-old with Asperger's syndrome may ask the checkout clerk for her address, and most likely will remember it, even months later.) They may have an exceptionally good memory for recalling facts and information.

Rett syndrome is typically diagnosed in girls. It is uncommon and characterized by a regression of skills after age 1 or 2. A key symptom is loss of hand skills, with the child often engaging in a hand-washing or wringing motion.

Childhood disintegrative disorder is quite rare, resulting in a regression of most skills previously developed. The child often becomes severely impaired in most areas, with no discernible cause.

There are many different levels of abilities and expectations for a child with autism spectrum disorder. Formal testing is difficult, as these children are very inconsistent in their willingness to "perform" for people, especially strangers. Children with milder forms may have normal or above-normal scores on IQ tests. We do know the brain is affected, but to what degree and in what way are hard to quantify with a number and seem to vary from child to child.

Higher-Functioning Autism/PDD Disorders

Related conditions on the higher end of the autism spectrum are PDD-NOS (pervasive developmental disorders, not otherwise specified), Asperger's syndrome, HFA (high-functioning autism), semantic-pragmatic language disorder (SPLD), nonverbal learning disorder (NLD), and hyperlexia. These are related disorders with fewer or less severe symptoms than classic autism. Therefore they may not be diagnosed in a child who is quite verbal until the child is of school age or an adolescent. Some professionals believe many scientific geniuses, once considered to have eccentric or antisocial personalities, in fact have a mild form of autism or PDD. Sometimes children with these disorders have a close relative with some other type of ASD/PDD. In other cases they may have been diagnosed initially as "autistic," but improved such that their symptoms became less severe. Since much of the diagnostic criteria and treatment discussions for these milder forms just started appearing in mainstream professional publications in the 1990s, professionals often miss these signs or misdiagnose them. Because there are subtle differences in the use of each of these milder PDD labels, professionals may sometimes disagree about which one to use.

Social Language Use in the Child with Mild Autism

Children with these disorders have difficulty using language in a normal way, primarily in social situations, called pragmatics. They may not understand verbal humor, and have difficulty interpreting facial expressions and idiomatic language. "You're a pain in my neck!" to them means they are hurting your neck. Eye contact may be inconsistent, and the child may stand too close or too far when talking to others. It is often difficult for these children to understand that others do not know what they are thinking, so their language often rambles and it is hard for the listener to know what the child is talking about. Often, playing with other children presents difficulties, as children with these disorders tend to play (and talk) in a fairly one-sided manner, expressing themselves but not really interested in the other child's response or interest.

Children with these disorders have difficulty processing what is spoken to them and may misinterpret what they hear. Sometimes they may speak with good sentence structure and sound quite normal. Others may talk a lot, but the sentence structure may be somewhat weak and confusing. ("Give me that only thing you put over it!") Usually children with these milder disorders have a very good vocabulary for naming or pointing to pictures, although they may have difficulty using the words (word retrieval) in a conversation. Often they are good readers, although they may not understand everything they read.

Often, children with PDD/autism display difficulty with attention span and so may also be treated for attention deficit disorder. In addition, they may be treated for obsessive-compulsive disorder, anxiety, or mood swings as their need for routine and sameness may sometimes be consuming. New medications for autism spectrum disorder/PDD are being researched and tested all the time. Some children who are intellectually high-functioning may be good candidates for cognitive-behavioral therapy (CBT), which has been shown to be a very effective intervention for these related mental health conditions.

Although there are differences between autism and PDD, they share many similar characteristics. The diagnosis is made by a psychologist, a physician, and/or a team of specialists (such as a speech-language pathologist) after interviewing the parents and teachers, observing the child, and administering some formal tests. The severity and nature of the behaviors exhibited help differentiate between or among some of the choices.

The Incidence of Autism Spectrum Disorders

The number of children with these disorders has been increasing at an alarming rate in the past ten years. It is the second most common childhood developmental disorder, with 1 of 150 children being affected.

Certainly my experience bears out this incredible increase. While we as professionals are doing a better job identifying children with milder forms of autism, the diagnostic criteria for classic autism have been consistent over many years and would not explain this increase. Many parents report that their children were developing normally until the use of an antibiotic or a vaccine between ages 15 to 24 months, leading some to believe there is a link to a breakdown or weakness in the immune system. However, research has not shown there to be a link between vaccines and autism. Others report noticing autistic-like behavior in their child from birth, leading some to believe it is caused by a virus during pregnancy. Still others point to a possible genetic link, since there is sometimes more than one child in a family with ASD. Another hypothesis is that it is caused by an environmental hazard, since it sometimes seems to occur in geographic pockets. There are also some reports of children with intestinal problems (usually diarrhea) whose autistic behaviors improve after the intestinal disorders are addressed, leading some to believe that there is an association between the digestive system and autism. At this writing it is widely believed that there are a variety of unknown causes for this disorder.

Many different therapeutic, educational, and pharmacological approaches are used to help children with ASD, depending on the most prevalent symptoms, severity, parents' philosophy, and financial resources. Many of these treatments help, but to a widely varying degree. Many are expensive or very time-consuming and may offer only minimal improvement. It is still somewhat difficult to predict which children will respond to which approaches, so sometimes it is a trial-and-error approach, with a combination of interventions often being most appropriate. Just as each child is different, so is there no universally accepted way of treating these children and, as of this writing, no "cure" for autism spectrum disorders.

Speech-Language Therapy for Children with Autism Spectrum Disorders

Speech-language therapy for children with ASD usually focuses on improving functional communication (such as the child's being able to tell someone he wants something or needs to go to the bathroom), improving interaction with other children (looking at the other child, standing at the appropriate distance, understanding facial expressions), understanding how to answer simple questions ("What is your name?" "Where is the ball?"), and initiating communication (such as learning how to initiate showing someone else something unusual the child has seen). Pronoun use is especially difficult for these children, so early therapy may practice using words such as *me* and *you*. For children with limited speech, therapists may use pictures at first to help the child learn to symbolically communicate. This is called the Picture Exchange Communication System (PECS). Because most autistic children have strong visual skills, therapy should use plenty of pictures paired with words. Using scripts helps the child learn rote social interactions ("How are you?" "Fine."). To help learn sentence structure, some children respond well to pairing some simple sign language with their words, especially for troublesome prepositions (*in, on, over*). The greatest challenge is helping the child learn to generalize and use the concepts learned in other situations. For example, the child needs to understand that "Open the door" can be used with other doors, not just the therapy room door. An excellent resource is *More Than Words: Helping Parents Promote Communication and Social Skills in Children with Autism Spectrum Disorder* by Fern Sussman for The Hanen Centre, a nonprofit agency. Phone (416) 921-1073, or access them at http://www.hanen.org.

As the children get older and more advanced, speech and language skills tend to focus more on language subtleties, including words with multiple meanings, idiomatic expressions, inferencing, humor, slang, and conversational skills. Social behavior—understanding it and using it— is the cornerstone of an intervention program for children with ASD, including understanding and using emotions, facial expressions, and body language. Recognizing what other people are thinking or feeling— and why—is a core area of difficulty for high-functioning children with ASD. This lack of perspective-taking is often at the heart of many social missteps for these children.

Inclusion

The 2004 IDEA laws (and research) favor educating children with disabilities in a normal classroom setting to the maximum extent possible, with separate special education classes or removal occurring in only the most severe cases. The law favors utilizing an aide and employing modifications if necessary in lieu of a segregated classroom. In fact the most important aspect of any speech or language program for a child with ASD is creating and facilitating opportunities for social interaction. More and more children with autism are being successfully integrated into regular classrooms—often because a parent initiates the placement. Children with ASD need a clear expectation of what to say and do in every social situation. It helps to practice these social rituals with peers who can respond more normally. Creating cue cards with pictures can assist the child in knowing how to respond to a variety of situations. However, the key to making inclusion work is adequate teacher training, classroom support (often an instructional aide is needed), special education supplementation (to go over important concepts, help the teacher modify the instruction and assignments, and help facilitate social skills), and realistic parental expectations. A very popular and respected model is the SCERTS program, developed by Barry Prizant et al. It stands for Social Communication, Emotional Regulation, and Transactional Support and emphasizes a holistic and functional approach to treating the child with ASD. Another popular program called TEACCH (see Resources for information about autism/PDD in appendix A) helps the child by organizing the classroom activities and routine in a visual way so that the child can understand and participate. The IEP team (which includes parents) decides what is right for your child. Inclusion provides an environment to learn and practice social language skills in addition to extending academic skills. Speech-language therapy should be part of this program. For children with milder problems, it may be more appropriate to conduct the therapy in small groups or directly in the classroom, or even at recess or in the cafeteria—all places that are typically challenging environments for children with ASD.

Parents should work closely with the teachers and help the child enjoy as many normal activities as possible. Keep to a routine. If you are not sure your child understands you, write down what you say as you say it. If your child is having difficulty understanding that he can swim *after* you go to the store, draw stick figures/pictures and number them with your sentences. (1) We are going to the store. (2) We will go swimming. Even though your child often seems distracted or turned away, information often "goes in." Autistic children have serious listening problems. When in doubt, write and draw!

Cerebral Palsy

Cerebral palsy (also known as CP) is a descriptive term for a group of disorders that affect the way a child moves. It is caused by brain damage that occurs during fetal development or at birth. Sometimes other learning problems are present as a result. Cerebral palsy is not progressive—that is, it doesn't get worse as the child grows up. It can affect one or more limbs, as well as the muscles on the face, and, with most disorders, there is a wide range of disability. With very mild cases, the child may have a limp; in more severe cases, the child needs to use a wheelchair.

There are several types of cerebral palsy, and an individual often has more than one type. With *spastic cerebral palsy,* the child's muscles make jerky movements and contract too hard. A child with *athetoid cerebral palsy* has involuntary contractions, which result in shaking or swinging of various parts of the body. Eighty percent of cerebral palsy cases are of these two types.

You can imagine how difficult it would be to speak if you couldn't move your mouth the way you wanted to. A child with cerebral palsy will have difficulty using the tongue and lips not only for speaking but also for chewing and swallowing. Involuntary drooling and grimacing often result as well. Although therapy will help develop and strengthen the oral-motor skills needed for talking, chewing, and swallowing, little can be done at this writing to undo the brain damage that causes the problem. There is a certain amount of acceptance that needs to come with a child who has cerebral palsy. The goal of therapy is not to cure the child but to make the most of the child's abilities.

One of the biggest problems children with cerebral palsy have is using their chest muscles and lungs to push out enough air, at the right time, for speaking. A lot of coordination is involved in this task. Many times the child will open her mouth but nothing will come out. Or she will run out of air before finishing the thought, ending in a whisper. Exercises to improve the strength and coordination of these muscles are important for a child with cerebral palsy.

The speech pattern of the typical child with cerebral palsy is described as dysarthric—a slurring, labored, imprecise manner of speaking characteristic of brain damage. Again, speech patterns can be improved with speech therapy to a certain extent, but the child will never have perfectly clear articulation. A good goal is for the child to be understandable to others.

A child with cerebral palsy tends to have a different voice quality as well. Because the muscles in the throat shape the voice, a child who over-contracts or has weakened muscles will most likely sound somewhat nasal or explosive. The pauses in the child's speech may sound like a stutterer's hesitation, but the lack of fluency is also due to the difficulty with controlling muscles.

Sometimes a child with cerebral palsy is affected severely. As a result, speech is simply not a feasible form of communication. A host of recent technological advances have created many more opportunities for a nonverbal child to communicate. With eye blinks or a touch, the child can operate many of the devices. When a child uses another form of communication, it is called *augmentative and alternative communication* (AAC). Today there are young adults with cerebral palsy who, although they are unable to speak, attend college and live very productive lives.

Cleft Palate

A *cleft palate,* a deformity that is present at birth, is a physical problem characterized by an opening on the roof of the mouth that leads into the nasal cavity. Children with a cleft palate sometimes also have a cleft of the lip. A cleft lip usually involves the top part of the lip, which seems split in half up to the nose. A child with a cleft palate can be at risk for developing middle ear infections, resulting in a temporary hearing loss. Teeth are often significantly misaligned, requiring extensive orthodontics. Until corrected with surgery or fitted with an appliance, a child with a cleft palate will have significant difficulty swallowing food or drinking.

Treatment of a child with a cleft palate requires extensive specialized care from a good craniofacial (skull and face) team at a hospital. The child may require several surgeries to repair the opening, but the doctors must wait to complete the task until the child has finished most, or all, growth. A surgeon, a dentist, a speech pathologist, an orthodontist, and a prosthodontist all need to work together on this team. The prosthodontist fits the child with an appliance called an *obturator,* which fits over the hole in the palate so the child can speak more clearly and eat more easily. This needs to be readjusted and replaced as the child grows. Some children use an obturator temporarily; others need one permanently because the tissue in the mouth or throat is not sufficient, even with surgery, for clear speech or easy swallowing.

A child with a cleft palate will need intensive speech therapy from a very early age. The hospital will usually make arrangements for this. Later, in the United States, the public school will provide therapy. The child's speech is characterized by a nasal quality, as though talking through the nose instead of the mouth. Certain sounds, such as *p, b, t, d, k,* and *g,* are difficult to pronounce. Often the child will make a snorting sound with the nose while talking. Many preschool-age children with cleft palates are extremely difficult to understand. Some children, despite the best medical attention and therapy, still speak with noticeable difficulty. Fortunately, new advances are occurring in the field every day.

Down Syndrome

Down syndrome is a specific form of developmental disability. It is genetic, not caused by something the mother did or didn't do during pregnancy. Having a child with Down syndrome is a higher risk when a woman gives birth over the age of 35 and a slightly higher risk when the father is 45 or older. As with most syndromes, there is a very wide range of ability within the Down syndrome population. Some children are merely "slow" and have a fairly typical childhood; others are severely disabled, unable to communicate easily or care for themselves. Most children with Down syndrome function in the mild to moderately intellectually disabled range.

A child with Down syndrome has certain physical traits that help the doctor make the diagnosis at birth. The head, ears, mouth, and nose of the child are somewhat smaller than those of a typical child. The eyelids are narrow and slanted. There are often white specks on the outside edges of the iris (colored) part of the eye. The top of the ear sometimes folds over slightly, and the inside of the ear, the canal, is narrow. Often children with Down syndrome have a tongue thrust, meaning their tongue protrudes when they speak and swallow. Lips get very dry and chapped. About 50 percent of children with Down syndrome have a crease across each hand, and about 40 percent have some kind of heart defect. These children are also prone to frequent middle ear infections and colds.

Because Down syndrome is nearly always identified at birth or shortly thereafter, important early intervention is possible. Parents in the United States and Canada can take advantage of programs that help stimulate the child's development in all areas from infancy. The child will be delayed in walking and crawling as well as talking. During infancy, therapy may be in the home or at a hospital. Preschool programs that combine these activities in a play-oriented setting are particularly effective.

It is becoming increasingly commonplace in the United States and Canada to educate children with Down syndrome in a regular classroom. This practice is called the *inclusion* model. However, the child will need much assistance and individualization to keep progressing with his or her own goals, which may be somewhat different from those of the other children. By being placed with typical children, the child will have good speech role models and more opportunity to practice speaking and communicating than when in a classroom with children who don't communicate well. Often this is most practical in the younger grades, but as the child gets older, he may feel socially isolated in regular classes.

Having friends and feeling they belong is also important to children with Down syndrome, so fostering friendships with intellectually disabled peers, including participating in the Special Olympics, is a wonderful gift for your child.

Children with Down syndrome may not necessarily need the usual speech therapy from a speech-language pathologist on an ongoing basis, but initially most children will benefit from intensive early intervention. Usually the SLP will come to the home, which is especially helpful for a variety of reasons. For one, it promotes good communication between the SLP and the parent, including strategies that would support the child's speech development, but it also allows the SLP to work within a child's familiar environment so that skills can be readily applied and functional. Often the parent and teachers can work together to provide the type of stimulation that will benefit the child most. The speech pathologist may be asked to act as a consultant or monitor. This is particularly true if the child's speech and language skills are functional and balanced with the other aspects of his or her development or once the child has reached a plateau in adolescence.

Some children with Down syndrome have specific speech or language problems that are more complex than a simple delay in development. A condition called hypotonia can occur, which typically results in feeding difficulties, tongue protrusion, short breathy phrasing, and an openmouthed posture. There are oral-motor programs that are designed to minimize the impact of hypotonia. One of my favorites was developed by Sara Rosenfeld Johnson, who also trains SLPs through her seminars; and there is a feeding program by Lori Overland, who specializes in feeding, speech, and language programs for children with Down syndrome. Both programs are available on DVD from talktools.net.

Another speech condition that sometimes occurs in children with Down syndrome is apraxia. Motor-planning and initiation can be disproportionately delayed in some children with Down. A great resource for improving articulation and speech in children with Down syndrome is any book, newsletter, or article written by Dr. Libby Kumin.

Because children with Down syndrome are prone to frequent ear infections and middle ear fluid, it is extra important to keep them tuned up and hearing well! Without good hearing, receptive and expressive language can stall even more, as can listening and attending in group settings.

The important thing to remember is there is no *one* right way to teach a child with Down syndrome. Each child is unique.

Hearing Impairment and Deafness

Deafness implies a child cannot hear sound at all, or very little, even with a hearing aid. *Hearing-impaired* means a child can hear some sound. Some children with mild hearing impairments function well with a hearing aid; others exhibit serious speech, language, and listening problems. Children with moderate to severe hearing impairments struggle with speaking clearly and comprehending speech. Children who have fluctuating hearing loss from chronic middle ear infections (otitis media) during infancy and preschool years are at risk for impairments of speech and language, which can create problems for learning and functioning in school. *Middle ear infections are the most common cause of acquired hearing loss in children from birth to 3 years of age.* Impairment can occur in one or both ears.

There are many other causes for hearing-related problems, ranging from a virus during the mother's pregnancy to a case of meningitis contracted by the child. Many times there is no known cause.

A child identified at birth as deaf or hearing-impaired is fortunate in many ways. Diagnosing deafness and hearing impairment as soon as possible is half the battle. Years ago we lacked the tools to test hearing until a child was several years old, but now, thanks to our new and sophisticated testing tools, we can even test a sleeping baby! Between one and three infants in one thousand are found to have hearing loss that requires intervention, and hearing loss is even more prevalent in babies who need intensive care. Research shows that babies identified with hearing loss that is treated at an early age can often have speech and language skills within normal limits by kindergarten.

If your doctor or audiologist has determined that your baby has a hearing loss, it is critical for you to become as knowledgeable and proactive as possible to take steps to minimize the effects of the loss, sooner rather than later, if your goal is for your child to speak as normally as possible. The audiologist is the specialist who will ultimately diagnose the hearing loss and recommend a course of action.

For most parents whose lives are rooted in the hearing world, there is typically a desire to maximize hearing, in order to develop oral speech and listening skills. The Alexander Graham Bell Association (www.agbell.org) provides invaluable information to parents of children with hearing loss, and can put you in touch with other parents and local resources to help you find the right programs and professionals to help your child, including auditory-verbal (AV) therapists or SLPs who specialize in this unique field. The key is to move quickly and make sure you get as much intensive early intervention as possible to maximize the very small window of learning time your child has to acquire speech and listening skills.

Children with even mild hearing impairments have problems with pronunciation. Certain sounds, such as *s, sh,* and *t,* may be difficult to hear, so the child may not pronounce them at all unless taught how. A sentence might sound like this: "My i-uh i nie" (My sister is nice). Sounds heard at the ends of words, which are harder to hear, are often left off. A hearing-impaired child's voice has a peculiar "sound" to it, as though it is coming from the back of the throat, and is deeper-pitched. In contrast, deaf children tend to have high-pitched voices. Sentence structures are typically characterized by the omission of small words (*the, a, is, to*). A sentence might be put together this way: "Boy rode horse." Aggressive speech therapy and proper amplification, as early as possible, will help improve these skills.

When listening, a child with even a mild hearing problem will have difficulty remembering directions or other information heard. When there is background noise, listening is difficult and tiring, so the child is often distracted. Learning phonics may be difficult because the child's discrimination for sounds is affected. Following an oral conversation may be confusing. Speech therapy for children with hearing problems also addresses improving their ability to comprehend and remember what is said.

As mentioned previously, a device called an FM system is particularly useful in helping a child with any permanent or temporary hearing problem function in the classroom (see chapter 7). In the United States, a child with a hearing impairment should have an FM system listed on the child's IEP, which means the school should pay for it. It is a basic piece of equipment that will help the child function successfully in the regular classroom and costs about $1,000, depending on the model and the needs of the child.

Hearing Aids

Today, hearing aids are either analog (traditional technology) or digital (newer technology). The digital aids are generally able to provide improved sound quality with less annoying amplification of background ambient noise and feedback (that screechy sound that happens at times when the hearing aid is in close proximity to certain objects or is moved a certain way). For many children with hearing loss, the consistent use of a hearing aid allows sufficient sound input for them to function quite well in most environments. The key is to make sure that molds are up to date, that testing is done regularly to ensure there have been no changes in hearing function, and that the aids themselves are maintained properly. You cannot simply buy a hearing aid and forget about it for a few years, because your child's ears change rather quickly. Last, I strongly recommend buying your hearing aid from the audiologist who tested your child and not from a hearing aid dispenser, who has extremely limited knowledge of hearing science aside from what is needed to sell and market the aids themselves. Most audiologists have a PhD and have undertaken rigorous training in the field. If at all possible, use their knowledge in fitting the ear molds and finding the best aid that will fit your child's hearing needs.

Cochlear Implants and Baja Devices

For children with profound hearing loss or whose hearing is still significantly impaired even with a hearing aid, a cochlear implant may be recommended. In fact, it is becoming more common to have a child use bilateral cochlear implants (*unilateral* refers to one ear; *bilateral* refers to two ears), which maximizes hearing and helps the child localize sound (i.e., to know which direction it's coming from) and hear better in background noise. A Baja device works slightly differently and is especially helpful for children with malformed or very small ear canals. It is not as common, but it can be very helpful. Both devices require an outpatient surgery, which, like any surgery, does have inherent risks. The child wears an external piece that is visible but often barely noticeable. When the devices are implanted early, and followed up with speech and auditory therapy and regular visits to an audiologist, there is a good chance your child may develop speech and language much like his peers. I have met quite a few children who are technically profoundly "deaf" but who through the use of a cochlear implant at a few months of age can chat away and converse like any other child with rather good functional hearing.

The other critical component is to make sure your child wears his hearing aid or implant every waking minute unless in water (bathing/swimming) or sleeping. In order to do their job, they have to be worn. I often meet parents who are concerned because their child isn't speaking or listening as expected, but when queried, they will admit that their child rarely puts on the hearing aid. They'd rather the child get therapy instead, but unfortunately it doesn't work that way. The child must wear the hearing aid or implant so the auditory pathways can learn to process auditory information—which is the necessary foundation for speech and language. If your goal is for your child to function successfully in a hearing classroom, he cannot afford to miss any time without the hearing aid or implant. We cannot make up for this by doing speech therapy, so from the beginning, your child needs to have the device on to have any benefit. If it's not comfortable, make sure the fitting is correct. Children grow quickly and need to have new molds made constantly. If finances are an issue, there are state and private programs that may be able to help you find ways to pay at a reduced rate or over time. Don't delay.

For some within the deaf community, hearing loss or deafness is not something they feel needs to be "fixed," nor is it seen as a disability. Using sign language is as natural for many who are deaf as speaking Italian is for those who live in Italy. It can be augmented with lipreading and other systems such as cued speech. For many, a combination of signing and speaking ("total communication") is best. The long-term goal of the total communication philosophy is for the child to be able to function in the deaf community as well as in the hearing community.

However, because we have such great early intervention in place and the ability to provide hearing through digital hearing aids and cochlear implants so efficiently, the number of children entering "deaf education" special education classrooms and becoming proficient in sign language in elementary and high schools has dramatically declined, with many of these children transitioning into regular classes with varying degrees of support, depending on whether or not there are other learning or cognitive issues involved (which often accompany children with hearing loss). In essence, with the advent of these devices, a child may be functionally deaf or hearing-impaired without them, but speak and listen somewhat like other children when they are on. The decision as to how to educate a child with profound hearing loss continues to be a parent's prerogative and a personal choice.

PKU

PKU is a disease that, if left untreated, causes brain damage. It is caused by the body's inability to process part of the protein called phenylalanine. Babies are routinely checked for this before leaving the hospital. However, it is important to test for this *after* twenty-four hours of life or the diagnosis may be missed. Symptoms include developmental delays, irritability, dry skin, and convulsions. The child may have a musty odor and is often blonder than his siblings. Treatment involves medication and a special diet, which must be strictly followed. Although rare, PKU should not be ruled out.

Traumatic Brain Injury

A traumatic brain injury (TBI) occurs when there is damage to the brain after birth from a specific event, such as a blow to the head, near drowning, choking, or deprivation of oxygen to the brain. Children with traumatic brain injuries display certain language and listening problems (aphasia) during their recovery and even permanently in many cases. The recovery period can last at least a year or even a little longer. It is often difficult for the parent of a child with a brain injury to see the child struggle to perform simple tasks that he did before with ease. At the same time, the parent can rejoice that the child's life was saved. Years ago, many children with TBI did not survive. Progress in a recovering child is often amazingly rapid, although a complete recovery is not always possible.

Children with TBI often display particular speech, language, and listening characteristics. They might do the following:

- Have difficulty concentrating or paying attention
- Have difficulty with listening skills: memory, comprehension, and processing
- Have difficulty talking about one subject; tend to ramble from thought to thought with little organization or sequence
- Have difficulty interacting in an appropriate way socially; may say things that are embarrassing or completely fictional
- Have difficulty putting complex or grammatical sentences together, especially at first
- Have difficulty thinking of the names of common objects (*anomia*)
- Have difficulty moving the lips, tongue, and jaw as desired
- Have difficulty pronouncing words with precision, mixing up syllables
- Use a monotonous pitch or odd intonation pattern when speaking

A child with a traumatic brain injury has other medical and therapeutic issues to deal with, aside from speech and language. Learning how to walk, tie a shoe, and adjust to such a drastic change in functioning are just a few tasks they must cope with. Children with traumatic brain injuries and their families work with a team of specialists that helps them along the long rehabilitative road. A neurologist, a psychologist, an occupational therapist, and a physical therapist are just a few of the members of the team.

How a child's brain thinks is called *cognitive functioning.* Attention span, memory, problem solving, and social judgment are cognitive skills. These are also important areas of relearning important to a child with a traumatic brain injury.

After a child with TBI has been released from the hospital or rehabilitation hospital, reentering school is possible with a great deal of support. Often the child does not understand that she is different. Denial is part of the brain injury. For this reason, the child may resist going to therapies or receiving special help. The parent and psychologist can help the child deal with these feelings of resentment.

The nature and amount of the therapy to address speech, language, and listening depend on the degree of the injury, the time elapsed since the injury, and the age of the child.

9
Answers to Your Questions

In this chapter, I answer the most common questions regarding speech, language, and listening problems that I have received over the years. I hope it answers yours!

Baby Talk

Q. My friends are giving me a hard time about using "baby talk" with my new baby. They say I should just talk normally, but it's hard for me to do that. I just seem to naturally get that goofy singsongy voice whenever I talk to her. Am I going to harm my baby's speech development this way?

A. No way! We call that "mother-ese" in the business. It is a very natural way for most women to communicate with their babies, and there is a reason why we have instincts to do that. Think about it—what do we do? We exaggerate the intonation ("Good MOOOORning!") and repeat ourselves quite a bit ("Do you want your bear? Yes? You want your bear? Here's your bear!") and talk to ourselves even though no one is responding. These are all perfect building blocks for developing speech. As your child begins talking, you'll want to eventually drop the baby names for things and use the more "grown-up" vocabulary and intonation. But for now, be as goofy as you want!

Pacifiers

Q. What do you think about pacifiers? I've heard they are really bad for babies and their speech.

A. I happen to think it's a good idea to at least introduce them to newborns, but I know not everyone agrees with me on this. Some babies will spit them out and that's fine, but some will latch on with gusto. Why do I recommend this? Because if there is a tendency to thumb-suck, it can hopefully satisfy that urge. With a pacifier, you have control and can take it away when the normal intense oral period is over, typically around 12 to 18 months of age. Thumbs are not so easy to get rid of. I would caution you to make sure you to use only the newborn size, though; nothing bigger. The large sizes take up too much space in the mouth and are unnecessary, even as your child grows. Reserve the pacifier for when your child is fussy or tired and needs something to chew on. But remember, you don't want it in his mouth all day long. Therein lies the problem. If your child has something stuck in his mouth for much of the day, it reduces the time he should be babbling or saying new words, so try to limit it to very brief periods during the day and for nighttime, but make a vow to lose every one of them after 18 months. It's easier than you think. Just one or two days of fussiness and it's over!

Baby's First Words

Q. My baby says "ma-ma-ma-ma" but she's not looking at me, and she seems to be saying it at various times. My parents keep asking if she's learned to talk yet or said her first word. Does that count?

A. Well, she's off to a good start with her babbling, but technically, no, that is not considered a first "word." Why? Because in order for it to be considered a true "word" your child needs to use it meaningfully in some kind of context. In the beginning, this is tricky to sort out since babies may in the course of babbling actually find themselves in some kind of situational context that may make it seem as if they are saying that word on purpose. Sometimes it takes a few times using it to really be sure. For example, let's pretend your daughter said, "Bah-buh" when you changed her diaper, and would repeat it over and over. Initially, you wouldn't be sure if that was a coincidence or not. So when you take out a diaper again, say, "What's that? Is it a dia-per?" If she smiles and says, "Bah-buh!" and consistently pairs the word with her diaper, that would be her first word.

Tongue Tie

Q. My baby seems to be tongue-tied. She has a hard time sticking out her tongue. It seems to be pulling on the bottom there, and when she cries the tip of her tongue bows in a little bit. What should we do about that?

A. Does your baby have a hard time with feeding? Is she choking or not able to eat the kinds of foods she should? When feeding issues become involved, it's helpful to have a consultation with either a lactation consultant (if you're breast-feeding) or a feeding specialist if your child is eating solids. Some feeding specialists are speech pathologists and some are occupational therapists. If there are no correlated feeding issues, I would wait a little bit. Sometimes the tissue under the tongue (the lingual frenulum) will stretch out a bit in time on its own. In other cases, the restriction may inhibit a child's ability to retract and lift her tongue comfortably and normally for sounds such as *r* or cause her tongue to be flat, so that tongue tip sounds (*l, s, n, t, d, z*) and palatal sounds (*sh, ch, j*) become affected. The operative word here is *comfortably*. I've had children in middle school and high school come to me with restricted frenulums who never had them clipped, and described how they feel their tongue is "moving in cement" all the time. Their speech often sounds just plain mumbly and indistinct, and after the procedure it is much clearer within a very short time. Just because a child can extend the tongue for a moment to demonstrate for a professional doesn't mean that position will be comfortable enough to maintain in steady conversation. The big question to ask is "How does it feel when you put your tongue up like that? Does it pinch or feel tight? If so, where?"

The good news is, often a child learns how to use a compensatory position for these sounds, which can sound just fine. If that isn't the case, and she develops associated speech difficulties and/or complains of it feeling "tight" or uncomfortable under her tongue, find a good private or hospital-based SLP who specializes in oral-motor or myofunctional therapy to have it checked. This often runs in families, so if you or your husband had it, there is an increased chance your baby will too, as well as other children in the family.

Some dentists know what to look for, but often they are not well versed in the effect of a restricted frenulum on speech and shy away from doing anything about it. You may need to have it clipped by an oral surgeon. I generally suggest waiting until age 3 or 4 to see how a child's speech develops if there are no feeding issues before going down that road. The procedure is very quick with a laser (five minutes), and there is no anesthesia, just a quick dab of a numbing solution under the tongue before the laser is used. No needles. The tongue is sore for a few days and you will need to have some Popsicles and acetaminophen around. If your dentist or oral surgeon insists on doing it the old-fashioned way with cutting and sutures, find someone with more updated laser equipment. The procedure is infinitely more painful—and the recovery longer—with traditional surgery.

Baby and TV

Q. My baby just loves to watch TV with me! We watch all my favorite shows together and even the morning news shows and baseball. My mother-in-law was visiting recently and made a face when I turned on the TV while I was feeding the baby. What's the harm? It's entertaining her and me.

A. Chances are your mother-in-law has been reading the current research and recommendations regarding TV, babies, language development, and attention span. Sorry to burst your bubble, but she's right. Babies and TV are not a good combination. The American Academy of Pediatrics strongly discourages any TV watching before the age of 2, and after that, fairly sparingly and with well-selected children's shows only. Watching TV is a passive activity and doesn't promote interactive speech and language development. Even when you are eating together, your attention should be on interacting, self-talking, and responding to your baby's noises and babbling. When you watch TV, you're both passively watching and that's not a good thing. Aside from that, watching TV at a young age can have an adverse effect on attention span, and limit the amount of physical activity your child gets. With preschoolers and school-age children, a little well-chosen TV is fine, but stick to educational channels, children's networks, and age-appropriate animal shows. Even better, get DVDs when she is older so that you can control the content. The bottom line is that keeping the TV on all day long as background company when you have a baby around is not healthy for her.

Babies and Sign Language

Q. I've seen books and even videos on sign language for babies. What do you think of them? I have a 10-month-old who is not talking and I'm considering introducing sign language. Would it slow down his speech?

A. It certainly would be logical to think that sign language might inhibit speech development, but actually, introducing signs and gestures can aid a child's language development and reduce his frustration. The key is to teach the sign and pair it with the verbal word for it, not to do it in silence. Have fun!

Raising a Bilingual Child

Q. We were raised in another country and speak another language. Now that we're in the United States, we'd like our child to be fluent in English, but we also want her to speak our native tongue. We plan to return home for visits, and we want to make sure she can communicate with our friends and relatives. Will this cause her to be confused?

A. Today many people are choosing to raise their children to speak more than one language. The latest research we have shows that introducing a second language at an early age will typically help your child become more proficient with a variety of language skills. The earlier, the better! It also allows a child to communicate with people from another culture, which in turn helps the child see the world from a different point of view. The nuances of language (how elders are addressed, how emotions are expressed, etc.) tell the child about what is valued in the culture. Children learn best from caregivers and parents who enthusiastically interact with them in the language in which they are most proficient and comfortable.

While exposure to two languages is often beneficial, sometimes the child's initial speech development may be slightly less advanced than that of a child who is exposed to only one language ("monolingual"). It also depends on how much interaction takes place in each language. Communication skills will tend to be strongest in the language spoken most frequently. It is generally felt that because the child is splitting or sharing her time learning two languages, the time spent talking in one language takes away opportunities to learn and grow in the other language. If you choose to raise your child in a bilingual home, there are some general guidelines you should follow:

• Keep the languages separate—that is, one parent or caretaker should speak one language, and someone else, the other. Avoid having the primary caretaker alternate speaking two languages or combine the two into one sentence or conversation. This kind of inconsistency makes it difficult for the child to learn which words go with which language.
• I've seen families speak the "school language" Monday through Thursday and their native tongue Friday through Sunday. This too seems to work well for children; the languages are compartmentalized enough

to keep the language systems apart from each other, but this system allows both parents to speak their native tongue at some point during the week. It also helps the parents practice their English skills.

• If at all possible, at least one parent or caretaker should be interacting daily with your child in the language spoken at school.

• Make sure you facilitate playdates not only with children who speak your native tongue, but also with children who speak the language of your new country. Interacting with peers is the single best way for your child to practice the other language in a natural way.

• A fun way to reinforce a second language is through songs, DVDs of familiar movies, and books.

• Once your child is in school, it's often harder to keep up the language of your native country. If at all possible, consider taking extended summer trips so your child has time to practice the language in a natural environment.

• For children who have mild or moderate speech delays and are receiving therapy, carrying over concepts and sounds that are addressed in therapy into your native language is helpful. For example, if the SLP is working on helping the child learn how to ask "where" questions, the parents should work on this same skill, in their native tongue, at home. Discuss it with your child's SLP. While some grammatical concepts and sound productions may not be used in your native tongue, there are many elements that are common to all languages.

For some children with significant speech and language delays, learning even one language is a challenge. Your child's speech language pathologist may request that the language spoken at home be consistent with the language used in therapy and in school, if at all possible, until the concepts are stabilized in one language. That is what we routinely used to advise years ago. Now, however, there are different opinions as to the wisdom of limiting the child to one language, regardless of the degree of the delay. My feeling is that for some children who are *severely* delayed and cognitively limited, it makes sense to focus primarily on the language that the child will be using in school, and with his peers, if the parents are able to speak it comfortably, to maximize the amount of functional language learned.

Raising a Trilingual Child

Q. We lived overseas for several years in a European country and our son picked up another language. We are from Asia and we spoke our native tongue as well. Now that we are moving to the United States our 3-year-old will soon be learning English. How can we keep up all three languages so he can be trilingual?

A. This is actually one of the most common questions I get, in one form or another. Sometimes there is a nanny who speaks one language, the parents speak another, and the child is schooled in yet another language. How does it all work? There are so many factors to take into consideration, there is no clear-cut answer to your question. Here are some of the issues to consider:

• What are your plans for where you will eventually live? Are you planning to move back to the same European country? Do you have friends and relatives the child will be regularly interacting with who speak that language? If so, keeping that language alive will be important. If not, without ongoing interaction and use, odds are that at his young age, he will likely lose that language.

• Is your child a quick language learner? If so, that's a plus. If not, trying to keep three linguistic balls in the air is a big challenge for a child with a speech delay and would likely prove too confusing and frustrating for him. I personally feel that for a child with a speech delay, learning three languages is not something I would encourage.

• In cases where a caregiver is speaking a third language to a child, the most important issue to consider is the amount of language interaction that is taking place. If the caregiver is very verbal, affectionate, and happy, your child may be able to pick up that language. Chances are, though, that he will learn to understand the basics of the language, but may prefer to respond in English or in his strongest language. My experience has been that it's rare for the child to be verbally fluent in these situations in a third language, but it does provide exposure. It also works best if the child is exposed to the caregiver's language from infancy, as it can be disconcerting for a preschooler or a toddler to be cared for by someone whom he doesn't understand and vice versa.

Adoption Issues

Q. *We are thinking of adopting, but are concerned about possible developmental issues. How common is it to have associated speech and language delays in adopted children?*

A. The likelihood of a child's having a speech and language delay depends upon the age of the child at the time of placement and the nature of the placement. If the child is the product of a healthy pregnancy and is placed as a newborn, there is no reason for concern and the child is no more likely to have a speech delay than any other child. The fact that a child is adopted in and of itself does not increase the risk for a speech or language delay.

If children are the product of a pregnancy marked by substance abuse or inadequate medical care, and/or were cared for in an extremely deprived environment for more than a year, they are at greater risk for learning and developmental disabilities, which could include a speech and language delay, as well as an attachment disorder. This is true for children from the foster care system in the United States as well as overseas. Children with attachment disorder exhibit delays with learning speech and language and have a difficult time desiring to initiate and use communication, even once they know what to do. Forming normal emotional bonds can be challenging, and their behavioral issues can be exhausting for the parents. That said, I have worked with preschool children who came from the direst of home conditions, abused to the point of hospitalization and delayed in all areas, yet several of them flourished in just a few years with lots of intensive early intervention, love, and support from their new families. In fact, one boy who had been diagnosed with severe intellectual disabilities (he could not even tell you his name at age 4) was in the top reading group by second grade! On the other hand, I've also seen many heartbreaking situations where children come to families as preschoolers or older from similar circumstances who struggle with language, behavior, and emotional control on an ongoing basis, despite lots of love, excellent resources, and therapies.

Speech Therapy and the Newly Adopted

Q. We just adopted a beautiful girl, age 3½, from a foreign country. She spoke only a few words in her native tongue when she was placed with us. We're wondering if she needs speech therapy to learn English or if we should wait and let her get acclimated.

A. Congratulations! This is a very exciting time for all of you. When a speech pathologist first examines a newly placed adopted child with speech delays, it is difficult to make a prognosis as to when or if the child will catch up. It varies from child to child. The younger the child, the greater the chance for rapid improvement. Generally, the longer the child is in an unsatisfactory living situation prior to her new placement, the greater the risk for serious or permanent developmental delays, including in speech and language. There is also the possibility that this child has a speech-language disorder and would have been delayed no matter where she was born or in what environment. Of course, limited stimulation would certainly make the situation worse.

When adopting any child, particularly an older child, your primary emphasis as the parent should be to help your daughter adjust emotionally to her new surroundings, especially in the first six months. Pressure to "catch up" through intensive therapies often backfires because the child has not had sufficient opportunity to develop a bond with the new parents. Take care not to compare your child with other children of the same age who were born in a healthy and loving environment. A child who arrives after three years of little interaction may be functioning more like an infant than a preschooler. It may take a year or two for the child to even begin to talk. Regardless, be careful to avoid making lifelong predictions based on the observations or tests just a few weeks or months after your child's arrival. Once your child has adjusted to her new home, it certainly makes sense to pursue whatever services she needs to grow and develop. We know that early intervention makes all the difference; just be sure it's not too much, too soon.

PECS for the Nonverbal

Q. Our son is 4 and still not talking, except for a bit of jibberish. He is developmentally delayed and may have apraxia; they are not sure. We want his speech therapy to focus on getting him to talk, but his SLP is suggesting we do something called "PECS." What is that, and do you think it's a good idea?

A. PECS stands for Picture Exchange Communication System. It was developed by Andrew Bondy and Lori Frost in 1985, and is at its core an augmentative communication strategy that requires the child to give or point to a picture or object. It is meant to help the child understand basic symbolic language and provide a simple way to communicate simple needs and wants. For example, this picture of a frog = this stuffed frog you are holding. By giving the card to you and seeking your attention, the child can communicate an idea. In fact, it's a great way to support the development of receptive and expressive language. A child who is nonverbal at 4 very much needs an alternative way to communicate, while you continue to support both receptive *and* expressive verbal language.

For very young children or those who are not yet comprehending pictures, the representation on the cards may need to be photographs or very realistic color drawings. There are also symbols from the Mayer-Johnson company (www.mayerjohnson.com) that are referred to as "icons" and produced by a program called Boardmaker, which is very popular. Adding a talking feature via an augmentative communication device so that when your child pushes a picture, the word is spoken via a recording can be especially helpful in associating the picture and spoken word. I like the simple ones by Mayer Johnson called Go Talk, such as Go Talk +9.

With a picture exchange system, make sure your child learns to get your attention (via a tap on the arm or some kind of sign or verbal noise, even if "Ahhh!") and make eye contact before handing them to you instead of handing you a card while looking away or dropping it on a desk in front of you. This way it sets up good habits and patterns for later greetings and initiations. There should be some kind of second step for the child to look at you for a response. For requests, I'm a big advocate of helping the child understand that there are several possible responses—yes, no, maybe, or after we do _____ [activity]. An automatic "yes" for anything requested can set the stage for expectations and rigid routines that can be hard to break later, but sometimes in the beginning you need to try for as many "yes" responses as possible so the child is motivated to continue using the system.

Preschool for the Speech-Delayed

Q. Our 3-year-old son is a bit speech delayed, just saying one- and two-word phrases. We take him for speech therapy twice a week. We're trying to decide if he should go to a preschool program this fall or perhaps wait until he's more verbal so he's not too frustrated. If he does go, what kind of program would you recommend?

A. Without knowing your son and the nature of his issues, this is a bit tricky to answer, so I'll have to give you some general information. Let's start with the question of whether or not he would benefit from going to a preschool program. I would vote a resounding yes to that question. One of the best things you can do for your child is have him in a social situation with his peers. It gives him more opportunities to apply the speech skills the SLP is working on in the most natural way, without a parent interpreting for him, and provides extended opportunities for interaction.

In terms of the type of program that would best suit him, ask his SLP, because that is who would have the most information about your specific child's needs. In general, though, with this kind of case, if he were my child, I would look for a language-based preschool program, staffed with skilled professionals in a small class, with a low teacher to pupil ratio.

Because your son is a bit behind at this point, I'd want every moment of the program to be focused on increasing his receptive and expressive language use. Doing so requires some extra training, and many teachers in local private preschools are simply not equipped to do this. Your local school district will likely have a classroom like this set up for preschoolers through the special education program, which would require an IEP and team meetings but is usually free or at very little expense to you.

Before enrolling him in the program I'd want the opportunity to sit in and see how the classroom is run. While a great special education preschool can be a life-changing and wonderful experience, a class staffed with ambivalent and burned-out teachers or children with severe behavioral problems or who have much more severe language delays than your own child are to be avoided. What you want to have is enthusiastic, dedicated (and hopefully experienced) teachers, coupled with children who are at the same level as your child, or a little above or slightly below. You want your child to have someone to talk to while there, since that is the whole purpose of going. These classes are usually three or four mornings a week for about three hours a day and have the benefit of a speech pathologist coming into the class or even a speech pathologist as the teacher.

In addition to a special education program, I'd also consider having him go a few mornings or afternoons a week to a private preschool with more typically developing peers. The purpose would be more social, to have strong peer models, and to get experience in larger group settings. Some children with delays can manage in regular preschools, and some need another year or so before they can be successful. It often depends on the attitude and philosophy of the preschool, as well as the training of the teacher. Whenever you can, though, attempt to have at least some portion of the week allotted to having your child interact with typically developing peers. Playdates in the park, gym classes, or arts and crafts lessons are a good start if he's not ready for the private preschool. What I would not want you to do is keep him home in the safety of your nest, away from any potential frustration, but also away from his peers. The other children are truthfully quite oblivious to speech difficulties at that age, and are more interested in playing.

ABA Therapy and Autism

Q. Our 29-month-old son was just diagnosed with autism. Our heads are swimming because we were given a rather long list of recommendations and we don't know what to do first. He is not yet speaking and can really not even sit still to do any kind of speech therapy. He runs in circles and screams quite a bit. They are recommending ABA therapy. What is it, and is it something you think would help our son?

A. ABA therapy stands for Applied Behavioral (or Behavior) Analysis. It is a type of intensive intervention that evolved from B. F. Skinner's work in behavioral psychology. It usually involves a big commitment of time (fifteen to thirty hours a week) and several different people coming into your home to work with your child. These are often trained college students who have an interest in a field related to pediatrics or autism. The nature of the therapy is one of using rewards and highly reinforcing activities to motivate your child to participate and achieve the skills being addressed. These skills are often initially related to imitating, pointing to simple pictures, making eye contact, sitting, and following simple directions, and are often advised for children such as your son who are demonstrating severe enough behavioral issues that they might benefit from it. Over time, the amount of reinforcement is decreased and the skills introduced are expanded. The research on the efficacy of ABA shows that for many children with autism spectrum disorders, it has been quite helpful. The reason you have so many recommendations is that early intervention for autism spectrum disorders indeed requires that you usually juggle many balls in the air at once: speech therapy, occupational therapy, ABA, a school program, and so on.

ABA is an adult-directed therapy, so a child who goes through ABA may be more able to attend to more teachers and other therapists in time, which is a good thing. The one caution I would give you is that once these basic skills are taught, there is some danger in that some children get to be "prompt-dependent." That is, they do a great job "performing," but only when rewarded and prompted by an adult. There comes a point where the emphasis needs to be on more natural communication and interaction, with less structure and adult initiation. The other caveat is that over time, some children do get burned out from the intensity of all their programs and begin pushing back and refusing to do any kind of therapy. I generally like ABA for younger children (ages 2 to 4) with moderate to severe symptoms of autism for a year or two, but prefer it be phased out once the child can participate successfully in other interventions or can transition to programs like SCERTS or RDI. I also find that Stanley Greenspan's Floortime Approach is a good match for very young children who are not ready for structured, adult-directed therapy. For more on these programs, see www.autismspeaks.org.

Gluten-Free, Casein-Free Diets, Supplements, and Autism

Q. We have a 28-month-old son who was diagnosed with autism last year. He is in a terrific program and is making progress in his ABA program, as well as with speech therapy and in his special education preschool. We've been hearing a bit about gluten-free, casein-free diets for these kids and how it helps their language and interaction. We're wondering, what do you think of them? And what about all those supplements?

A. A gluten-free, casein-free diet means your child cannot have anything with wheat, barley, rye, oats, and other specific foods (gluten) or dairy products (casein). There are more and more tasty substitute products being developed, so this diet is getting easier to implement. It is felt that the proteins in these ingredients cause children with autism to have adverse changes in their brain and body. In our pediatric speech pathology practice, there have been a few instances where we have seen noticeable improvements in children on this diet. These are situations when the diet was the only variable that had changed in the preceding few weeks. Did it cure their autism? No, but the improvements in eye contact, level of interaction, and attention span, and the decrease in irritability were well worth the effort and adjustment it took for the families to eat this way and were noticed by everyone who saw the child. The success stories we've observed with GFCF diets have involved children with secondary digestive discomforts, including chronic diarrhea.

On the other hand . . . we've also seen many more children on this diet whose parents reported *some* subtle improvements in behavior or language, but in working with the children we did not truly notice improvements that could not be explained by other factors, such as the intensive therapies the child was receiving. We also have found that it is common for families to abandon the diet after about six months because there is no observable change at all and the diet presented too great a challenge to implement with not enough reward. In other words, the success stories we have observed have been the exception rather than the rule in our experience, with many more children having more subtle changes or none at all. Of course, there's always the possibility that not all families have followed the diet as diligently as others or whose child needed something slightly different. It's hard to say. There is still a lack of good research out there on the effectiveness of the GFCF diet, so I can only tell you what I've seen in many years of working with children on the autism spectrum. That said, if it were my child, I would talk to a skilled nutritionist in this area, try the diet, and stick with it for a good three to six months, including trying several of the variations, to see if it helped. If it did, I'd continue with it.

In the case of nutritional supplements, we also see a similar spread of success stories, with many people using the GFCF diets in conjunction with supplements such as fish oil and/or omega-3 fatty acids. However, some supplements and doses are not healthy for your child, so it is critical that you work with someone who has a nutrition/medicine background and not just consult a clerk from the health food store or the Internet. Remember, these supplements are not approved by the FDA. Just because they are "over-the-counter" in no way means they are necessarily safe, especially for a young child with a fragile system. Studies show that some supplement and vitamin bottles may not even include the ingredients on the label or in the strength indicated.

I'd suggest talking with your doctor, reading up on these topics, and visiting some Web sites, including Defeat Autism Now (www.defeat autismnow.com) and Generation Rescue (www.generationrescue.org), to find practitioners who specialize in this diet and can recommend supplements if it's something you are open to trying.

PDD versus Severe Anxiety Disorder

Q. We just had the second professional evaluation of our 3-year-old son. Now we are totally confused! The first team told us our son had PDD, and the second doctor is telling us our child has severe social anxiety and language delays, but is not on the autism spectrum. Should we get a third evaluation? How does this information impact the planning we have for our son? Should we pull him out of his ABA program? Help!

A. In cases where the child's diagnosis is clear-cut, there is usually agreement among professionals. However, there does seem to be a difference in the use of terminology, particularly when a child has a mild case or just a handful of symptoms. I find that some professionals prefer to use the term PDD-NOS (Pervasive Developmental Delay—Not Otherwise Specified) for children with milder symptoms, while some may prefer the term HFA (High-Functioning Autism). This is one of the reasons the *DSM* is attempting to better clarify these terms in its 2013 edition. A social anxiety disorder tells us that your child is very apprehensive and perhaps resistant to interacting with others, particularly in new situations with unfamiliar people. In reality, this is also true for children with autism spectrum disorders. The difference between the two is a qualitative one. That is, the child with autism has many more associated behaviors surrounding rituals, routines, sensory issues, echolalia, rigid preferences, a lack of initiation and eye contact, et cetera, which are observed across most settings. The child with a social anxiety disorder may function rather normally in the comfort of her home or with familiar people. The social and language components are a huge part of autism, but it is indeed possible to have social language delays or a social anxiety disorder coupled with a speech delay and yet not have autism spectrum disorder.

In cases where the symptoms fall into a "gray area," some professionals may decline to formally diagnose a child with autism at all because the child's symptoms are not consistently observed or as pervasive as they would expect. As a result, it is not uncommon for parents to seek several opinions and to find that each professional has a slightly different diagnostic label. Add to that the fact that your child may act differently at each appointment, so the professionals may see him at his best *or* at his worst, depending on his mood, the time of day, if he's getting over a cold or just woke up. This variation in performance often accounts for the lack of agreement among professionals. I would guess in your child's case, he may have acted slightly different during the appointments or that the training of the professionals may cause them to lean one way or the other. A physician or a team may perhaps prefer the term autism spectrum disorder whereas a psychologist or a psychiatrist may view it through a different lens and call it a social anxiety disorder. Your child's case may very well be a little of both. This of course can result in even more confusion for you.

So what to do? I'd read up on both diagnoses and see if one fits what *you* observe in your child, since you see him the most. In the case of the social anxiety disorder, does it run in the family? If so, the chances are increased that there may be some validity to the diagnosis. It may take some time to really know for sure which it is, but certainly working with someone who can give your child support who has a strong language background but also has worked with social anxiety would be helpful.

Speech Delay and Kindergarten

Q. Our daughter is speech delayed. Should we send her to kindergarten? She will be 5 in July.

A. Without knowing your child and the extent of the speech delay, it is difficult to answer this question. Research shows that retention (not promoting a child to the next grade) is usually not an effective strategy because there are social and emotional consequences to it that can sometimes offset whatever academic gains are made. That said, I've seen cases where children have been detained in lower grades (kindergarten or first grade) where the child matured and seemed to be quite successful in later years. However, in your child's case, she hasn't actually started school. "Speech delayed" can mean many things. If the issue is simply articulation, I'd want to know if she has strong phonemic awareness skills or not. Her speech pathologist should be able to tell you. How is she socially? Can she sit and attend a whole-group lesson for fifteen to twenty minutes? Does she have frequent tantrums or refuse to do class-work sometimes? How are her fine motor skills? Does she have sufficient vocabulary and receptive language to understand stories and instruction? If the issue is related to receptive and expressive language lags, your child's SLP and preschool teacher may have opinions as to her readiness. A child with strong social skills, attention span, phonemic awareness, fine motor skills, and basic alphabet and number knowledge will probably do fine in kindergarten, despite the speech difficulties. However, there are associated risk factors with speech delays that sometimes make it challenging for a child to begin kindergarten on time unless there is good support in the classroom and modifications are made. If she has weak-nesses in some of the areas discussed above, you may want to give her more time and start the following year.

If you do decide to delay kindergarten, you may want to look into a "junior kindergarten class" for children who are not ready to go to kindergarten but perhaps socially are beyond the typical preschool curriculum. Another option is to move her to a different preschool so she doesn't feel like she "stayed back" and repeated the same curriculum. Having the same toys, same teachers, same stories, and same lessons may not be terribly helpful or fun and may give her the impression that she failed, so a fresh place with new materials, teachers, games, and activities may be a better choice.

Scheduling Speech Therapy at School

Q. We are struggling with scheduling our third-grade son for speech therapy at school. The school SLP wants to pull him from recess, but he is balking, yet we don't want him to miss academic work. What should we do?

A. Ah, scheduling woes! It's really a no-win situation, isn't it? You either pull him from the fun classes and have him resent it, or pull him from the academic classes and risk having him fall further behind. This is one reason why more and more SLPs are "pushing in" to classes and providing interventions right in the classroom, often to several children at once, or even doing whole-class lessons. However, it's not always feasible or appropriate to do, depending on the nature of the therapy itself. It is also why private therapy is so popular for those who can afford it. If your child does need to go to therapy during academic periods, it's important that you work with the teacher to minimize the effects of going out for services, including making sure he doesn't get extra homework that he doesn't know how to do in order to make up the classwork that he missed. Having extra work on top of the speech therapy isn't fair, nor is being tested on information presented while he was in therapy, and sadly it happens just due to oversight. Often the SLP is trying to schedule a number of compatible children together, many of whom attend several therapies. It is nearly impossible to satisfy each child's individual requests, so your child's time may be driven by logistics that are out of everyone's control.

Coordinating School-based SLP and Private Services

Q. Our private SLP and school-based SLP hardly ever communicate. What can we do? Does it make sense to have two different people working with our son?

A. With the sheer number of children on both their caseloads, this isn't surprising. Finding a mutually convenient time during a workweek may be next to impossible. Instead, I'd gently request that they shoot for an annual or semiannual "touching base" phone call or e-mail, but with ongoing weekly communication, perhaps in the form of a shared notebook. The notebook could contain pictures and descriptions of sounds your child is working on or language concepts. The other SLP can make a comment or add info as well. It usually is more beneficial if there is at least some coordination of goals and strategies when one or more speech pathologists is working with a child. Within the same private office or school, it is much easier to check in with each other and coordinate, but two totally different locations make it difficult.

If your child has articulation goals, it is important to have a game plan so your child isn't getting too many new sounds thrown at him at once. Likewise, with stuttering there are a variety of programs that reference various techniques with specific lingo, so it could be confusing to have too many cooks in the kitchen in this regard. Sometimes it may be a good idea to pick one SLP and avoid having your child get mixed messages. However, if there are social difficulties or academic challenges due to the speech or language disorder, having a school-based SLP working with the classroom teacher can be a great asset; likewise, having a private SLP who can do more individualized instruction can be beneficial at the same time.

The Persistent *R* Sound Problem

Q. Our 10-year-old daughter has been in speech therapy to fix her r sounds for four years and it's not any better. What should we do?

A. That's about three years too long, frankly. It sounds like one or more of the following is happening, and only you know which they are.

- Your daughter is not terribly unhappy with her speech. Changing a speech pattern requires a bit of motivation. Does she really want to change it?
- Let's say she *does* want to change it. Does she set aside the time to practice the activities sent home? If not, the therapy won't be helpful.
- She may enjoy going to speech therapy because it's fun and gets her out of a class, and thus is not anxious to finish therapy.
- She has an underlying auditory problem and can't "hear" the differences between the correct and incorrect sound and so either she can't produce it clearly at all, or she can, but it doesn't sound "right" to her, so it's not generalized.
- She has underlying oral–motor placement issues that make it difficult (not impossible) for her mouth to produce the sound with the usual strategies.
- Her speech pathologist is not very skillful in treating *r* distortions and could benefit from some further training.
- Her attendance at speech therapy is not frequent or intensive enough for her to make substantial progress. We know that more frequent sessions (two times a week), even if just for twenty to thirty minutes at a time in some cases, are more effective than one long session a week. Are there many holidays, illnesses, or breaks that are disrupting her progress?

In order to see change, you will need to sort out which of the above situations are contributing to the delay in your daughter's case and make changes accordingly. In the event that it's a lack of motivation and that she's able to produce a clear *r* at the word level, you may want to consider setting short-term goals for her in cooperation with her SLP, including her spontaneous use of the corrected *r* in conversation. Some kind of reward for meeting each goal may help motivate her.

Making an *S* without Front Teeth

Q. Our son just lost his front teeth. Can he make an s sound?

A. He should be able to still make an *s* sound if he could do it before. For some children, it seems to be more of a challenge, but in particular if your son has a tongue thrust (where the tongue protrudes between the teeth and pushes out when swallowing), the missing teeth can make the situation worse. Over time, those top teeth may resist emerging because of that pressure, so it becomes a vicious circle.

Speech Therapy: How Often?

Q. How often should children be getting speech therapy?

A. It really does depend on the child and the nature and severity of the problem itself. For children with moderate to severe articulation disorders and apraxia, frequency is critical; usually two or three times a week is best if feasible. Other times, related intervention may be delivered by many people, so isolated speech therapy may be less necessary. For example, your child's reading specialist may work on phonemic awareness, the classroom teacher may be great at working on expressive language through writing and show-and-tell (for mild delays), and the special education teacher may be working on improving social language skills in a lunchtime "friends" group. In other words, if many people are involved and contributing to your child's program, there may be less need for isolated, traditional "speech therapy" per se, and once a week may be just fine, especially if there is good communication with you and the classroom teacher.

Speech Therapy: How Long Does It Take?

Q. My 4-year-old son will be starting speech therapy soon. He has trouble expressing himself and is hard to understand. How long will it take for him to catch up?

A. This is probably one of the most common questions SLPs are asked. The truth is, we really don't know precisely how long it will take, and unfortunately for some children, the difficulties are such that they may not realistically ever "catch up." While we try our best to maximize each child's potential, there is a limit to what we can achieve, and there are no surefire guarantees. A few of the factors that contribute to the equation are the severity of the problem, the skills of the SLP, the motivation and cooperation of the child, the amount of home practice and carryover of the activities suggested, the consistency and frequency of attendance, the physical and intellectual limitations of the child, and the fact that sometimes other difficulties evolve over time that were not as noticeable or as much of a concern at the time of the initial evaluation. For example, sometimes the child comes to us for an articulation difficulty, but we find that the auditory processing of spoken language is weak, which in turn fuels difficulties in reading and spelling. These are much more complex issues, so while the initial articulation difficulty may be worked out, other skills may continue to require intervention.

Typically, simple articulation problems can be remediated in a matter of months, but trouble with certain sounds (e.g., *r* or lateral *s*) can be persistent and hard to correct and can take a year or longer of therapy or even longer. Children with developmental delays, severe articulation disorders, and autism spectrum disorders may need direct intervention throughout their childhood. (See the next question.) Many times, it takes working with a child for some time in order to get a sense of their rate of progress before we can make an educated guess as to how much progress should realistically be expected in a given amount of time. However, please know that it is impossible to precisely answer that question with any certainty, so an SLP should not be "promising" to cure or fix your child in a specified time. Ballpark guesses based on experience and working with your child over time are likely as close as we can get to answering that question.

Speech Therapy: When to End Services

Q. We have a son who is almost 13. He's been in speech therapy since he was little for receptive and expressive language problems, articulation, auditory processing, and even pragmatic (social) language use. He's made enormous progress, but continues to be behind his peers in all these areas and still struggles in academics. At what point do you phase out therapy?

A. At this age, isolated therapy may or may not make much of an impact if it's not tied to something he's currently learning or will readily use. Sometimes children with language disorders and weaknesses are better served by tutoring in specific areas, such as reading and writing, or with content areas, such as science and social studies, since reading comprehension and lecture-style learning are often difficult. You may find your child takes in and learns the information more effectively with small-group or one-to-one support. What are the areas that are presenting the most difficulties? It's important to prioritize and be fairly focused with the therapy goals. Many times at this age the social component becomes much more prominent than when they were younger and may require an SLP with a different set of skills. It might also be a good idea to take a break from formal therapy during the school year and use the summer months to do some intensive work in these areas. If your son is balking and you don't see much improvement—and you've tried a good variety of therapy methods, programs, and motivators—it's okay to step back from getting formal therapy, even if some deficits remain. At that point, the focus should be on compensating for the difficulties and finding the right academic environment and support for your child to be successful.

APPENDIX A

Resources

The following organizations and agencies may be able to give you additional information about your child's speech, language, or listening problem, or direct you to a local agency that can help you.

For information about speech-language-hearing issues in the United States:

American Speech-Language-Hearing
   Association (ASHA)
2200 Research Boulevard
Rockville, MD 20852
(800) 638-8255
www.asha.org

Web site for Baby Development Info:
www.Babycenter.com

In Canada:

The Canadian Association of Speech-
   Language Pathologists and Audiologists (CASLPA)
920-1 Nicholas Street
Ottawa, ON K1N 7B7
(613) 567-9968
(800) 259-8519
e-mail: caslpa@caslpa.ca
www.caslpa.ca

The Hanen Centre
Suite 515 -1075 Bay Street
Toronto, ON M5S 2B1
(416) 921-1073
www.hanen.org

In Australia:

Speech Pathology Australia
11-19 Bank Place, 2nd floor
Melbourne VIC 3000
+61 3 9642 4899
www.speechpathologyaustralia.org

In Asia:

www.speech-language-
   therapy.com/Asia.htm

For information about any kind of disability and parents' rights in the United States:

The Council for Exceptional
   Children
1110 North Glebe Road,
   Suite 300
Arlington, VA 22201
(888) 232-7733
www.cec.sped.org

Disability Rights Education and
   Defense Fund
2212 Sixth Street
Berkeley, CA 94710
(800) 348-4232
www.dredf.org

Education Resources Information
    Center (ERIC)
National Institute of Education
U.S. Department of Education
Washington, DC 20208
(800) 538-3742
www.accesseric.org

National Dissemination Center for
    Children with Disabilities (NICHCY)
1825 Connecticut Avenue NW, Suite 700
Washington, DC 20009
(800) 695-0285
www.nichcy.org

**Magazine for families and parents of
children with disabilities:**
Exceptional Parent
eparent.com

For information about assistive
listening devices (including FM
systems and soundfield systems):

Custom All-Hear
(800) 355-7525
customallhear.com

Phonic Ear
(732) 560-1220
www.phonicear.com

Lightspeed Technologies
11509 SW Herman Road
Tualatin, OR 97062
(800) 732-8999
(503) 684-5538
www.lightspeed-tek.com

For information about attention
deficit disorder:

Children and Adults with Attention
    Deficit Disorder (CHADD)
8181 Professional Place, Suite 150
Landover, MD 20785
(800) 233-4050
www.chadd.org

National ADD Association
1788 Second Street, Suite 200
Highland Park, IL 60035

(847) 432-ADDA
mail@add.org
www.add.org

For information about
augmentative/alternative
language technology:

Alliance for Technology Access
1304 Southpoint Boulevard, Suite 240
Petaluma, CA 94954
www.ataccess.org

For information about
autism/PDD:

Autism Society of America
7910 Woodmont Avenue, Suite 300
Bethesda, MD 20814
(800) 3-AUTISM
(301) 657-0881
Autism-society.org

Autism Research Institute
4182 Adams Avenue
San Diego, CA 92116
www.autism.com

Generation Rescue
www.generationrescue.com

For information about raising
bilingual children:

Bilingual family newsletter:
Multilingual Matters Ltd.
www.multilingual-matters.com

For information about cerebral
palsy:

National Easter Seal Society
233 South Wacker Drive, #2400
Chicago, IL 60606
(312) 726-6200
nessinfo@seals.com
www.easterseals.com

United Cerebral Palsy Association
1660 L Street NW, Suite 700
Washington, DC 20036

(800) 872-5827
www.ucp.org

For information about cleft palate and other facial deformities:

American Cleft Palate-Craniofacial
    Association
1504 East Franklin Street, #102
Chapel Hill, NC 27514
(919) 933-9044
www.acpa-cpf.org

For information about the deaf or hearing impaired:

Alexander Graham Bell Association for
    the Deaf and Hard of Hearing
3417 Volta Place NW
Washington, DC 20007
(202) 337-5220
www.agbell.org

American Society for Deaf Children
800 Florida Avenue NE, #2047
Washington, DC 20002
(717) 703-0073
www.deafchildren.org

Computer software designed for speech and language improvement:
Laureate Learning Systems, Inc.
110 East Spring Street
Winooski, VT 05404
(800) 562-6801 for free demo CD
www.LaureateLearning.com

Multimedia resources:

Software for learning nouns and verbs:
Great Action Adventure, available from
    several vendors, including
    www.autismcoach.com

Videomodeling software that teaches social language use:
www.modelmekids.com

DVDs for videomodeling of play behaviors:
www.teach2talk.com

www.watchmelearn.com

DVDs to demonstrate activities parents can do at home to promote listening and expressive language development for toddlers and preschoolers:
Available from Laura Mize, MS, CCC-SLP,
    who also has a great Web site with
    lots of helpful tips.
www.teachmetotalk.com

DVDs on feeding therapy and oral-motor techniques:
Lori Overland: *Feeding Therapy.*
    Available at www.talktools.net.
Sara Rosenfeld Johnson: *A Three-Part
    Treatment Plan.* Available at
    www.talktools.net.

Companies that publish speech and language materials, including games, picture cards, and software:
www.autismcoach.com
www.lakeshorelearning.com
www.linguisystems.com
www.mayerjohnson.com
www.proedinc.com
www.socialthinking.com
www.superduperinc.com

To subscribe to CEC Smart Brief, a great free e-newsletter with cutting-edge special education stories and research:
www.smartbrief.com/cec/

For information about Down syndrome and intellectual disabilities:

Association for Children with Down
    Syndrome
4 Fern Place
Plainview, NY 11803
(516) 933-4700

The Arc of the United States
www.thearc.org

National Down Syndrome Society
(800) 221-4602
www.ndss.org

Childhood Apraxia of Speech (CAS):
www.apraxia-kids.org

For information about learning disabilities:

Learning Disabilities Association of
    America (LDA)
4156 Library Road
Pittsburgh, PA 15234
(412) 341-1515
ldanatl@usaorg.net
www.ldanatl.org

International Dyslexia Society
40 York Road, 4th floor
Baltimore, MD 21204
(410) 296-0232
www.interdys.org

Phonemic awareness training software:
Earobics
(888) 242-6747
www.earobics.com

Fast ForWord
Scientific Learning Corporation
(888) 358-0212
www.scilearn.com

For information about PROMPT technique providers for childhood apraxia of speech:

(505) 466-7710
www.promptinstitute.com

For information about stuttering:

Stuttering Foundation
3100 Walnut Grove Road, Suite 603
P.O. Box 11749
Memphis, TN 3811-0749
(800) 992-9392
www.stutteringhelp.org

For information about recovery from traumatic brain injury:

Brain Injury Association of America
(800) 444-6443
www.biausa.org

For information about voice disorders:

Voice Foundation
1721 Pine Street
Philadelphia, PA 19103
(215) 735-7999
www.voicefoundation.org

To contact the U.S. government offices that handle special education queries:
OSERS
Office of Special Education and
    Rehabilitative Services
400 Maryland Avenue SW
Washington, DC 20202-0498
(202) 245-7459
www.ed.gov

APPENDIX B

Suggested Reading

On speech-language development:

Baron, Naomi S. 1993. *Growing Up with Language: How Children Learn to Talk.* Cambridge, Mass.: Perseus Press.

Manolson, A. 1992. *It Takes Two to Talk.* Toronto: Hanen Centre.

Of general interest to parents of children with disabilities:

Canfield, Jack, Mark Hansen, Heather McNamara, and Karen Simmons. 2007. *Chicken Soup for the Soul: Children with Special Needs: Stories of Love and Understanding for Those Who Care for Children with Disabilities.* Deerfield Beach, Fla.: HCI.

Greenspan, Stanley, Serena Weider, and Robin Simon. 1998. *The Child with Special Needs: Encouraging Intellectual and Emotional Growth.* Reading, Mass.: Addison-Wesley.

Wright, Peter, and Pamela Darr Wright. *Wrightslaw: Special Education Law,* 2nd ed. 2007. Hartfield, Va.: Harbor House Law Press.

Of interest to parents of children with autism spectrum disorders:

Attwood, Tony. 2008. *The Complete Guide to Asperger's Syndrome.* London: Jessica Kingsley.

Gutstein, Steven, and Rachelle Sheeley. 2002. *Relationship Development Intervention with Young Children.* London: Jessica Kingsley.

Hogdon, Linda A. 1999. *Solving Behavior Problems in Autism: Practical Supports for School and Home.* Troy, Mich.: Quirk Roberts Publishing.

Notbohm, Ellen. 2005. *Ten Things Every Child with Autism Wishes You Knew.* Arlington, Tex.: Future Horizons.

Prizant, Barry, Amy Wetherby, Emily Rubin, and Amy Laurent. 2005. *The SCERTS Model: A Comprehensive Educational Approach for Children with Autism Spectrum Disorders.* Baltimore: Brookes Publishing Company.

Siegal, Bryna. 2003. *Helping Children with Autism Learn: A Guide to Treatment Approaches for Parents and Professionals.* New York: Oxford University Press.

Of interest to parents raising bilingual children:

Steiner, Naomi, Susan Hayes, and Steven Parker. 2008. *7 Steps to Raising a Bilingual Child.* New York: AMACOM.

Zurer Pearson, Barbara. 2008. *Raising a Bilingual Child.* New York: Living Language.

Of interest to parents of children with apraxia, oral-motor, or articulation difficulties:

Bahr, Diane. 2010. *Nobody Ever Told Me (or My Mother) That!: Everything from Bottles and Breathing to Healthy Speech Development.* Arlington, Texas: Sensory World.

Dougherty, Dorothy. 2005. *Teach Me How to Say It Right: Helping Your Child with Articulation Problems.* Oakland, Calif.: New Harbinger Publications.

Flanagan, Maureen. 2008. *Improving Speech and Eating Skills in Children with Autism Spectrum Disorders.* Shawnee Mission, Kan.: Autism Asperger Publishing Company.

Johnson, Sara Rosenfeld. 1999. *Oral-Motor Exercises for Speech Clarity.* Tucson, Ariz.: Talktools.

Marshalla, Pamela. 2004. *Oral-Motor Techniques in Articulation and Oral-Motor Therapy.* Anaheim, Calif.: Marshalla Publishing.

Of interest to parents of children with auditory and language processing disorders:

Bellis, Teri James. 2003. *When the Brain Can't Hear: Unraveling the Mystery of Auditory Processing Disorder.* New York: Atria.

Gaulin, Cindy. 2000. *Language Processing Problems.* Bloomington, Ind.: Xlibris.

Hamaguchi, Patricia McAleer. 2001. *It's Time to Listen,* 2nd ed. Austin, Tex.: Pro-Ed.

————. 2003. *A Metacognitive Program for Treating Auditory Processing Disorders.* Austin, Tex.: Pro-Ed.

Heymann, Lois Kam. 2010. *The Sound of Hope: Recognizing, Coping with, and Treating Your Child's Auditory Processing Disorder.* New York: Ballantine Books.

Swain, Deborah Ross, and Donna Geffner. 2007. *Auditory Processing Disorders: Assessment, Management and Treatment.* San Diego, Calif.: Plural Publishing.

Of interest to parents of children with delayed speech:

Agin, Marilyn, Lisa Geng, and Malcolm Nicholl. 2003. *The Late Talker (What to Do If Your Child Isn't Talking Yet).* New York: St. Martin's Press.

Apel, Kenn, and Julie Masterson. 2001. *Beyond Baby Talk: From Sounds to Sentences— A Parent's Complete Guide to Language Development.* New York: Three Rivers Press.

Dougherty, Dorothy, and Diane Paul. 2007. *Talking on the Go.* Rockville, Md.: ASHA Publications.

Feit, Debbie. 2007. *The Parent's Guide to Speech and Language Problems.* New York: McGraw-Hill.

Of interest to parents of children with a hearing impairment:

Cole, Elizabeth, and Carol Flexer. 2007. *Children with Hearing Loss: Developing Listening and Talking Birth to Six.* San Diego, Calif.: Plural Publishing.

Estabrooks, Warren. 2006. *Auditory-Verbal Therapy and Practice.* Washington, D.C.: Alexander Graham Bell Association for the Deaf and Hard of Hearing.

————. 2000. *50 Frequently Asked Questions about Auditory Verbal Therapy.* Toronto: Learning to Listen Foundation.

Schwartz, Sue. 2007. *Choices in Deafness: A Parent's Guide to Communication Options,* 3rd ed. Bethesda, Md.: Woodbine House.

Of interest to parents of children with complex neurobiological disorders:

Kutscher, Martin. 2005. *Kids in the Syndrome Mix of ADHD, LD, Asperger's, Tourette's, Bipolar, and More!* London: Jessica Kingsley.

Of interest to parents of children with Down syndrome:

Groneberg, Jennifer Graf. 2008. *Roadmap to Holland: How I Found My Way Through My Son's First Two Years with Down Syndrome.* New York: NAL Trade.

Kumin, Libby. 2003. *Early Communication Skills in Children with Down Syndrome: A Guide for Parents and Professionals.* Bethesda, Md.: Woodbine House.

Skallerup, Susan. 2008. *Babies with Down Syndrome: A New Parents' Guide.* Bethesda, Md.: Woodbine House.

Of interest to parents of children who stutter:

Ainsworth, Stanley, and Jane Fraser. 2008. *If Your Child Stutters: A Guide for Parents,* 7th ed. Memphis, Tenn.: Stuttering Foundation.

Of interest to parents of picky eaters:

Ernsperger, Lori, Tania Stegen-Hanson, and Temple Grandin. 2004. *Just Take a Bite.* Arlington, Tex.: Future Horizons.

Of interest to parents of children with social-cognitive and pragmatic deficits:

Winner, Michelle Garcia. 2009. *Thinking About You Thinking About Me.* San Jose, Calif.: Think Social Publishing.

Of interest to parents of children with autism who are seeking information about the impact of food and nutrition on their children:

Strickland, Elizabeth. 2009. *Eating for Autism: The 10-Step Nutrition Plan to Help Treat Your Child's Autism, Asperger's, or ADHD.* Cambridge, Mass.: Da Capo Press.

Of interest to parents of children with sensory integration disorders:

Ayres, A. J. 2005. *Sensory Integration and the Child: Understanding Hidden Sensory Challenges.* 25th anniversary edition. Santa Rosa, Calif.: Crestport Press.

Bell, Lindsey, and Nancy Peske. 2005. *Raising a Sensory Smart Child.* New York: Penguin.

Kranowitz, Carol Stock. 2005. *The Out of Sync Child,* rev. ed. New York: Perigee
————. 2006. *The Out-of-Sync Child Has Fun: Activities for Kids with Sensory Processing Disorders.* New York: Perigee.

Kranowitz, C. S., S. Szklut., L. Blazer-Martin, E. Haber, and D. I. Sava. 2001. *Answers to Questions Teachers Ask About Sensory Integration: Forms, Checklists, and Practical Tools for Teachers and Parents,* 2nd ed. Las Vegas: Sensory Resources.

Wetherby, A. M., and Barry Prizant. 2000. *Children with Autism Spectrum Disorders: A Developmental, Transactional Perspective.* Baltimore: Paul H. Brookes.

Williams, M. S., and S. Shellenberger. 2001. *Take Five! Staying Alert at Home and School.* Albuquerque: TherapyWorks.

Williamson, G.G. and M. E. Anzalone. 2001. *Sensory Integration and Self-Regulation in Infants and Toddlers: Helping Very Young Children Interact with Their Environment.* Washington, D.C.: Zero to Three.

Index